Unlocking the Chinese Realm

Unlocking the Chinese Realm

Apostle David O. McKay and Latter-day Saint Encounters in East Asia, 1852–1921

Reid L. Neilson

Greg Kofford Books
Salt Lake City

Published in the USA.

ISBN: 978-1-58958-831-8 (paperback)
Also available in ebook.

Greg Kofford Books
P. O. Box 1362
Draper, UT 84020
www.gregkofford.com
facebook.com/gkbooks
twitter.com/gkbooks

Library of Congress Cataloging-in-Publication Data

Names: Neilson, Reid L., 1972- author
Title: Unlocking the Chinese realm : Apostle David O. McKay and Latter-day Saint encounters in East Asia, 1852-1921 / Reid L. Neilson.
Description: Salt Lake City : Greg Kofford Books, [2026] | Includes bibliographical references and index. Summary: "In Unlocking the Chinese Realm, historian Reid L. Neilson offers a comprehensive account of Latter-day Saint early encounters with China and its surrounding regions. Spanning from Brigham Young's 1852 call for missionaries to Hong Kong through Apostle David O. McKay's 1921 dedicatory prayer in Peking, the book traces nearly seventy years of evolving religious aspiration, cultural encounter, and global vision. Drawing on diaries, reports, and periodical accounts, Neilson illuminates how McKay's prayer symbolically "turned the key" to China, consecrating the nation and its people to receive the restored gospel while reflecting broader Western attitudes toward the East at the dawn of the twentieth century. Blending biography, theology, and global religious history, Unlocking the Chinese Realm situates McKay's mission within a longer narrative of Latter-day Saint engagement with East Asia-from early Hawaiian and Californian contact with Chinese migrants to later apostolic rituals of dedicating lands in preparation to share the gospel. With detailed analysis and rare archival sources, Neilson reveals how McKay's 1921 act echoed across generations of church leaders and members, shaping the faith's hopes for China and its diaspora well into the modern era. This deeply researched study opens new perspectives on Mormonism's international expansion and the sacred geography of global Christianity"-- Provided by publisher.
Identifiers: LCCN 2025049637 (print) | LCCN 2025049638 (ebook) | ISBN 9781589588318 paperback | ISBN 9781589588325 ebook
Subjects: LCSH: McKay, David O. (David Oman), 1873-1970--Travel--China | Church of Jesus Christ of Latter-day Saints--Missions--China--History
Classification: LCC BX8617.C6 N45 2026 (print) | LCC BX8617.C6 (ebook)
LC record available at https://lccn.loc.gov/2025049637
LC ebook record available at https://lccn.loc.gov/2025049638

For Barbara and Stan Shakespeare as well as
the members of the Montgomery Chinese Branch

Under the century-old limbs and green leaves of this—one of God's own temples—with uncovered heads we supplicated our Father in Heaven, and by the authority of the Holy Melchizedek Priesthood, and in the name of the Only Begotten of the Father, turned the key that unlocked the door for the entrance, into this benighted and famine-stricken land, of the authorized servants of God to preach the true and restored Gospel of Jesus Christ. . . .

Acting under appointment of the Prophet, Seer, and Revelator, and by virtue of the holy Apostleship, I then dedicated and set apart the Chinese realm for the preaching of the Glad Tidings of Great Joy as revealed in this Dispensation through the Prophet Joseph Smith.

—David O. McKay, January 9, 1921, Peking

Contents

Illustrations

Preface

Nine decades after the 1830 organization of The Church of Jesus Christ of Latter-day Saints (hereafter "the church"),[1] its First Presidency (the top governing body) made an assignment that would prove historic for the church's fledgling history in China. The Ninety-First Semiannual General Conference had come and gone in early October 1920, and the Latter-day Saints had enjoyed hearing dozens of sermons from senior church leaders, including church president Heber J. Grant, his counselors, Anthon H. Lund and Charles W. Penrose, and many from the Quorum of the Twelve Apostles. It was a spiritual three-day gathering at the Tabernacle on Temple Square in Salt Lake City, and though general conferences often provided opportunities for general authorities to make major announcements, no such statements were made. That would change within the week.

On Thursday, October 14, 1920, the First Presidency and the Quorum of the Twelve Apostles met for their weekly meeting in the Salt Lake Temple. During their discussion, the church leaders assigned one of their own—forty-seven-year-old Elder David O. McKay—to embark on a yearlong, around-the-world fact-finding trip to the missions, schools, and branches of the church, beginning in the Pacific Isles. McKay was a relatively junior apostle (situated in the middle of the Quorum of the Twelve in terms of seniority, and fourth-youngest in terms of age) and was currently serving as the church's commissioner of education and as general superintendent of its Sunday schools.[2] His comparative youth coupled with extensive leadership experience made him an obvious choice for undertaking a protracted assignment with a demanding schedule. That

1. In 2018, The Church of Jesus Christ of Latter-day Saints updated its official style guide, which the Associated Press has since adopted. Observers are encouraged to use the full name of the church the first time it is referenced, and "the church" for shortened references, instead of "Mormon Church" or "LDS Church." See Church Newsroom, "Style Guide—The Name of the Church."

2. In order of seniority (the order in which each apostle was called to his position), the Twelve Apostles were Rudger Clawson, Reed Smoot, George Albert Smith, George F. Richards, Orson F. Whitney, David O. McKay, Anthony W. Ivins, Joseph Fielding Smith, James E. Talmage, Stephen L. Richards, Richard R. Lyman, and Melvin J. Ballard. *Ninety-First Semi-annual Conference* (1920), 1.

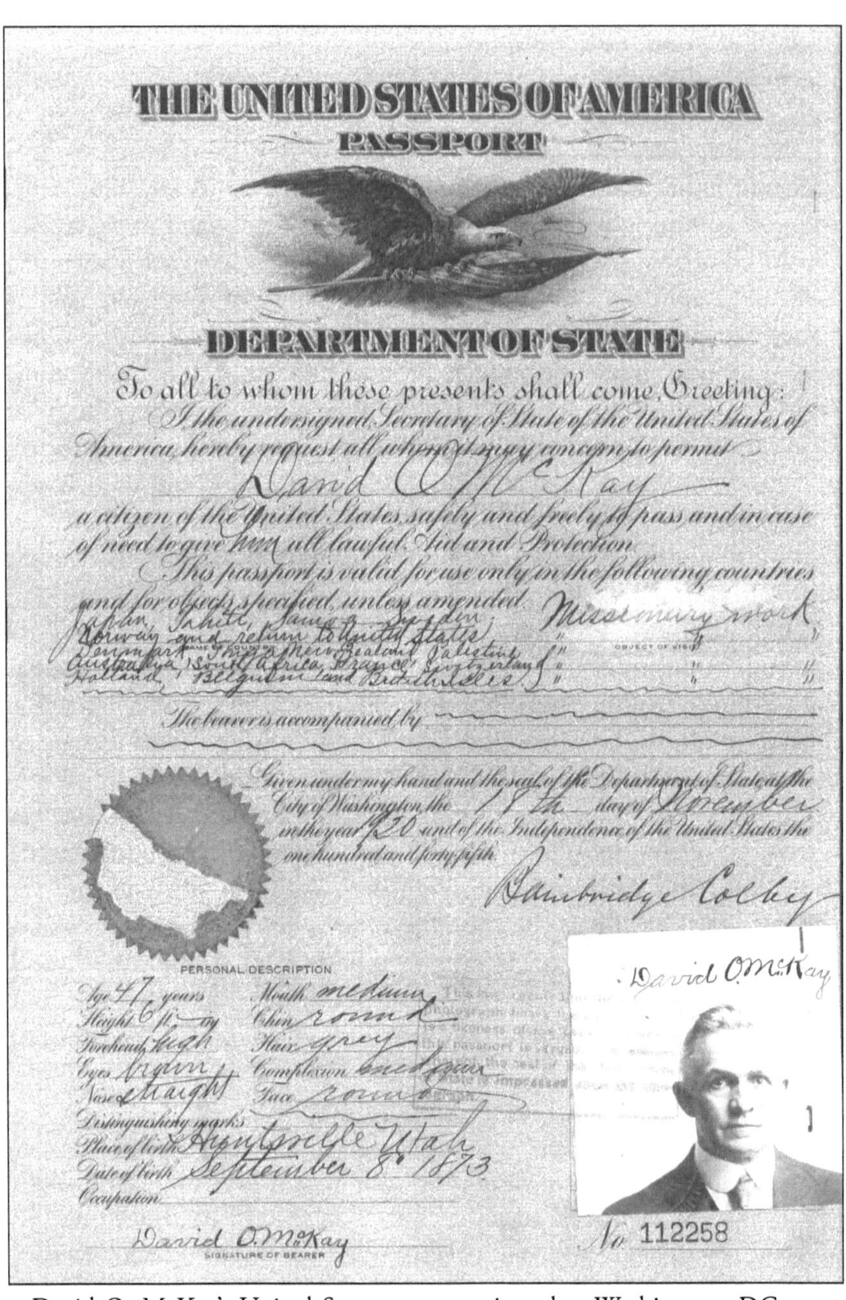

THE UNITED STATES OF AMERICA

PASSPORT

DEPARTMENT OF STATE

To all to whom these presents shall come, Greeting:

I the undersigned, Secretary of State of the United States of America, hereby request all whom it may concern to permit

David O. McKay

a citizen of the United States, safely and freely to pass, and in case of need to give him all lawful Aid and Protection.

This passport is valid for use only in the following countries and for objects specified, unless amended.

NAME OF COUNTRY	OBJECT OF VISIT
Japan, Tahiti, Samoa, Sweden, Norway and return to United States	Missionary work
Denmark, Tonga, New Zealand, Palestine	"
Australia, South Africa, France, Switzerland	"
Holland, Belgium and British Isles	"

The bearer is accompanied by

Given under my hand and the seal of the Department of State at the City of Washington the 18th day of November in the year 1920 and of the Independence of the United States the one hundred and forty-fifth.

Bainbridge Colby

PERSONAL DESCRIPTION

Age 47 years
Height 6 ft — in
Forehead high
Eyes brown
Nose straight
Mouth medium
Chin round
Hair grey
Complexion medium
Face round
Distinguishing marks
Place of birth Huntsville Utah
Date of birth September 8 1873
Occupation

David O. McKay

SIGNATURE OF BEARER

David O. McKay

No. 112258

David O. McKay's United States passport, issued at Washington, DC, on November 18, 1920. Courtesy Church History Library, The Church of Jesus Christ of Latter-day Saints.

evening, McKay met with William C. Spence, the church's transportation agent, to begin planning his global itinerary.[3] The following morning, Grant called fifty-year-old Hugh J. Cannon, president of the Liberty Stake (a geographical area of a dozen or so congregations) in the Salt Lake Valley and the son of the late First Presidency member George Q. Cannon, to accompany McKay on his lengthy journey.

Soon after, Grant announced McKay and Cannon's upcoming mission to a reporter with the church-owned *Deseret News.* Grant explained that he had earlier hoped to make such a tour of the Pacific missions himself while he had been serving as the inaugural president of the Japanese Mission (1901–1903), but when he proposed such a journey to the First Presidency, they had not approved it. By 1920, as president of the church, sixty-three-year-old Grant was pleased to be calling a younger man to achieve his earlier dream: "Now Elder McKay is to take the trip which I then advocated. He will make a general survey of the missions, study conditions there, gather data concerning them, and in short, obtain general information in order that there may be some one in the deliberations of the First Presidency and the Council of the Twelve thoroughly familiar with actual conditions."[4]

The church president also invited McKay to consider offering an apostolic country dedicatory prayer for the Chinese people while touring East Asia. "Before we left home, President Grant [had] suggested that when we were in China, if we felt so impressed, to set the land apart for the preaching of the Gospel. As Peking [Beijing] is really the heart of China, we had concluded that this would be an appropriate place to perform this sacred and far-reaching duty," McKay noted of this special assignment in 1920.[5]

Dedicatory Prayers and Sacred Sites

In Latter-day Saint practice, the church's apostles offer a ritualized prayer to dedicate a nation to God for the preaching of the church's doctrines and faith. As noted in this volume's epigraph, Elder David O. McKay proffered an official blessing in Peking, by assignment from President Heber J. Grant. "Under the century-old limbs and green leaves . . . with uncovered heads we supplicated our Father in Heaven, and by

3. "Two Church Workers Will Tour Missions of Pacific Islands," *Deseret News,* October 15, 1920.

4. "Two Church Workers Will Tour Missions of Pacific Islands."

5. David O. McKay, Diary, January 9, 1901.

Hugh J. Cannon and David O. McKay in light-colored travel suits while on their world tour, 1921. Courtesy Church History Library, The Church of Jesus Christ of Latter-day Saints.

the authority of the Holy Melchizedek Priesthood, and in the name of the Only Begotten of the Father, turned the key that unlocked the door for the entrance, into this benighted and famine-stricken land," McKay noted in his diary on January 9, 1921, of his prayer among cypress trees in a Chinese garden. "Acting under appointment of the Prophet, Seer, and Revelator, and by virtue of the holy Apostleship, I then dedicated and set apart the Chinese realm for the preaching of the Glad Tidings of Great Joy."[6] However, in the century since McKay formally prayed to commence Latter-day Saint evangelism among the Chinese, the church has not sent its young elders and sisters to mainland China as proselyting missionaries.

Thirty-five years ago, two members of the church's Quorum of the Twelve Apostles, Russell M. Nelson and Dallin H. Oaks, visited China by assignment, like McKay before them. When they returned to Utah they clarified the church's status in the People's Republic of China, which remains the status quo to this day. "'When will China be opened?' This question has been asked of Church leaders for years," a journalist for the *Church News* reported. Nelson and Oaks "have a simple and direct response, which may be surprising to many Church members: 'The door to China is already open!'" The church's reporter continued: "But it's not open in the way that most members think. There are no plans for sending missionaries to China, and there will be no Church proselyting in that country. But branches [congregations] of the Church have already been established in the cities of Beijing, Shanghai and Xi'an, and many Chinese citizens have joined the Church during their studies in the United States and elsewhere."[7] In 2020, independent Latter-day Saint demographer Matt Martinich claimed that the church has membership in most major Chinese cities, despite the fact that it "operates under significant legal restrictions in the PRC, and there remains no stakes in the PRC at present."[8]

The church does have a formal and acknowledged presence in China, as well as chapels, temples, and missionaries in neighboring Taiwan, Hong Kong, and Macau. Moreover, Latter-day Saint missionaries do

---

6. McKay, Diary, January 9, 1921.

7. "China: Two apostles visit, assured that religious freedom exists and people are free to worship as they choose," *Church News*, January 28, 1989. For more on Nelson's engagement with the Chinese people, see Sheri Dew, *Insights from a Prophet's Life*, 132–36, 142–47, 165–70, 205–7, 302–4. See also Spencer J. Condie, *Russell M. Nelson*, 215–32.

8. "Eight New Temples Announced—Analysis," Growth of The Church of Jesus Christ of Latter-day Saints (blog).

teach interested overseas Chinese investigators around the world. When referring to the Chinese diaspora, I have relied on the following scholarly characterization. "An overseas Chinese person is defined here as a Chinese person who resides outside the Chinese mainland, Hong Kong, Macau and Taiwan," sociologists Duley L. Poston Jr. and Juyin Helen Wong clarify. "Chinese emigrants began to move to other Asian countries, particularly Southeast Asia, more than 2000 years ago. Large numbers of Chinese migrated from China to virtually every other country in the world during the 19th century and early 20th century. By around 2011, there were over 40.3 million overseas Chinese residing in 148 countries."[9] A decade ago, the church launched an official website, www.mormonsandchina.org, to provide information for this growing number of Chinese nationals who join the church while living abroad and for church leaders who minister to these converts.[10]

Despite current ecclesiastical restrictions, there *is* an episodic early history of the church in the "Chinese realm" and among the overseas Chinese, stretching back 170 years. That is the story told in this book.

The first half of this volume focuses on the events leading up to David O. McKay's 1921 dedication of the Chinese realm. Chapter 1 begins in 1852, when Brigham Young, Joseph Smith's successor as president of the church, assigned several Latter-day Saint men living in pioneer Utah Territory to be missionaries in faraway Hong Kong, which had recently become an Asian colony of the British Empire. Relying on firsthand accounts, especially those of James Lewis, I chronicle these men's short-lived mission to East Asia. Chapter 2 documents early Latter-day Saint encounters with East Asians on the other side of the Pacific Ocean, in Hawaii, California, and Utah during the second half of the nineteenth century. I borrow the themes of *meeting* and *migration* from religious studies scholars Thomas A. Tweed and Stephen Prothero to help make sense of these interactions in the Hawaiian Islands and Intermountain West. In 1901, nearly sixty years since the church had last sent missionaries to East Asia, the First Presidency determined to open the Japanese Mission, with apostle Heber J. Grant as its inaugural leader. Chapter 3 tells the story of early Latter-day Saint evangelism in Japan, including the experience of two of its seasoned

9. Duley J. Poston Jr. and Juyin Helen Wong, "The Chinese Diaspora," 349, 362–63. See also Peter S. Li and Eva Xiaoling Li, "The Chinese Overseas Population"; and Lynn Pan, *The Encyclopedia of the Chinese Overseas*.

10. "New Church Website Will Help Chinese Nationals, Church Leaders Around the World," Church Newsroom.

missionaries as they toured mainland China in 1910 to evaluate prospects for the church among the Chinese, which they recommended against.

The book's second half begins with a theological overview to help prepare readers better understand and appreciate the importance of apostolic keys to Latter-day Saints and why the First Presidency sent David O. McKay to Peking in 1921. "Unlocking the Doors to All Nations," the subject of Chapter 4, is a history and analysis of country dedicatory prayers, an ordinance or ritual performed by Latter-day Saint apostles. Chapter 5 explains what McKay was doing and saying as he knelt within the Forbidden City, offering a prayer on behalf of the Chinese realm. I have contextualized the words of his formal blessing within the history of China at that time of devastating famine and poverty. My closing chapter chronicles the "echoes" or reverberations of McKay's 1921 dedicatory prayer language in subsequent Latter-day Saint thought and church ceremonies in East Asia.

Finally, I have featured several core primary sources as appendices to this volume. Appendix A is a transcription of Hosea Stout's report on the China Mission in the Salt Lake Tabernacle in December 1853, reproduced here from the original Pittman Shorthand for the first time. Alma O. Taylor's 1910 report to the First Presidency following his fact-finding mission throughout China is Appendix B. David O. McKay's apostolic dedicatory prayer offered in Peking in 1921 is featured in Appendix C. McKay's traveling companion, Hugh J. Cannon, offered his own perspective and history of this historic event in the pages of a number of Latter-day Saint periodicals, which is printed as Appendix D. McKay's personal essay on the conversion and religious life of Ah Ching, an overseas Chinese Latter-day Saint living in Samoa, is featured as Appendix E. Lastly, I have compiled a chronology of the church in East Asia, from 1852 to 2025, as Appendix F. Hopefully these appendices help readers better appreciate the thinking and writing of these keys figures in this emerging story between the Latter-day Saints and the Chinese.

Acknowledgments

Over the past several decades, I have explored and developed many of the themes and conclusions in this monograph in the articles, chapters, and books referenced below. I want to thank the editorial and production teams who helped prepare my previous publications, which benefit this present work. Portions of this book previously appeared in a similar or revised form in three books and four articles.[11] As I researched and wrote these publications on the history of the Latter-day Saints and East Asia, I was also able to present my evolving ideas at many academic conferences and historical gatherings.[12] I am thankful for the conference committees

---

11. Reid L. Neilson, "Alma O. Taylor's 1910 Fact Finding Mission to China"; Laurie F. Maffly-Kipp and Reid L. Neilson, eds., *Proclamation to the People: Nineteenth-Century Mormonism and the Pacific Basin Frontier*; Reid L. Neilson, "Turning the Key That Unlocked the Door: David O. McKay's 1921 Apostolic Dedication of the Chinese Realm"; Reid L. Neilson, *Early Mormon Missionary Activities in Japan, 1901–1924*; Reid L. Neilson, "Traveling and Standing Ministers: The Commandment to Travel (or Not) in the Joseph Smith Era Revelations"; Reid L. Neilson, "Early Mormon Missionary Work in Hong Kong: The Letters of James Lewis to Apostle and Church Historian George A. Smith, 1853–1855"; and Reid L. Neilson and Carson V. Teuscher, eds., *Pacific Apostle: the 1920–21 Diary of David O. McKay in the Latter-day Saint Island Missions.*

12. Reid L. Neilson, "The 1910 China Fact Finding Mission of Elder Alma O. Taylor," annual symposium of the Joseph Fielding Smith Institute for Latter-day Saint History, Brigham Young University, 2000; "The Japan Mission: First Efforts, 1854–1900," annual symposium of the Joseph Fielding Smith Institute for Latter-day Saint History, Brigham Young University, 2001; "Making Waves in a Sea of Faith: Mormonism at the 1893 and 1993 World's Parliament of Religions," Omnibus Lecture Series, L. Tom Perry Special Collections, Harold B. Lee Library, Brigham Young University, 2005; "Joseph Smith and Nineteenth-Century Mormon Responses to Asian Religions," The Worlds of Joseph Smith: An Academic Symposium at the National Taiwan University, Taipei, 2005; "Terrestrial Crossings on the Mormon Periphery: David O. McKay and Hugh J. Cannon's 1920–1921 Globetrotting Adventure," annual meeting of the Mormon History Association, Salt Lake City, Utah, 2007; "Representing Mormonism in the White City: America's Despised 'Religion' at the 1893 World's Parliaments of Religions," annual regional meeting of the American Historical Association, Honolulu, Hawaii, 2007; "Nineteenth-Century Mormonism and the Pacific Basin Frontier," conference on Pacific Worlds and the American West, American West Center, University of Utah, Salt Lake City, 2008; "Neither White nor Black: The Evolving Evaluation of Asians in Twentieth-Century Mormon Theology," annual regional meeting of the American Academy of Religion, Denver, Colorado, 2008; "Turning the Key That Unlocked the Door: David O. McKay's 1921 Apostolic Dedication of the Chinese Realm," annual meeting of the Mormon History Association, Sacramento, California, 2008; "In His Own Words: Hosea Stout's 1853 Missionary Adventures in Hong Kong," annual Church History Symposium, Brigham Young University, 2011; "Errand to the World: The 1852 Mormon Missionary Conference," annual meeting of the Mormon History Association, Calgary, Canada, 2012; "Unlocking the Doors

and others who allowed me to share my scholarship at these domestic and international gatherings.

I am also grateful for the support of my colleagues and friends who have allowed me to share my working drafts in these various venues and for their valuable feedback that helped me improve the published versions. The librarians, archivists, and professional staffs of the L. Tom Perry Special Collections; the Utah Valley Regional Family History Center and the Harold B. Lee Library at Brigham Young University; the Church History Library of The Church of Jesus Christ of Latter-day Saints; the Special Collections and the J. Willard Marriott Library at the University of Utah; and the Research Library and Collections at the Utah Historical Society—all provided helpful guidance and access to needed primary source documents, historical images, and secondary research along the way. I am grateful for their professional talents and personal goodness and desire to help me with my historical project on China. In retrospect, I have spent much of my academic career following in the footsteps of one of my mentors, Professor R. Lanier Britsch, and his scholarship on the history of the church in Asia, including China.[13]

I dedicate this book to my maternal aunt Barbara and uncle Stanley Shakespeare and their fellow teachers of the China Teachers Program of the David M. Kennedy Center for International Studies at Brigham Young University. Barb and Stan taught English to their Chinese students in Qingdao and Beijing for four school years as volunteers. Their love of all things China was contagious to all of us nephews and nieces as we read their weekly emails.

On a personal note, my wife Shelly and I were assigned to preside over the Washington DC North Mission from July 2019 until July 2022, as mission leaders. We took our five children—Johnny (then 15), Kate (13), Ally (9), Whitney (6), and James (3)—with us to live near our nation's capital. Our domestic mission and ecclesiastical area supported four

---

to all Nations: Early Latter-day Saint Country Dedicatory Prayers as a Ritual of Reconciliation," annual meeting of the Global Mormon Studies Association, Mexico City, Mexico, 2024; and "From Parowan to the Pacific: The Overland Travel of China Missionaries from Southern Utah to Southern California in 1852," annual meeting of the John Whitmer Historical Association, St. George, Utah, 2024.

13. See R. Lanier Britsch, *From the East: The History of the Latter-day Saints in Asia, 1851–1996*; and Reid L. Neilson, "Foreword," in R. Lanier Britsch, *Moramona: The Mormons in Hawaii* (2nd ed.).

languages besides English: Spanish, French, American Sign Language, and Chinese. Each of these languages had their own congregations within our mission boundaries. Missionaries were called to our mission with these various language assignments, including many young sisters serving at the Washington DC Temple Visitors' Center, where people of many nationalities toured on a regular basis.

On our first Sunday in Maryland, we attended church meetings at the Kentlands Chapel, which is in suburban Gaithersburg, Montgomery County. We were pleasantly surprised to discover that our English-speaking Kentlands Ward shared the red brick, colonial-style chapel with the Chinese-speaking Montgomery Chinese Branch, housed within the Washington DC Stake.[14] Years earlier, local church leaders had blended the two neighboring units' modest youth and Primary programs to help bolster both. Each Sunday morning, the Montgomery Chinese Branch would gather for sacrament meeting in Mandarin, then our youth and younger children would gather together for instruction and songs in English, and then the Kentlands Ward would conclude with its own sacrament meeting in English. I was delighted that our children would be able to interact with Asian American Latter-day Saints at church every week. Our missionaries served in this branch and were important contributors to its ongoing stability and success.

In May 2022, just months before we concluded our missionary service, the members of the Montgomery Chinese Branch gathered at the Kentlands meetinghouse to celebrate their church unit's thirtieth anniversary. The day's events included a series of activities, including a more formal meeting complete with a slideshow of past leaders, members, and missionaries. Lunch was served, and there were wonderful musical numbers and testimonies presented to the audience. Authors Po Nien (Felipe) Chou and Benjamin K. Tsai published and distributed a new history of the ecclesiastical unit, *Montgomery Chinese Branch: Voice of the Chinese Saints in Washington DC, 1992–2022* for the anniversary commemoration.[15]

That day I thought of the prayer of Elder David O. McKay in 1921, as he dedicated the Chinese realm for the preaching of the gospel a century earlier, and how those prophecies were being partially fulfilled among

14. In December 2021, church leaders renamed the Montgomery Chinese Branch as the Montgomery Mandarin Branch and transferred it from the leadership of the Washington DC Stake to the Seneca Maryland Stake, after nearly thirty years.

15. Po Nien Chou and Benjamin K. Tsai, *Montgomery Chinese Branch*.

overseas Chinese Latter-day Saints in the Washington, DC metropolitan region. During the celebration, I felt inspired to finish what I began to publish portions of back in 2000—a narrative history of the church's early efforts to bring the gospel of Jesus Christ to the Chinese, from the days of Joseph Smith to the apostolic dedication by McKay in 1921. I determined that, after my mission, I would revisit my previous scholarship on Latter-day Saint evangelism in East Asia and produce a monograph that told this story. Accordingly, I also dedicate this volume to the members of the Montgomery Chinese Branch in Maryland.

In 2022, I started a new chapter in my career as the Assistant Academic Vice President of Religious Scholarly Publications at Brigham Young University (BYU). It has been a pleasure to collaborate with the leadership and staff in the Office of the Academic Vice President, including professors C. Shane Reese (now our university president), Justin Collings, Michael Barnes, Renata Forste, Larry L. Howell, Kendra Hall Kenyon, Brad L. Neiger, and Richard Osguthorpe, along with Kera Kilpatrick and Kris Nelson. It has also been wonderful to work closely with professors Steven C. Harper, Jared W. Ludlow, J. B. Haws, W. Justin Dyer, and Scott C. Esplin across campus, all longtime friends from Religious Education years ago. Most of all, I am thankful for the goodness of my family members Shelly, Johnny, Kate, Ally, Whitney, and James in Bountiful, Utah.

My longtime collaborator and valued friend, Nathan N. Waite, with whom I coedited *A Zion Canyon Reader* (2014) and *Settling the Valley, Proclaiming the Gospel: The General Epistles of the Mormon First Presidency* (2017) is to be thanked for his editorial work on this volume. Nate improves every manuscript he touches, and I am grateful for his professionalism and ability to help authors like me communicate more clearly with our readers.

This is my third book publication with Greg Kofford Books, the first being (with coeditor Aaron McArthur) *The Annals of the Southern Mission: A Record of the History of the Settlement of Southern Utah* (2019), and the second being *Elias—An Epic of the Ages: A Critical Edition* (2025). I am grateful for the press's founder and namesake, Greg, who has created an important venue for Latter-day Saint scholarship. He is to be thanked for underwriting such a productive publishing house. The longtime managing editor there, Loyd Isao Ericson, and his editorial and production team have been incredible to work with on these several book projects. He has an eye for important manuscripts that deserve to see the light of day and add to our understanding of the Latter-day Saint experience. *Domo arigato gozaimasu!*

In hindsight, the seed for this volume was planted during the winter semester of my freshman year at Brigham Young University. On March 12, 1991, Elder Dallin H. Oaks of the Quorum of the Twelve Apostles spoke on "Getting to Know China" in a campus-wide devotional address. As he concluded his remarks, he encouraged the students gathered in the BYU Marriott Center to "open our minds and our hearts to the people of this ancient realm and this magnificent culture. We must understand their way of thinking, their aspirations, and their impressive accomplishments. We must observe their laws and follow their example of patience. We must deserve to be their friends."[16] In documenting early Latter-day Saint forays into the Chinese realm, this book is my modest response to Oaks's encouragement to "get to know China."

Finally, I feel it important to acknowledge that North American Latter-day Saints whose lives and quotes are presented here sometimes participated in the stereotyping of Asian people and their cultures. The racialized language and tropes they employed were all too common in their day. In more recent times, President Russell M. Nelson has called on church members to "lead out in abandoning attitudes and actions of prejudice" and "promote respect for all of God's children."[17]

Reid L. Neilson
Bountiful, Utah
Summer 2025

---

16. Dallin H. Oaks, "Getting to Know China," 100. For more on Oaks's involvement with the church and China, see Richard E. Turley Jr., *In the Hands of the Lord*, 213–14, 288–90.

17. Russell M. Nelson, "Let God Prevail," 94.

CHAPTER ONE

James Lewis and the Early China Mission in Hong Kong

"In 1852 I was called on a mission to China with Hosea Stout and Chapman Duncan," James Lewis reminisced late in life. "This was the great trial of my life, in poverty with three helpless children, another was expected any day. I felt my weakness like Sampson shorn of his locks, but my trust was in God my Heavenly Father."[1] Born in Maine on January 12, 1814, Lewis first heard of The Church of Jesus Christ of Latter-day Saints and the persecutions of its members after finding employment in Missouri in 1840. He believed in their teachings and was baptized and ordained an elder, an office in the church's priesthood, in February 1842 in Keokuk, Iowa.[2] In 1847, he married Emily Jennison Holman in St. Louis, Missouri.[3] He was one of the many Latter-day Saint pioneers who relocated to the West, traveling with the Silas Richards wagon company in 1849; a year later, he was sent to southern Utah to help in an effort to mine iron in Parowan.[4] When Iron County, Utah, was established, Lewis was nominated and elected as county recorder, and he also served as second lieutenant in the Iron County militia's cavalry company. A school was started in Parowan in 1851, and Lewis was listed in that year's census as a teacher.[5]

Leaving his young, pregnant wife and three (almost four) children behind in a pioneer settlement in southern Utah was just the beginning of Lewis's challenges as a Latter-day Saint missionary. Lewis and his companions were unable to effectively evangelize among the native Chinese, and the British and other expatriates stationed in Hong Kong would not accept their message. In addition, the foreign environment made it difficult for the missionaries to keep in good spirits. "The heat of the atmosphere was very oppressive. Being reduced in bad health, owing to change of diet,

1. James Lewis, "Autobiography of James Lewis," 3, Church History Library.

2. Lewis, "Autobiography of James Lewis," 2.

3. Lettie Young Swapp, "Biography of Emily Jennison Holman Lewis," 7, Church History Library.

4. Lewis, "Autobiography of James Lewis," 1–3.

5. Morris A. Shirts and Kathryn H. Shirts, *A Trial Furnace: Southern Utah's Iron Mission*, 35, 74, 78, and 107.

the manner of preparing it, &c., our spirits were, becoming depressed, and not perceiving a cheering ray of hope in all our labors," Lewis reminisced after returning home from China.[6] Despite the missionaries' lack of success in China, however, their mission was representative of the greater Latter-day Saint endeavor to spread the message of Christianity (Matt. 28:16–20) before the anticipated Second Coming of Jesus Christ, which they believed was soon.

The August 1852 Special Missionary Conference

When scholars of North American religion and historians of the American West think of mid-nineteenth-century Latter-day Saints, they often picture Joseph Smith, martyred and buried in Nauvoo, Illinois, and Brigham Young, his prophetic successor, leading the first group of Latter-day Saint pioneers to the Great Salt Lake Valley using ox-drawn wagons. The Mormon Exodus, numbering about seventy thousand pioneers over two decades, has become an American migration epic. But by 1852, just five years after Young, the "American Moses," led his fellow Latter-day Saints to begin settling the valleys of the Intermountain West, the global distribution of Latter-day Saints was actually much more European by birth than American.

Although the Latter-day Saints gathered the church's earliest years in New York, Ohio, Missouri, and Illinois, they imagined their religion becoming a global faith spreading far beyond the American borders. Since first evangelizing in England in 1837, Latter-day Saint missionaries had enjoyed tremendous conversion results in the region. In 1843, a year before his martyrdom, Smith charged members of the Quorum of the Twelve Apostles in Nauvoo, Illinois, saying, "Don't let a single corner of the earth go without a mission."[7] Before his death, he had called a handful of elders to evangelize in the nations of Australia, India, South America, Germany, Russia, Jamaica, and Tahiti; some fulfilled their missions while others did not. It would be left to these apostles, including Smith's successor, Brigham Young, to expand Latter-day Saint missionary work beyond the British Isles. They were responsible for personally leading the church's errand to the world in the ensuing decades. Between 1849

6. James Lewis to George A. Smith, December 12, 1854, reprinted as "Items of the China Mission," *Deseret News*, January 4, 1855.

7. Joseph Smith, History, vol. D-1, 1539; Joseph Smith, Journal, April 19, 1843, in Andrew H. Hedges et al., *Joseph Smith Papers, Journals, Volume 2*, 370.

and 1851, Young assigned Latter-day Saint leaders and laity to preach in Italy, France, Scandinavia, the Sandwich Islands, and Chile for the first time. "While most of these initial attempts had limited success, they do reveal that Brigham Young and his associates took very seriously the scriptural injunction to carry the gospel" to all the world, historian David J. Whittaker concludes.[8]

Latter-day Saint leaders and members alike kept busy divining the signs of the times during the middle of the nineteenth century. Consumed with millenarian fever, they were convinced that Christ's Second Coming was at the door. Not long after the first pioneers entered the Salt Lake Valley, political and social revolutions broke out in Europe, first in Sicily and then in France, Germany, Italy, and the Austrian Empire. These continental revolutions intensified the feeling that humankind was living on borrowed time. Alarmed church leaders debated where to send missionaries to raise the warning voice.[9] In a general epistle to the church in September 1851, Young and his counselors in the First Presidency referred to the revolutions exploding all across the globe and hinted that they might call missionaries soon to China and Japan, "which for ages have sat in darkness."[10]

By 1852, just fifteen years after the first Latter-day Saint apostles traveled to England, the 50,000-member American church had evolved into a largely British religious tradition. Its center of gravity, although not its headquarters, had shifted across the Atlantic Ocean to the potteries and industrial centers of the United Kingdom. That year there were at least 10,000 Latter-day Saints in the Utah Territory, and nearly 2,000 in the rest of North America; 32,500 in the British Isles and more than 1,600 in the rest of Europe, and 2,000 in other areas of the globe.[11]

The church's ongoing development into a transnational religious movement accelerated in the summer of 1852, when the First Presidency planned a special missionary conference in the newly constructed adobe Salt Lake Tabernacle on the temple block. Over the weekend of August 28–29, church leaders made two landmark announcements over the

---

8. See David J. Whittaker, "Brigham Young and the Missionary Enterprise," 90–91; and Reid L. Neilson and Nathan N. Waite, *Settling the Valley, Proclaiming the Gospel: The General Epistles of the Mormon First Presidency*, 114.

9. See Craig Livingston, "Eyes on 'The Whole European World': Mormon Observers of the 1848 Revolutions," 78–112.

10. "Sixth General Epistle of the Presidency of the Church of Jesus Christ of Latter-day Saints," *Millennial Star* 14, no. 2 (January 15, 1852): 17–18, 25.

11. Brandon Plewe, "State of the Church in 1852," 234–36.

Brigham Young was the president of The Church of Jesus Christ of Latter-day Saints who called several missionaries to China in 1852. Ambrotype taken in 1850 by Marsena Cannon. Courtesy Utah State Historical Society.

pioneer pulpit: a flurry of global mission assignments[12] and a spirited defense of plural marriage.[13]

The timing of this unprecedented evangelism conference was strategic: by holding it in the summer heat, the First Presidency would be giving the newly called missionaries time to travel over the mountain passes to the west and east before the winter snows limited their travels.[14] During the Saturday afternoon session, the First Presidency assigned about one hundred Latter-day Saint men to evangelize in distant lands, the largest cohort of full-time missionaries in the church's three-decade history.[15] Elders were called to labor in the European nations of Ireland, Wales, France, Germany, Berlin, Norway, Denmark, and Gibraltar; in Cape of Good Hope, Africa; in North America, specifically Nova Scotia, the West Indies, British Guiana, Texas, New Orleans, St.

---

12. See Reid L. Neilson and R. Mark Melville, *The Saints Abroad: Missionaries Who Answered Brigham Young's 1852 Call to the Nations of the World.*

13. Peter Crawley, *Descriptive Bibliography of the Mormon Church, Volume Two*, 354–57. See David J. Whittaker, "The Bone in the Throat: Orson Pratt and the Public Announcement of Plural Marriage," 293–314; Kathryn M. Daynes, *More Wives Than One: Transformation of the Mormon Marriage System, 1840–1910*; and Sarah Barringer Gordon, *The Mormon Question: Polygamy and Constitutional Conflict in Nineteenth-Century America*, 22–23.

14. Church leaders also held their regular fall general conference meetings on October 6–8, 1852. See "Minutes of the General Conference . . . ," *Deseret News*, October 16, 1852.

15. *Minutes of Conference* was initially published as a *Deseret News* extra in Salt Lake City, Utah, on September 14, 1852. Ten days earlier, the first newspaper mention of the historic gathering was printed: "The Special Conference," *Deseret News*, September 4, 1852. The initial "extra" was republished in a regular newspaper edition as "Minutes of Conference," *Deseret News*, September 18, 1852, about three weeks after the event.

Louis, Iowa, and Washington, DC; and in the isles of the Pacific, namely Australia and the Sandwich (Hawaiian) Islands. Church leaders also assigned a number of men to commence missionary work in the Asian nations of Hindustan (India), Siam (Thailand), and China.[16]

Latter-day Saint men were startled to learn that they had been called to preach in distant lands far across the ocean, and their wives and children were just as surprised. James Lewis was assigned to China that August with three other elders—Hosea Stout,[17] Chapman Duncan,[18] and Walter Thomson[19] (who was called shortly after the conference)—and all were as shocked about their East Asian assignment as the other newly called

16. For a biographical register of all missionaries called in the August 1852 special conference, see Neilson and Melville, *The Saints Abroad*, 317–62.

17. Hosea Stout (1810–1889). Born September 18, 1810, in Mercer Co., Kentucky; son of Joseph Stout and Anna Smith. Married Samantha Peck, January 7, 1838. Baptized in Caldwell Co., Missouri, August 24, 1838. Wife died, November 29, 1839. Appointed clerk of high council in Nauvoo, Hancock Co., Illinois, March 8, 1840. Married Louisa Taylor, November 29, 1840. Participated in plural marriage. Elected colonel of fifth regiment, second cohort in Nauvoo Legion, June 23, 1843. Selected as chief of police in Nauvoo by October 1844. Ordained an elder, October 4, 1844. Ordained a president of eleventh quorum of the seventy, October 8, 1844. Migrated with Brigham Young company to Great Salt Lake Valley, arriving September 23, 1848. Appointed attorney general of the provisional state of Deseret by March 1850. Served mission to China, 1852–53; wife and infant son died, January 1853. Neilson and Melville, *The Saints Abroad*, 357.

18. Chapman Duncan (1812–1900). Born July 1, 1812, in Barnet, Caledonia Co., Vermont, or Bath, Grafton Co., New Hampshire; son of John Duncan and Betsy Taylor Putnam. Baptized in Jackson Co., Missouri, December 1832. Married Rebecca Rose, May 1835. Participated in plural marriage. Appointed to serve mission to Virginia, April 1844. Appointed to second quorum of the seventy, October 8, 1844. Migrated to Great Salt Lake Valley in Willard Richards company, arriving October 17, 1848. Served mission to China, 1852–53. Neilson and Melville, *The Saints Abroad*, 327.

19. Walter Thomson (1825–1877). Born August 10, 1825, in Barony, Glasgow, Scotland; son of John Thomson and Margaret Thomson. Baptized January 4, 1841. Married Agnes Ross in Rowe, Dunbarton, Scotland, November 13, 1847. Served as clerk of Glasgow conference, 1849–50. Emigrated with wife and two children from Liverpool, England, arriving in New Orleans, Louisiana, March 20, 1851. Migrated to the Great Salt Lake Valley in Morris Phelps company, arriving September 26–October 1, 1851. Ordained a seventy, February 22, 1852. Called on mission to China, but fell ill and stayed in California, 1852–53. Neilson and Melville, *The Saints Abroad*, 358.

Hosea Stout was one of several men called by Brigham Young as a missionary to China in 1852. Courtesy Utah State Historical Society.

missionaries were at theirs. "Today was the Special Conference held for the purpose of sending Elders abroad. There was about 80 or 90 chosen to day to go forth to different parts of the world," Stout noted in his diary. (The total number called was 108.) "Myself, James Lewis, Walter Thompson [*sic*], and Chapman Duncan were chosen to go to China. The brethren who were chosen all manifest a good spirit and seem to have the spirit of their Calling."[20] Duncan, another seasoned pioneer, had faced mob violence in Missouri in the 1830s, and like Stout, he had traveled in Utah in 1848.[21] Thomson, on the other hand, had only arrived in Utah from his native Scotland a year before. Lewis and Duncan were both living in the southern Utah settlement of Parowan and were not at the conference.[22] The four men had families to worry about, and Lewis and Stout both had a child on the way.[23] Nevertheless, these called-upon men were willing to serve as missionaries to China.[24] "That was the way things happened in Utah. You could be an

20. Hosea Stout, Diary, August 28, 1852, Church History Library.

21. Chapman Duncan, "Biography of Chapman Duncan," 3–11, 31–40, Church History Library.

22. James Lewis had been a county recorder, and Chapman Duncan had been serving as a tithing clerk in Parowan. Elijah Elmer arrived in Parowan on September 12 from Salt Lake with news that they were going on missions. Donald G. Godfrey and Rebecca S. Martineau-McCarty, *An Uncommon Common Pioneer: The Journals of James Henry Martineau, 1828–1918*, 18; Henry Lunt, "Life of Henry Lunt and Family, Together with a Portion of His Journal," 54; and Shirts and Shirts, *Trial Furnace*, 74, 244.

23. Swapp, "Biography of Emily Jennison Holman Lewis," 9.

24. Though Walter Thomson was unable to join these three missionaries in Hong Kong, he served in the British Mission in 1875. He worked as recorder in Weber County, Utah, where he died in 1877. Neilson and Melville, *The Saints Abroad*, 358.

ordinary man," historian Laurel Thatcher Ulrich explains, "then, all of a sudden, you were sent off to save the world."[25]

The following day, August 29, Elder Orson Pratt openly acknowledged and defended the Latter-day Saint practice of plural marriage for the first time in the church's history. The unconventional marital arrangement had been instituted by Joseph Smith more than a decade earlier and was conducted with increasing openness by Latter-day Saint men and women in the intervening years. Though polygamy in Utah was no secret to the nation, the church's candid admission helped ratchet up tension that would lead to conflict with the United States government for more than fifty years. "From then on, Church leaders publicly endorsed the practice as a fundamental, even defining, aspect of Mormonism and integrated the practice into a broader vision of Mormon political philosophy," historian Christine Talbot argues. "The open practice of plural marriage added new dimensions to Mormon doctrine that, combined with earlier controversies, produced an insurmountable distance between Mormon and white middle-class Protestant Americans."[26] The doctrine's public promulgation would also present long-term challenges to Latter-day Saint elders called to preach during the second half of the nineteenth century—a painful theme that emerged often in their personal letters and subsequent narratives, including the writings of those assigned to China.[27]

The 1852 global missionary assignments came at a tenuous time, while the Latter-day Saint pioneers were barely surviving in their desolate Great Basin kingdom.[28] Limited financial and human resources, coupled with competing institutional projects, required church leaders to make seemingly impossible decisions. The question of how to fulfill their divine mandate to "build Zion" at home and to "warn the nations" abroad, while at the same time meeting the temporal and spiritual needs of the Saints and building temples to provide eternal blessings to the living and dead, weighed heavily on the hearts of church leaders settled in the Great Salt Lake Valley. It would be an ongoing tension throughout the pioneer period.[29] "Missionaries were expanding the work worldwide, opening one new

---

25. Laurel Thatcher Ulrich, *A House Full of Females: Plural Marriage and Women's Rights in Early Mormonism, 1835–1870*, 239.

26. Christine Talbot, *Foreign Kingdom: Mormons and Polygamy in American Political Culture, 1852–1890*, 33.

27. See Ulrich, *House Full of Females*, ch. 10.

28. Neilson and Waite, *Settling the Valley, Proclaiming the Gospel*, 11–13.

29. Neilson and Waite, 1–31.

land after another, although long-term efforts were gradually focusing on a few fruitful countries," historical cartographer Brandon Plewe explains.[30]

Brigham Young and his fellow Latter-day Saint leaders counseled together to find the proper balance between their church's colonization and evangelization programs. These two represented competing but also complementary priorities. Converts baptized through missionary work would gather with their families to Zion, bringing with them the means to help colonize Utah and aid their fellow pioneer Saints. These new immigrants could later serve as missionaries themselves, often in their former homelands, and convert others, ensuring that there was always a growing number of settlers at home and missionaries abroad. Prioritizing temporal and spiritual imperatives with limited human and financial resources required the wisdom of biblical Solomon. Any adult man they assigned to help settle the Latter-day Saint villages springing up throughout the Intermountain West meant one less missionary they could send abroad to teach and gather new converts to Zion. The Latter-day Saints considered anyone who had not received baptism under proper priesthood authority, at home or abroad, among those needing salvation. Young's calling of over one hundred men in August 1852 to win converts across the globe exemplifies the Latter-day Saint missionary impulse.

The Nineteenth-Century Church and the Pacific Basin Frontier

The Latter-day Saints established their new church headquarters in pioneer Utah Territory, but in the Pacific they were moving around on a regular basis, interacting with native peoples, European and American merchants and missionaries, and voyagers from East Asia.[31] This was especially true in the early nineteenth century, a time of US–Pacific trade expansion when the imperial competition for ports and local loyalties was fiercely competitive. A close look at the early growth and development of the Latter-day Saints and their activities in the Pacific world reveals a great deal about the early history of the church as well as wider historical trends.[32]

30. Plewe, "State of the Church in 1852," 243.

31. See Laurie F. Maffly-Kipp and Reid L. Neilson, *Proclamation to the People: Nineteenth-Century Mormonism and the Pacific Basin Frontier*.

32. For bibliographies on the Latter-day Saints in the Pacific world, see James B. Allen, Ronald W. Walker, and David J. Whittaker, *Studies in Mormon History, 1830–1997: An Indexed Bibliography*; David J. Whitaker, "Mormon Missiology:

In principle, the church was to be a global religious tradition, a message for all. In reality, the church's missionary program unfolded fitfully during the nineteenth century, especially in the Pacific Basin frontier. Much of the uneven nineteenth-century missionary deployment was due to Latter-day Saint racial and theological attitudes as well as logistical constraints. While American Protestants evangelized almost exclusively in non-Christian, non-Western nations, the Latter-day Saints focused their resources on the Christian, North Atlantic world. Between 1830 and 1899, church leaders called and set apart more than 12,000 full-time missionaries. Specifically, they assigned 6,444 church members (53 percent) to evangelize throughout the United States and Canada and designated 4,798 (40 percent) to missionize in Europe, concentrating on Great Britain and Scandinavia. Church authorities sent the remaining 803 elders and sisters (7 percent) to the peoples of the Pacific. Of these, they allocated less than 1 percent of their missionary force to Asia. Aside from Africa, no other inhabited continent received fewer resources from early Latter-day Saint leaders.[33] In short, they allocated not even a tithe of their missionaries to the Pacific Basin frontier during the nineteenth century.[34]

A few Latter-day Saints began evangelizing in Australia and French Polynesia during the early 1840s, and in a March 1849 letter to church members, apostles Parley P. Pratt and Franklin D. Richards noted that one elder had returned the previous October from evangelizing in the South Pacific and noted that there were already twelve hundred Pacific Islander Latter-day Saints. The same letter announced Pratt's intention to lead a fresh Latter-day Saint charge into the Pacific world, attempting to establish additional Latter-day Saint outposts in the Pacific, including one in the Pacific Rim nations: "Parley P. Pratt may accompany them to the Islands

---

An Introduction and Guide to the Sources," 507–17; Grant Underwood, "Latter-day Saints in the Pacific: A Bibliographic Essay," 293–305; Russell T. Clement, *Mormons in the Pacific: A Bibliography*; Reid L. Neilson, "Mormonism and the Japanese: A Guide to the Sources," 435–44; Robert H. Slover II, "Resources in the Church Historian's Office Relating to Asia," 107–18; and Kahlile B. Mehr, Mark L. Grover, Reid L. Neilson, Donald Q. Cannon, and Grant Underwood, "Growth and Internationalization: The LDS Church Since 1945," 199–228.

33. The exception was South Africa, where missionaries evangelized among the white population. See Armand L. Mauss, *All Abraham's Children: Changing Mormon Conceptions of Race and Lineage*, 212–66, for an explanation of the reasons why the Latter-day Saints traditionally avoided Black Africa.

34. Gordon Irving, *Numerical Strength and Geographical Distribution of the LDS Missionary Force, 1830–1974*, 9–15.

or to Chili [*sic*] with a view to establish the Gospel in South America, Australia, New Zealand, China, Japan, the various groups of the Pacific Islands, or to each or either of these places as the way may open up."[35] Brigham Young championed sending elders to southern and southeastern Asia during the 1850s, and when the First Presidency established the Pacific Mission in 1851, they called Pratt as the mission's first president.

By the spring of 1851, Pratt was in Pacific missionary mode. "I left Great Salt Lake City for the Pacific, on a mission to its islands and coasts," he recalled in his autobiography. After traveling down the Southern Route (Old Spanish Trail) through Las Vegas to the port of San Pedro and up the California coast to San Francisco, where he set up mission headquarters, Pratt penned a letter to one of the missionaries already serving in French Polynesia. "Eight of us are here, and will go to the Sandwich Islands and elsewhere as the way opens and the Spirit directs. . . . Several young men are with me who will go to Chile and Peru in due time. Bishop Murdock will also go soon to the English Colonies in New Zealand, Van Dieman's Land, or New Holland, if the Lord will."[36] The apostle subsequently authored a pamphlet—*Proclamation! To the People of the Coasts and Islands of the Pacific; of Every Nation, Kindred and Tongue*—addressed to Christians, Jews, and pagans, or "those who are not Christians, but who worship the various Gods of India, China, Japan, or the Islands of the Pacific or Indian Oceans," making clear the expansive scope of his evangelical undertaking.[37] Although Pratt exhibited interest in spreading the gospel to the nations of China and Japan, he was never personally involved in assigning missionaries to any Asian lands.[38]

It is clear from Pratt's personal writings that he envisioned his church's Pacific Mission encompassing the nations and peoples of the entire Pacific

---

35. Parley P. Pratt and Franklin D. Richards to Orson Pratt, March 9, 1849, reprinted as "An Epistle of the Twelve to President Orson Pratt, and the Church of Jesus Christ of Latter-day Saints in the British Isles," *Millennial Star* 11, no. 16 (August 15, 1849): 246–47.

36. Parley P. Pratt, *Autobiography of Parley P. Pratt*, 343, 354–55. See also David J. Whittaker, "Parley P. Pratt and the Pacific Mission: Mormon Publishing in 'That Very Questionable Part of the Civilized World,'" 58–59.

37. Parley P. Pratt, *The Essential Parley P. Pratt*, 152, 156.

38. See A. Delbert Palmer and Mark L. Grover, "Hoping to Establish a Presence: Parley P. Pratt's 1851 Mission to Chile," 115–38; and Matthew J. Grow, "A Providential Means of Agitating Mormonism: Parley P. Pratt and the San Francisco Press in the 1850s," 158–85.

Basin. During his two terms as mission president, which spanned the years between 1851 and 1855, Pratt oversaw the continued expansion of the church in the Americas, Polynesia, and Australasia. Interestingly enough, Pratt never ventured far beyond the California coast, with the notable exception of his fact-finding mission to Chile in 1851. But his legacy and promotion of the enterprise had a significant impact well beyond his tenure as Pacific Mission president. He provided the inspiration and institutional imprimatur for the dozens of other missionaries who crisscrossed the Pacific on behalf of the church, before he was murdered in 1857.

Departure for the Pacific Basin Frontier

After the August 1852 missionary conference, James Lewis, Hosea Stout, Chapman Duncan, and Walter Thomson began preparations to leave for China. Of the 108 men called to the mission field at the August 1852 church gathering, thirteen others were assigned to labor in Asia—nine in India and four in Siam. The elders were given two months to get their affairs in order, and before departing, they were given priesthood blessings to fulfill their new missionary assignments by apostles who promised evangelistic success in the months and years ahead.[39] In late October 1852, the four missionaries bound for China joined the other elders called to the Pacific Basin frontier, South Asia, and South America and began their journey.[40]

---

39. Stout, Diary, October 16, 1852.

40. Thirty-eight elders set out together for the Pacific ports of California to reach their assigned missionary fields: *China* (Hong Kong): Hosea Stout, James Lewis, Chapman Duncan, and Walter Thomson; *Hindoostan* (India): Nathaniel Vary Jones, Amos Milton Musser, Samuel Amos Woolley, Richard Ballantyne, Robert Hodgson Skelton, William Fotheringham, William Furlsbury Carter, Truman Leonard, and Robert Owens; *Siam* (Thailand): Chauncey Walker West, Sterne Lawrence Hotchkiss, Elam Luddington, Levi Savage Jr., Benjamin Franklin Dewey; *Australia*: Augustus Alvin Farnham, William Hyde, Burr Frost, John Hyde, Josiah Wolcott Fleming, Paul Smith, James Graham, John Sunderlin Eldredge, Absalom Porter Dowdle, and John Warren Norton; and the *Sandwich Islands* (Hawaii): William McBride, Ephraim Green, Edgerton Snider, James Lawson, Thomas Karren, Nathan Tanner, Redick Newton Allred, Reddin Alexander Allred, Benjamin Franklin Johnson. For biographical sketches of these missionaries see "Appendix 2: Missionaries Called in the August 1852 Special Conference," in Neilson and Melville, *The Saints Abroad*, 317–62.

The company followed the Southern Route or wagon road (roughly modern-day Interstate 15) from Salt Lake City through the fledgling settlement of Parowan and the springs of Las Vegas and southward to the Latter-day Saint colony of San Bernardino, California, where they arrived exhausted and famished on December 3. "The elders were happy to see once again a well-organized community of Saints. San Bernardino was a thriving community surrounded by many acres of rich and fertile farmland," historian R. Lanier Britsch describes. "Church members there were very kind to the missionaries; they took them into their homes, fed them, and gave them every comfort they could provide. For twelve days the group rested and wrote letters home."[41] The missionaries also sold their wagons and horses and sent the proceeds to their destitute families back in Utah, thus "starting without purse or scrip as did the Apostles of Christ, to preach the restoration of the Gospel through the Prophet Joseph Smith," in Lewis's words.[42] The San Bernardino Saints also donated money to help pay for the elders' eventual passage to their mission fields.

The group of about forty missionaries then made their way to Los Angeles and the neighboring Pacific port of San Pedro by early January 1853, where they secured passage on a ship north up the California coast to San Francisco. Unfortunately, Walter Thomson became ill and was unable to join his three companions any further on their mission to China. James Lewis wrote to apostle George A. Smith in Utah that he and the rest of the missionaries arrived in San Francisco in mid-January "after a short sojourn at San Bernardino, in good health and spirits." He then noted how the various smaller groups of missionaries secured passage on vessels that would take them to India, Siam, the Sandwich Islands, and Australia.[43]

Two elders in this traveling company—James Brown and Elijah Thomas—were assigned to *British Guiana* (Guyana) on the northern Caribbean coast of South America. They joined this group of missionaries heading to San Bernardino, California, before traveling further south for the port of San Diego. There they boarded a ship bound for the Isthmus of Panama, which they crossed to reach their mission field in the British colony bordered by Venezuela and Brazil. "The Gospel in the United States, &c.," *Millennial Star* 15, no. 14 (April 2, 1853): 216–17.

41. R. Lanier Britsch, *From the East: The History of the Latter-day Saints in Asia, 1851–1996*, 14–15.

42. Lewis, "Autobiography of James Lewis," 3.

43. James Lewis to *Deseret News*, February 28, 1853, reprinted as "Elders Correspondence," *Deseret News*, April 30, 1853.

In his letter from San Francisco to the apostle in Salt Lake City, Lewis further shared his limited understanding of an ongoing political and military rebellion then consuming China and the positive influence he mistakenly anticipated it would have on their forthcoming evangelism in East Asia. "The China missionaries will leave March 1st [1853] for Hong Kong, and from information from that country, the way seems opening for the Gospel by the revolutions which are going on in some of the districts, overthrowing idolatry and establishing the belief in God," Lewis wrote.

> This is going on independent of any missionary effort, and the results are in the future relative to the good it may produce to that people, and I judge with some degree of certainty that the Lord is preparing the way for the fullness of the Gospel to go forth among this strange, and till within a few years, comparatively unknown people. If ever there was a time, since the rise of this church, for the saints to rejoice, 'tis the present; for we realize the rapid spread of the gospel in all lands, whither the Elders have been sent; and although the powers of evil keep pace with the truth, yet the onward march of the power and work of God is felt in almost every land and clime beneath the sun.[44]

However, within months of landing in Hong Kong, Lewis and his companions would better appreciate the negative impact of political revolution in China and how it would help to thwart their evangelistic ambitions in China.

Lewis and his fellow China-bound missionaries remained in San Francisco nearly two months, preparing and fundraising for the passage to Hong Kong. They would be the final group to begin their Pacific voyage to their mission assignments. Compared to San Bernardino, there was not as strong a Latter-day Saint presence in the Bay Area. Some Saints had arrived in San Francisco in 1846 onboard the *Brooklyn* and helped build up the town, but most of them left in 1848 for Utah just as the California Gold Rush began. Beginning in 1849, thousands of Chinese immigrants arrived in San Francisco to work in the gold mines and elsewhere, inhabiting the communities that had previously been home to many Latter-day Saints. Twenty thousand Chinese arrived in 1852, and sixteen thousand arrived in 1854, but after that the number of immigrants decreased to a few thousand per year until the late 1860s.[45]

---

44. James Lewis to *Deseret News*, February 28, 1853.

45. William E. Homer, "San Francisco, California," in *Encyclopedia of Latter-day Saint History*, 1066–67; and Thomas W. Chinn, ed., *History of the Chinese in California: A Syllabus*, 22.

Not surprisingly, Lewis described these Chinese immigrants and their growing Chinatown in San Francisco to church leaders in Utah: "In California there are about 75,000 Chinamen, generally in San Francisco and the mines. They are called the best cooks, washers, and servants in that country. They are capable of performing, and enduring more labor and fatigue than any other people in that land;—have no spirit to retaliate for the many insults and injuries they receive." Lewis further described to Elder George A. Smith:

> In San Francisco whole streets are occupied by them. They have their own hotel keepers, wholesale and retail merchants, grocers, and physicians. In fact they do their own business, independent of others. After obtaining sufficient to make them independent at home, they usually return. They take little or no notice of strangers, only when for their interest; are greatly addicted to gambling, and have gaming establishments and houses of prostitution publicly open day and night, like their neighbors. Thousands of women are brought from China to this market, hired by the more wealthy of their own countrymen, for ten, and often three dollars per head for each year. On any money advanced for outfit or passage, if not paid the first year, it doubles the second on principal and interest. Young females of from 14 to 16, as well as children, are bought in China at from 30$ to 50$ each, and brought to California to swell the already enormous amount of crime, prostitution, degradation, and corruption.[46]

While waiting in San Francisco, Lewis and his companions tried to learn more about the Chinese people, their language, culture, and religion in preparation for their coming missionary labors in Hong Kong. "I visited many of their leading men, to ascertain if possible, the situation of their country, and gather books, to forward the work in which I was engaged; but I found they were not disposed to give any information, and seemed surprised that we were desirous of knowing anything about them, tho' few could speak English so as to be understood." Lewis sympathized with the plight of the immigrant Chinese who were poorly treated by many of the white residents in the city. "I found the Chinese in California with a prejudice of feeling," he wrote, "caused by their ill treatment from its citizens, which is not confined to miners, but includes their legislators. They are traduced, vilified, and abused on every hand. Yet they thrive, increase, and will ere long wield a powerful influence, particularly relating

---

46. James Lewis to George A. Smith, June 3, 1854, reprinted as "Chinese in California," *Deseret News*, June 22, 1854.

to trade." Despite their different culture and lifestyles, the Latter-day Saint elder found the Chinese people to be intelligent and morally advanced.[47]

Finally, on March 9, 1853, weeks after the other missionaries departed for their Pacific Basin mission fields, Lewis and his companions boarded the *Jan Van Hoorn*, a Dutch bark. Their transpacific voyage to Hong Kong had begun.[48]

Arrival in Hong Kong

After about fifty days at sea, the Latter-day Saint missionaries' ship entered the Victoria Harbor, which separates Hong Kong Island and the Kowloon Peninsula on the South China Sea. The city was scarcely a decade old, having been established in 1841 by Great Britain as a strategic overseas colony following the First Opium War. For decades China had been the main supplier of tea to British consumers, which created an unsustainable trade deficit. The British determined to offset this imbalance in commerce by exporting addictive opium to the Chinese, which they produced in their poppy fields in India. The Chinese then countered the devastating effects of the opium trade by destroying the British's inventory stored in Canton. This conflict led to the British establishing Hong Kong as an offshore colony, which would provide a strategic location to continue to oversee military and economic activities in southern China. Finally, in June 1843, the Chinese government allowed foreigners to engage in open trade at five of their ports on coastline of the South China Sea and relinquished control of Hong Kong to the British (which would remain in their possession until 1997).[49]

In the three decades previous to the foreign trade wars with China in the early 1840s, Christian missionaries had established a foothold in China, especially Canton. Protestant evangelists from America and England had begun learning Chinese and establishing Christian schools and hospitals, which resulted in the conversions of some of their East Asian associates. These same missionaries benefited from the treaties of 1842 and 1844 with the Chinese government, which allowed greater privileges for their religious work. "The Protestants, although confined almost exclusively to Hong Kong and the five treaty ports, were preparing for further expansion by producing literature, experimenting with

47. James Lewis to George A. Smith, June 3, 1854,.

48. Stout, Diary, March 2 and 9, 1853.

49. Stephen L. Prince, *Hosea Stout: Lawman, Legislature, Mormon Defender*, 205.

missionary methods, and acquiring a body of foreign agents trained in the language and experienced in the customs of the country," describes missiologist Kenneth Scott Latourette of the mid-nineteenth century in China, including Hong Kong. "The Protestant communities, while totaling only a few hundred, were increasing rapidly. Starting from such small beginnings, Protestants were making proportionally a more rapid growth than were the Catholics." But they were still operating on the margins of Chinese society and limited in their scope of activities. They did not have full flexibility to penetrate into mainland China with their Christian message, instead being circumscribed to the treaty port cities. "For more than a generation missionaries were to face the opposition of a political, intellectual, social, and religious structure which seemingly had in it no room either for them or for their message," Latourette concludes.[50]

The Latter-day Saint missionaries arrived in East Asia during this challenging era for western Christians and their religious enthusiasm. "We landed at Hong Kong on the 28th of April, having arrived in the harbor the day before," James Lewis wrote of their arrival in East Asia. "After considerable search, we found a room to occupy which had formerly been used for stowing treasure, double barred and bolts, with privilege of eating with the owner, at the rate of one dollar per day each. This being the only chance, our luggage was moved ashore." Like his fellow missionaries, Lewis was intrigued by the sights and scenery of the Chinese settlement: "The harbor seems little more than an open roadstead, where vessels remain a short time and proceed up the river to Canton, which is 90 miles from this point. From the harbor the city presents quite a handsome appearance, as it is situated at the base of a high mountain, which protects it from a strong southwest wind which prevails the most of the year."[51]

But Lewis was unimpressed by the Chinese grifters who greeted their ship and tried to take advantage of the newcomers, reporting, "Upon our arrival, the vessel was immediately covered with Chinese either for one pretense or another, designing, however, to steal everything they could carry away, for they have the character of being the most skillful thieves in the world, or at least a portion of them." He also noted the value of Hong Kong to the British government and military. "This place is of considerable importance in many respects. The island was ceded to the English

50. Kenneth Scott Latourette, *A History of Christian Missions in China*, 226–27, 270.

51. James Lewis to George A. Smith, November 25, 1854, reprinted as "Chinese Mission," *Deseret News*, December 14, 1854.

at the time peace was ratified after the war. Here is the residence of the governor general of China, and is the great military post in China, and is the terminus of the line of steamers which bring the overland mail from the home government, monthly."[52] He wrote in the same letter that he saw a copy of the *New York Herald* in Hong Kong just twenty-nine days after it was published in New York City, on the other side of the globe.

Lewis also noted the military presence of British soldiers in Victoria, the de facto capital of Hong Kong during the British colonial period. "Here are quartered about 1,000 or 1,200 troops of the lower order of English regiments made up of Irish and Scotch, though mostly Irish, with a regiment from the island of Ceylon (blacks). Owing to the heat of the climate, they are only allowed out of barracks in the evening from six to eight o'clock, when they throng the places of prostitution, made so easy of access by license from authority," Lewis described in a letter. "The city of Hong Kong has probably 10,000 inhabitants of a motley mixture of all nations; of these, it is said, 6,000 are licensed prostitutes. There are about 250 English aside from the troops stationed here; they are the aristocratic nabobs, who reside in that country to make a fortune, and retire from business as soon as this is accomplished."[53]

The Utah missionaries spent the next few days securing lodging and feeling overwhelmed by the high rents they encountered. "We found that unless a man had wherewith to pay his way at quite a high price, he could have the exquisite pleasure of starving," Lewis explained. The missionaries were grateful for the offer by British resident George Dudell, who agreed to let them live rent free for up to three months. Lewis continued, "Our room was in the third story of an old decayed mansion, a portion of which had fallen down; but, as this was our only chance, we felt quite at home after our removal."[54] Soon they moved to complimentary rooms at the Canton Bazaar in Victoria, where they hired a Chinese servant to help with their domestic duties.[55]

With their room and board secured for the time being, Lewis and his companions determined to commence missionary work among the residents of Hong Kong. "The next business was to find a place to preach; after trying, we found our only chance was the street. Previous to this, we had visited the American consul, Mr. Anthony, who treated

52. James Lewis to George A. Smith, November 25, 1854.
53. James Lewis to George A. Smith, November 25, 1854.
54. James Lewis to George A. Smith, December 12, 1854.
55. Stout, Diary, May 4 and 5, 1853.

us respectfully, saying he knew our principles, and presumed we should have poor success in China," Lewis wrote. "Yet he would extend to us all the protection he could; thought we should not be molested, should have to preach in the streets; did not seem to desire we should renew our visit. We visited a number of clergymen of the Baptist and Methodist order, but aside from courtesy it was a mere blank. Our only dependance was in the God of Israel, who sent us; for, thus far, nothing presented any encouragement."[56] During the rest of May, the elders held a series of public preaching meetings in Hong Kong, which elicited little interest from the British or Chinese residents.

On May 16, 1853, James Lewis and his companions wrote to church president Brigham Young seeking advice: "Do not feel that we are discouraged or cast down, for we only want the proper element to act on to assure success. The people are remarkably friendly and courteous, but care nothing for religion or missionary activities. We long to hear from you, to receive comfort and counsel."[57] But they knew that they would not receive a response from their prophet in Salt Lake City for many months, given the primitive state of pioneer mail to and from Utah. By early June, just weeks later, the elders lost hope of any missionary success in Hong Kong. "Paul-like we can truly say that the spirit speaketh expressly, that we preach the gospel no more in Asia for the present," Hosea Stout lamented in his diary, paraphrasing the ancient apostle's words found in Acts 16:6. The elders planned to return to California, where they hoped to "await the orders of the First Presidency, and the dictates of the Holy Spirit to yet learn by what means the Lord will open, to introduce the gospel successfully in this benighted land."[58]

Early Latter-day Saint Evangelistic Practices in South and East Asia

Across South and Southeast Asia, the handful of Latter-day Saints assigned in 1852 struggled in their missionary efforts before abandoning their foreign posts. Their evangelizing practices did not meet the expectations of the Indians and other Asians they encountered, who often hoped to benefit financially from their association with Westerners. The elders

56. James Lewis to George A. Smith, December 12, 1854.

57. Hosea Stout to Brigham Young, May 16, 1853, Brigham Young Office Files, Church History Library.

58. Stout, Diary, June 9, 1853.

also lacked the necessary language skills to work among the non-English-speaking masses outside of the British cantonments. Unlike their counterparts in North America and Western Europe, who relied on the financial generosity of church members and strangers in their mission fields, the Latter-day Saint elders in India, Siam, and Burma found the people destitute and philosophically unwilling to underwrite their missionary endeavors. These missionaries also suffered from pitiable living conditions, sickness, inadequate medical care, and lack of transportation. In all, they converted only about seventy people, many of them expatriate Europeans, before returning to Utah within a few years.[59]

The missionaries assigned to China were even less successful. James Lewis, Hosea Stout, and Chapman Duncan arrived in Hong Kong during the Taiping Rebellion, a Chinese civil war that lasted from 1850 until 1864 on mainland China.[60] The conflict originated with a Chinese man named Hong Xiuquan, who had read some tracts left by Christian missionaries and had a vision that led him to believe he was the younger brother of Jesus Christ. Hong established a religious community, the Taiping Tianguo, that forbade opium and alcohol and that pooled all resources into a community fund. He and his followers, known as God worshippers, spread throughout southeast China, preaching their unique form of Christianity, combating Confucian ideas, and seeking to overthrow the Qing dynasty. Western societies initially favored the idea of a Christian group overthrowing Chinese traditions, but they became less enthusiastic when they observed the eccentricities of the Taiping group. The Taiping Rebellion ended in 1864 with the death of Hong Xiuquan.[61]

Lewis explained his understanding of the political and military situation in his letter to apostle George A. Smith:

> The present revolution is to throw off the Tartar yoke, and return to the religion of their Fathers, (however upon this point there is much speculation.) Yet it is confidently asserted that the present leader of the rebel party claims to be inspired by his Father, (the Almighty) with revelation to rid his

59. Britsch, *From the East*, 8–42.

60. Jonathan D. Spence, *The Search for Modern China*, 171–80. See also Thomas H. Reilly, *The Taiping Heavenly Kingdom: Rebellion and the Blasphemy of Empire*.

61. Spence, *The Search for Modern China*, 171–80.

> country of the Tartars; and it is reported by the missionaries that he believes in visions, dreams, &c.[62]

In a letter to Brigham Young, Hosea Stout described the missionaries' precarious political situation: "The foreigners in Shanghai have formed themselves into an armed neutrality to be ready for the worst—not knowing what may happen. There is a great deal of excitement in all the trading posts. The troops here are held in readiness to act as occasion requires." Even though American warships had arrived in the East China Sea, the missionary from Utah judged China "in a state of excitement, very unsafe to penetrate to the interior." The same went for other foreign settlement ports dotting the East and South China Sea.[63] To make matters worse, Hong Kong's natural climate added to the elders' discouragement. Unaccustomed to the sticky humidity, scorching temperatures, and heavy rains, the elders found it difficult to hold outdoor meetings.[64]

Furthermore, the Latter-day Saint elders' attempt to impose the church's routine "Euro-American missionary model"[65] proved disastrous. The church's 1853 foray into Hong Kong helps historians better appreciate why the normative Latter-day Saint approach was so poorly suited to evangelize non-Christian, non-Western peoples. Moreover, its struggles help historians see why the later Japan Mission would likewise flounder. The early Asian missions struggled to engage their Eastern audiences, leading church leaders to eventually shutter both operations. So how did three major components of the missionary model—missionary training, financial arrangements, and evangelistic practices—affect the outcome of the early mission to Hong Kong?

The Latter-day Saint elders called to China in August 1852 were expected to evangelize the Chinese without any missionary preparation. These men were farming in their fields in Utah one day and designated as their church's official representatives to the world's most populous nation the next. They learned of their missionary assignments to China at the same time as—or later than—everyone attending the church conference. Although the missionaries may have been enthusiastic while in Utah, the trio's evangelistic zeal dissipated once they arrived in China. This was seemingly due to their lack of preparation for extended missionary life

62. James Lewis to George A. Smith, February 16, 1855, reprinted as "China Mission," *Deseret News*, March 14, 1855.

63. Hosea Stout to Brigham Young, May 16, 1853.

64. James Lewis to George A. Smith, December 12, 1854.

65. See Reid L. Neilson, *Early Mormon Missionary Activities in Japan*, ch. 3.

in Asia. When the elders sailed into the Hong Kong harbor, they were struck by the foreignness of their new environment. "We arrived all well, in a strange land and among strange people," Lewis recounted. "We did not find a cordial welcome."[66] Stout similarly described to Brigham Young their tenuous situation as foreigners in China: "We are strangers in a strange land where darkness covers the earth and gross darkness the people. Here we find a people situated differently from others we have seen and less likely to receive the gospel."[67]

The three elders' biggest problem was that none of them spoke Cantonese, the Chinese dialect prevalent in the Canton region of southern China, including Hong Kong. The elders assigned to labor in China were seemingly expected to evangelize the Chinese without any missionary training, including language acquisition.[68] Unlike the Western European Latter-day Saint missions that were staffed primarily by native-speaking immigrants, there was seemingly not a single Chinese Latter-day Saint convert until 1854 in Hawaii.[69] So church leaders had to call non-Chinese-speaking men to the Hong Kong mission field. Unlike the Protestant missionaries who arrived in China confidently anticipating studying the language for years, the Latter-day Saint elders despaired at the prospect. All three men were wholly unprepared to preach in the local language. "China is divided into many provinces, each province having a different dialect, not understood by the others," Stout lamented to Brigham Young. "Their written language is uniform and understood by all, having different sounds to the same character, but the same meaning. Their words are monosyllables and are represented by complex characters."[70]

In the elders' defense, it is unclear if they were actually planning to evangelize the Chinese-speaking locals or if they instead hoped to convert English-speaking expatriates living in the British colony. For example, when the first Latter-day Saint missionaries landed in the Sandwich Islands in 1850, just two years earlier, they initially focused their attention on the English-speaking Caucasian settlers. It was only after these efforts failed that some of the missionaries felt inspired, and obligated, to preach

66. Lewis, "Autobiography of James Lewis," 4.
67. Hosea Stout to Brigham Young, May 16, 1853.
68. Hosea Stout to Brigham Young, May 16, 1853.
69. R. Lanier Britsch, *Moramona: The Mormons in Hawaii*, 90.
70. Hosea Stout to Brigham Young, May 16, 1853.

to the Hawaiian natives. Nonetheless, other missionaries abandoned the Hawaiian Mission rather than learn the local language.[71]

Regardless of their initial intentions, the elders in Hong Kong quickly realized their linguistic quandary and anguished over the prospect of learning Chinese. "Our object now was to gather all the information we could concerning the language of the Chinese, of their manners and customs," Lewis explained to George A. Smith. "They seemed anxious to know why we came to that country to teach them, when those who could understand and speak our language would not believe us. What reason we had to expect them to believe what we told them, when they could not understand us."[72] The Latter-day Saints' lack of language training also limited their ability to understand and appreciate the surrounding Chinese culture. Their diaries and letters make it clear that they gained most of their information from English-language newspapers and from conversations with other foreigners in Hong Kong. It is possible that some of the information they received was actually misinformation, especially information obtained from other Euro-American missionaries who did not want the Latter-day Saints to remain in the East Asian region. Clearly, the elders from Utah were unprepared to thrive, or even survive, in Chinese culture.[73] They realized they needed to hire a Chinese teacher in order to reach the Chinese population of Hong Kong, especially since the small English-speaking populace expressed little interest in their message.[74] But Chinese language tutors did not come cheap, and the Latter-day Saints had limited means.

Accordingly, the Latter-day Saints in Hong Kong also suffered as a result of their financial arrangements. Whereas traveling "without purse or scrip" (Luke 22:35) gave biblical legitimacy to the elders in Christian North America and Western Europe, the same Euro-American missionary practice proved to be a major liability in Asia. The Latter-day Saints found the cost of living in Hong Kong prohibitive and the price of Chinese tutors beyond their meager funds. "To our astonishment we found it as costly living here as in San Francisco. We are totally without means of

---

71. Britsch, *Moramona*, 13–17. See also Donald R. Shaffer, "Hiram Clark and the First LDS Hawaiian Mission: A Reappraisal."

72. James Lewis to George A. Smith, December 12, 1854.

73. James Lewis to George A. Smith, June 3, 1854, reprinted as "Chinese in California," *Deseret News*, June 22, 1854.

74. James Lewis to George A. Smith, November 25, 1854, reprinted as "Chinese Mission," *Deseret News*, December 14, 1854.

support by labor, a prospect truly gloomy, causing a complete breakdown of our morale had we not evidence within us that we were sent of God to establish the gospel here," Stout reported to Brigham Young. "The lowest cost of a Chinese teacher will be about twenty dollars a month. We can see no way of sustaining ourselves so as to learn the language."[75] The elders expected financial contributions from the local people, but the Hong Kong residents were unmoved and withheld their funds. The Chinese and Euro-American inhabitants looked down on the Latter-day Saints because of their hapless financial condition, in contrast to the financially independent representatives of other Christian faiths. Attempting to live by this New Testament financial system was a major stumbling block to their evangelism of the Chinese in Hong Kong, and the approach contributed to the Latter-day Saints' stint in China being so short, whereas before, during, and after their time there, American Protestants continued to build up Chinese churches in East Asia.[76]

Traditional Latter-day Saint evangelistic practices also added to the elders' lack of success among the residents of Hong Kong. Unlike other Euro-American Christian representatives in Asia, the Latter-day Saints did not try to set up schools or offer any social services. As millenarians, the Latter-day Saints instead focused their efforts on broadcasting the message of Christ's restored primitive church and his pending Second Coming. The three men initially attempted to canvass local residents to drum up interest in their message, one of the mainstays of Latter-day Saint missionary work in the Atlantic world. The Chinese were not impressed; few of the people they encountered had any desire to discuss religion, and the vast majority refused to engage in spiritual conversations, especially with mendicant missionaries. "Upon other topics they were free and sociable, but felt to wonder at our presumption in endeavoring to establish our doctrines in Asia under the circumstances in which we placed ourselves; for they looked upon any person in a dependent position as worthy of no regard whatever, and beneath their notice," Lewis wrote. Whereas other Protestant missionaries "were received with courtesy and respect, . . . the servants of the Lord were despised, their company not desired, and their doctrine unheeded even by the lowest caste of the English and America population."[77]

---

75. Hosea Stout to Brigham Young, May 16, 1853.

76. Spence, *The Search for Modern China*, 172–76; and Latourette, *A History of the Expansion of Christianity*, 6:361–63.

77. James Lewis to George A. Smith, February 16, 1855.

When street contacting and the door-to-door approach proved ineffective in Hong Kong, the Utah elders next tried preaching meetings. Initially, English-speaking soldiers and other foreigners attended the Latter-day Saint gatherings out of curiosity, but that soon changed. "The people seemed satisfied yet they said it was not what they expected to hear, for they anticipated an expose of spiritual wives [plural marriage] and so forth," Lewis recalled. As a result, their listeners lost interest when the elders taught more traditional Christian doctrines. To make matters worse, the editors of the English-language newspapers began publishing articles demonizing the church and polygamy—a job made easier by the ironic fact that the doctrine of plural marriage was first publicized during the same general conference the previous year in which the China Mission was announced. "Our congregations in the meantime were reduced to a cipher—no one attending. We then began to visit the people individually, so that we might clear our garments, and bear a faithful testimony, after having traveled so far," Lewis described, alluding to the apostle Paul's publicly shaking out his clothing to declare that his listeners' sins would fall on their own heads. "Our endeavors to teach the way of life and salvation was unheeded by the Americans and English [in Hong Kong]."[78]

Halting Evangelism in Hong Kong

It took only about six weeks in Hong Kong for the three Latter-day Saint elders to give up hope of any future success among the Chinese residents or British expatriates. Again and again, the Latter-day Saint Euro-American missionary model floundered in non-Christian, non-Western Hong Kong. The missionaries from Utah were totally discouraged and at a loss as to how to proceed. "We feel that we have done all that God or man can require of us in this place," Hosea Stout mourned. "We have preached publicly and privately as long as anyone would hear and often tried when no one would hear."[79] Lewis further explained, "The heat of the atmosphere was very oppressive. Being reduced in bad health, owing to change of diet, the manner of preparing it, &c., our spirits were, becoming depressed, and not perceiving a cheering ray of hope in all our labors. . . . Our books were loaned, and returned without thanks; . . . The soldiers turned away because of their officers, and we seemed alone."[80]

78. James Lewis to George A. Smith, December 12, 1854.
79. Stout, Diary, June 7, 1853.
80. James Lewis to George A. Smith, December 12, 1854.

When the British and other expatriates in Hong Kong failed to get an "exposé" on plural marriage but instead heard about "the first principles of the gospel, of the re-organization of the church and kingdom of God," Lewis wrote, "they felt disappointed."[81] Less than two months after arriving in Hong Kong, Lewis, Stout, and Duncan determined to temporarily abandon their missionary labors to the Chinese in East Asia.[82]

It was a combination of factors, then, that doomed the missionary effort—the contemporaneous Taiping Rebellion made their message politically inexpedient, the harsh tropical climate drained away their optimism, their inability to localize traditional missionary practices made it impossible to connect with their intended audience, their lack of language and cultural training impeded communication, and their anachronistic financial arrangements made day-to-day survival uncertain.

In contrast, the Latter-day Saints did enjoy evangelistic success with some peoples of the Pacific Basin frontier during the second half of the nineteenth century. But these were Pacific Islanders, not Asians. Protestant and Catholic missionaries had largely colonized and Christianized the Hawaiians of the Sandwich Islands and Māori of New Zealand prior to the arrival of the Latter-day Saint missionaries. Therefore, these and other peoples of the South Pacific were not as religiously or culturally distant as the inhabitants of Asia. The Latter-day Saint elders and sisters in Polynesia and Australasia were able to overcome the weakness of the Euro-American missionary model in the Pacific world, as historian Laurie F. Maffly-Kipp helps us understand. Unlike in Hong Kong, the Latter-day Saint evangelistic practices meshed well with the traditional islander cultures. The Latter-day Saint style of preaching and worshipping was less formal than that of other American churches. As opposed to the Protestants, who relied on books to help teach the natives, the Latter-day Saints emphasized the telling of stories, the singing of hymns, and the enjoyment of the gifts of the Spirit. The natives took pleasure in their cultural continuities with the Latter-day Saints. The personal backgrounds and lack of missionary training of the Latter-day Saint missionaries actually worked to their advantage, unlike in Hong Kong. In contrast to the Protestants, with their learning and apparent refinement, the visitors from Utah lacked formal learning and the attendant risk of appearing arrogant. The Latter-day Saint missionaries were

81. James Lewis to George A. Smith, December 12, 1854.

82. Stout, Diary, June 9, 1853; and Hosea Stout, James Lewis, and Chapman Duncan to Brigham Young, August 27, 1853, Brigham Young Office Files, Church History Library.

also so poor that they had to live like the natives, unlike the Protestants, who kept their distance from the locals and were unwilling to adopt their food or habits. The islanders, unlike the Chinese, were impressed with the humility of the Latter-day Saints, who treated them with greater respect than other Euro-Americans. Living with the locals also enabled the Latter-day Saints to quickly acquire the local languages and learn customs. The Latter-day Saints were persecuted by other Christian groups, including the Protestants. Paradoxically, this maltreatment set the American Latter-day Saints apart from the Christian establishment in the eyes of some Pacific Islanders. As "outsiders" they became insiders abroad.[83]

Yet the reverse was true in Hong Kong for the Utah missionaries. Although there were many British and other white residents there, making the Latter-day Saints cultural insiders, their message and practices set them apart in negative ways, and they were met with indifference. "After having visited the people, and, as far as possible, introduced the subject of our mission, we were politely informed, in most instances, that they did not wish to hear of our religion, and desired no reference to the subject," Lewis noted in a letter to George A. Smith lamenting their own poverty and lack of financial stability. "But the servants of the Lord were despised, their company not desired, and their doctrine unheeded by even the lowest caste of the English and American population."[84]

Finally, on June 22, 1853, James Lewis, Hosea Stout, and Chapman Duncan took passage on the *Rose of Sharron* from the British colonial outpost in East Asia and began their return voyage to San Francisco.[85] After two months crossing the Pacific Ocean, they arrived on August 23. Eager for news from their families and church leaders in Utah, they disembarked and sought out their fellow Latter-day Saints in the city. Stout was devastated to learn that his wife, Louisa, and their newborn child had both passed away earlier that January in Salt Lake City, seven months previous. Word had never reached him in Hong Kong. "Let those who have drank of this bitter cup respond to my feelings and drop a tear of compassionate sympathy with me in this hour of my deepest mourning," he lamented in

---

83. Laurie F. Maffly-Kipp, "Looking West: Mormonism and the Pacific World," 48–56. See also Laurie F. Maffly-Kipp, "Assembling Bodies and Souls: Missionary Practices on the Pacific Frontier," 51–76; and R. Laurence Moore, *Religious Outsiders and the Making of Americans.*

84. James Lewis to George A. Smith, February 16, 1855.

85. Stout, Diary, June 22, 1853.

his diary that first day back on land.[86] The following day, the three missionaries "held a council" and determined that Stout should return to Salt Lake City "with the letters and papers we brought from Hong Kong and make report of our doings and the situation of affairs in China, to the President [Brigham Young], and learn his will in relation to our future course," according to Stout. It was also decided that Lewis and Duncan would remain in northern California "and act as the Lord opens the way."[87]

Just days after the three missionaries disembarked in San Francisco, and just before Stout began his journey to Salt Lake City, the Hong Kong elders met fellow Latter-day Saints Cyrus Canfield and Edward Wade. Several months earlier, during the April 1853 general conference, church leaders in Utah assigned Canfield and Wade to join Lewis and his companions in China.[88] In fact, the First Presidency and Quorum of the Twelve had recently discussed the possibility of calling additional apostles so that they could send one to oversee missionary work in China. They debated if they had the authority to ordain other apostles, with Parley P. Pratt and Brigham Young offering their opinions that there could be extra-quorum apostles. Young explained, "We want to send a man to China and send him as an Apostle to build up the Kingdom there and then go thro [*sic*] to the end."[89] Ultimately, church leaders did not end up calling a special apostle to China to dedicate the land for the preaching of the gospel. Instead, they called the two additional missionaries who now encountered the returning missionaries in San Francisco. In Stout's words, these new missionaries "had come thus far and meeting us thus returning are left in the same uncertainty that we are not knowing what to do."[90]

With the original 1852 China mission halted, neither Canfield nor Wade continued on to East Asia. Determined to receive counsel from Young, Stout journeyed to Southern California by boat, where he was rejoined by Lewis in the Latter-day Saint colony of San Bernardino in Southern California. While there, on October 25, 1853, the returning elders finally received Young's reply to the letter they had sent from Hong Kong on May 16.[91] Together the two returning missionaries then followed

86. Stout, Diary, August 23, 1853.

87. Stout, Diary, August 24, 1853.

88. "Minutes of the General Conference," *Deseret News*, April 30, 1853.

89. Thomas Bullock, Minutes (LaJean Carruth shorthand version), April 17, 1853; Historian's Office general church minutes.

90. Stout, Diary, August 26, 1853.

91. Stout, Diary, October 25, 1853.

the southern route north across the Mojave Desert and the wilderness of the West to Salt Lake City.

Brigham Young had written on September 30 that he "hasten[ed] to answer by the return mail, being well aware of the anxious desire of the Elders on Missions to receive even a few lines from home." After reading of Stout's discouragement, the church president urged patience and long-suffering in their new assignment in Hong Kong: "[You] are constantly remembered in our prayers, and you are doubtless too familiar with the operations of breaking new ground, to be cast down by a long and tedious beginning among strangers, and must be aware that you simply require patience & perseverance, with the exercise of what faiths and obedience you can obtain." Young concluded, "You are at liberty to finish your mission, and go to any other point, or return home, wherever and whichever the spirit may dictate."[92] But by this time, however, Stout, Lewis, and Chapman were already back on American soil and heading home.

Young would soon learn that the Hong Kong mission had been halted. On October 31, the church president wrote to Augustus Farnham, one of the missionaries called in 1852 to labor in New South Wales (Australia), reporting, "The missionaries to China are on their way home, not having been able to accomplish much, so far as I have learned."[93] Despite discouraging challenges in China, however, Young was not giving up on his global millenarian vision, including taking the gospel to the Chinese, like those immigrants living in California and Hawaii.

Returning Home to Utah

In late October 1853, the *Deseret News* provided Latter-day Saints in Utah with a similar update on the elders assigned to Hong Kong as they were making their way back to Zion: "A portion of our Chinese missionaries . . . are in California, striving for a chance to get home. Latest rumor says, the President of the mission, Hosea Stout, was at San Bernardino, and will be in this winter." Then, likely relying on the missionaries' earlier letter to Brigham Young from Hong Kong, the paper editorialized on their struggles: "*Cause*—No door open for the Gospel in China. The rebellion, so called, absorbs the attention of every soul, and no time to attend to

92. Brigham Young to Hosea Stout, September 30, 1853, Hosea Stout Papers, Church History Library.

93. Brigham Young to Augustus Farnham, October 31, 1853, Church History Library.

anything else." The editors continued: "From all reports that we have seen, it is reasonable to infer that a complete and total revolution is in progress for all of China, and that all old forms, ceremonies, customs and laws, oft said to be older than the world, are about to be changed; and if so, the progress of nations, for good or evil, will be the consequence." The paper concluded, "We pity the nations who will not receive the Gospel, when the Elders of Israel have compassed sea and land, without purse or scrip, to carry it to them."[94]

Lewis and Stout finally departed from San Bernardino for Salt Lake City on November 3, 1853. After crossing over the rim of the Great Basin near modern-day Cedar City, Utah, Lewis was reunited with his loved ones in nearby Parowan. "Here Elder Lewis met his wife and family all well and rejoicing to meet him once more," Stout wrote in his diary that evening. "How different will be my return home."[95] He had been dreading his own homecoming for months since hearing of the death of his wife and newborn. Back in July, facing the harsh reality of his situation when he returned home, he had written, "I gazed upon the sad wreck of all my hopes in silence while my heart sank within me and those around could not refrain from mingling their tears with mine for a few moments when we all hastily withdrew from a place so full of sad recollections as my *HOME*."[96] While Lewis remained with his loved ones in southern Utah, two weeks later Stout arrived in Salt Lake City "at home or what more properly might be said where once was my home."[97] He had been gone for fourteen months, since the previous October. That same day, he met with Brigham Young and reported on his short-lived mission to China. He spent the rest of December reconnecting with his other children and loved ones in the Salt Lake Valley. Stout also was called upon to speak to government and church groups on his recent missionary labors in Hong Kong, including a sermon in the Salt Lake Tabernacle on Christmas Day 1853.[98] The original missionaries called to China in 1852 would not return to Hong Kong to evangelize. Lewis settled back into life in Parowan, Utah, and his two missionary companions similarly resumed their lives among their fellow Latter-day Saints in California and Utah.

---

94. "China," *Deseret News*, October 29, 1853.

95. Stout, Diary, November 25, 1853.

96. Stout, Diary, August 23, 1853.

97. Stout, Diary, December 8, 1853.

98. Stout, Diary, December 19, 23, and 25, 1853. See Appendix A, herein, for a transcription of Stout's remarks in the Tabernacle.

CHAPTER TWO

Early Latter-day Saint Encounters with East Asians

In April 1854, the First Presidency of The Church of Jesus Christ of Latter-day Saints issued their Eleventh General Epistle to church members worldwide and provided an update on evangelism efforts of those men called to evangelize around the world in 1852. Of the original three men called to East Asia, they reported, "Br[other]s. Hosea Stout, James Lewis, and Chapman Duncan, returned from the China mission, after having arrived at Hong Kong, and without effecting any impression, or establishing the standard of truth in that mighty empire. This is owing to the disturbed state of the country, which hindered them penetrating the interior, and acquainting themselves with the manners, customs, and in some degree the language of the people."[1] This marked the end of early Latter-day Saint evangelism in China.

Church leaders would not send additional missionaries to East Asia for another five decades following the early disappointments in Hong Kong in 1853.[2] When they finally did in 1901, it would be to the Japanese, not the Chinese. Moreover, they allowed almost a century to pass after James Lewis and his companions labored in Hong Kong before they again assigned elders to evangelize in that British colony in 1949. "The mission to China cannot be assessed as anything but a complete failure," historian R. Lanier Britsch concludes. "The missionaries were as well aware of this as any later observer."[3] Nevertheless, he expresses admiration for Lewis and

---

1. Brigham Young, Heber C. Kimball, and Jedediah M. Grant, "Eleventh General Epistle of the Presidency of the Church of Jesus Christ of Latter-day Saints, to the Saints in the Valleys of the Mountains, and those scattered abroad throughout the Earth, greeting," *Deseret News*, April 13, 1854.

2. In 1855, Latter-day Saint missionaries returning from evangelizing in India passed through Hong Kong on their return voyage to California and then to Utah. They recorded the baptism of "a young female of our party, which I presume is the first baptism here for many centuries." But this was a Native American and not a Chinese convert. See Hugh Findlay to Franklin D. Richards, June 26, 1855, reprinted as "Foreign Correspondence: China," *Millennial Star* 18, no. 38 (September 22, 1855): 607.

3. R. Lanier Britsch, *From the East: The History of the Latter-day Saints in Asia, 1851–1996*, 37.

his fellow intrepid elders who left pioneer Utah to evangelize the Chinese under such difficult circumstances.

Similarly, while chronicling the first century of the Latter-day Saint movement in 1930, Assistant Church Historian B. H. Roberts made an audacious declaration about the missionaries called in August 1852: "Thus did the Church of the Latter-day Saints in these years . . . seek to fulfill the initial obligation given to that church in the very opening of the New Dispensation, namely, to preach the gospel of the kingdom to every nation, and kindred, and tongue, and people." He continued his claim with one long laudatory sentence, which begs contemplation (and scrutiny) by anyone studying nineteenth-century Christian missiology in America:

> And if the numerical and financial strength of the church be taken into account, or rather its weakness in these respects be taken into account, and if the circumstance of the location of the saints in an undeveloped and comparatively isolated country in the mountain interior of America be also considered, it will render these missionary enterprises the most wonderful manifestations of Christian zeal and enthusiasm—the largest and most earnest service undertaken, within the same space of time, for God and man, since the days of the apostles of the early Christian church.[4]

Like other evangelical Americans, Latter-day Saints encountered Chinese and Japanese people and their faith traditions both at home in the Intermountain American West and in the broader Pacific world. To help tell the story of Americans and Asians meeting each other at various sites around the globe, especially in the Pacific world, religious studies scholars Thomas A. Tweed and Stephen Prothero suggest two terms: *meeting* (including literary, artifactual, and interpersonal) and *migration*, which I will explain below.[5] These themes are well suited to help explore early Latter-day Saint interactions with East Asia. Latter-day Saints played host to Asians in Utah and sent missionaries among them in the Pacific. These meetings, though limited in scope, were an important basis for the Latter-day Saint evaluation of East Asians. While church members initially focused their attention on the Chinese people, the Japanese captured their greater interest by the turn of the twentieth century. In contrast to

4. B. H. Roberts, *A Comprehensive History of the Church of Jesus Christ of Latter-day Saints, Century One*, 4:75–76.

5. Thomas A. Tweed and Stepehn Prothero, *Asian Religions in America: A Documentary History*, 1–12. They also use a third term, *mapping*, to further describe this cultural encounter. See Reid L. Neilson, "Joseph Smith and Nineteenth-Century Mormon Mappings of Asian Religions," 209–20.

Protestants, who actively evangelized Asians in their midst, the Latter-day Saints generally did not until the beginning of the twentieth century, due to theological and logistical concerns.

Catholics and Protestants in the Pacific World

Scholars have increasingly analyzed the Pacific world, from the west coast of the United States and South America, across the Pacific Islands from Hawaii to Tahiti, down to New Zealand and Australia, and up to Japan, as a distinctive region with a unified history.[6] Historians have only recently begun to document and analyze the breadth and depth of these events.[7] Far from the "empty" space that historians have sometimes described, the Pacific has been alive with movement and contact for hundreds of years. Although this history included the exchange of goods, ideas, and religious faiths, it was also fraught with competition and tension. On the heels of the age of discovery, European powers sought to expand their influence and dominion around the globe. The Pacific world, newly discovered to Europe, became the military, financial, and spiritual battleground of ongoing feuds and imperialistic ambitions. Religion played a key role in motivating and justifying European expansion in the Pacific region, and each imperialist nation brought a distinct approach to missionizing the territories it claimed.

Spanish Catholics, emboldened by the 1493 papal decree dividing religious jurisdiction for much of the world between Portugal and Spain, determined to transform the Pacific Basin frontier into Catholic territory. They were successful in their evangelical ambitions in Guam, the Philippines, and Mexico, including what is now California and the American West. Dutch missionaries also made their way to the Pacific world but often engaged in lucrative trade opportunities rather than evangelism. Russian Orthodox missionaries turned their attention to the Inuit, Yupik, and Aleut peoples in modern-day Alaska. British Anglicans appeared in the Pacific Rim by the beginning of the nineteenth century, moving quickly to colonize Australia and New Zealand. Although the Spanish, Portuguese, and Dutch had enjoyed a presence in Asia for hundreds of years, British missionaries did not begin evangelizing in Asia until

6. Matt K. Matsuda, "The Pacific," 758–80. See also Arrell Morgon Gibson, *Yankees in Paradise: The Pacific Basin Frontier.*

7. See Laurie F. Maffly-Kipp, "Eastward Ho! American Religion from the Perspective of the Pacific Rim," 127–48.

the start of the nineteenth century. The London Missionary Society, organized in 1795, focused much of its energies on Christianizing the Down Under natives. They soon expanded their missionary outreach to the isles of the South Pacific, including Tahiti, where they found measurable success among the islanders. The British were followed by French Catholics, who arrived in the South Pacific during the 1840s. By 1886 the French had displaced the British from parts of Polynesia, yet seemed content to maintain the colonies they established rather than expand.[8]

American Protestants were latecomers to the Asia-Pacific world. During the eighteenth and early nineteenth centuries, they were preoccupied with more pressing domestic concerns, including westward expansion and the evangelism of Native Americans and displaced Africans in the United States. The American Protestant missionary encounter with the peoples of the Pacific Basin frontier began in 1810 when congregational leaders in New England met to form the American Board of Commissioners for Foreign Missions, a group that soon became the dominant American missionary organization. Two years later the organization sent missionaries to South Asia but later determined to begin full-scale missionary work in the Sandwich Islands (Hawaii). During the next several decades these missionaries experienced tremendous success as they Christianized and westernized the Hawaiian natives and expanded the political influence of the United States into the middle of the Pacific. American Protestants reached East Asia in about 1830, years after the British Anglicans. In 1829, the American Board of Commissioners for Foreign Missions sent Elijah Bridgman, David Abeel, and Peter Parker to educate and provide medicine to the Chinese, as well as teach them the good word. By the mid-nineteenth century, various American Christian groups were laboring in the treaty port cities of Hong Kong, Canton, and Shanghai. It would not be until the 1870s that Protestant representatives began active missionary work in neighboring Japan.[9]

The American missionary movement in the Pacific Basin frontier differed in several ways from the larger European Christianizing effort. First, a wide variety of American Protestants spread into the region, mirroring the plethora of Protestant sects and denominations back home. Next, American evangelical groups made their way to the Pacific at various

8. Gibson, *Yankees in Paradise*, 263–68.

9. Kenneth Scott Latourette, *History of the Expansion of Christianity*, 300–69, 382–411. See also Winburn T. Thomas, *Protestant Beginnings in Japan: The First Three Decades, 1859–1889*.

points throughout the 1800s. Third, unlike the Europeans, who generally focused on a particular area in the Pacific, the Americans eventually encompassed the entire Pacific Rim. Lastly, American missionaries spread Western culture in the region more than any European nation.[10]

By the end of the nineteenth century, the three Ms of American civilization—militaries, merchants, and missionaries—had spread across the Pacific Rim. But it was missionaries, more than any other group, who moderated the exchange of information and representation between Americans and Asians.[11] These men and women were the ones who had left their North American homelands to interact and engage with the peoples of other lands, cultures, and religions. The missionaries became the moderators of information and evolving attitudes with their fellow religionists back home. Historian Grant Wacker argues that "the missionaries' perceptions moved from abhorrence to grudging admiration to varying degrees of approval of the ethical and religious ideals of the peoples among whom they worked" during this era.[12] This resulted in greater openness to the true claims and moral contributions of non-Christian faiths in the decades to come.

Latter-day Saints Meet East Asians

It is unlikely that Joseph Smith, the founding leader of the Latter-day Saint religious tradition, ever meaningfully encountered East Asians during his lifetime. Born in 1805, Smith spent his childhood and youth on farms in Vermont, New Hampshire, and New York, isolated from the larger world of Pacific Rim commerce and travel. When he was eight years old, Smith was sent to an aunt and uncle in Salem, Massachusetts, to convalesce after a leg operation. By the early nineteenth century, Salem was a major hub of Chinese trade with North America, and it is possible that a young Joseph Smith passed by Chinese sailors working along the seaport docks. Salem was also home to a large collection of Asian artifacts,

10. Gibson, *Yankees in Paradise*, 266–84. See also Laurie F. Maffly-Kipp, "Assembling Bodies and Souls: Missionary Practices on the Pacific Frontier," 51–76; and Neil Gunson, *Messengers of Grace: Evangelical Missionaries in the South Seas, 1797–1860*.

11. William R. Hutchison, *Errand to the World: American Protestant Thought and Foreign Missions*, 1.

12. Grant Wacker, "A Plural World: The Protestant Awakening to World Religions," 256.

collected and housed in a renovated bank building by the East India Marine Society, which was founded in 1799 and is the forerunner of today's celebrated Peabody Essex Museum.[13] As a curious young boy, Smith may have visited the burgeoning museum—by that time one of Salem's leading attractions—to pass the time while his leg healed. If so, he was briefly exposed to Asian culture through its treasures and relics. Smith's only other youthful encounter with the Pacific Rim would have been through his father, who disastrously attempted to sell Vermont ginseng to a Chinese trading company that prized it for its medicinal properties.[14]

Even as an adult in rural antebellum America, Smith had extremely limited, if any, opportunities to learn about the East. The Latter-day Saint leader spent his life in the interior of New England, in the landlocked Western Reserve, and in Missouri and Illinois on the western American frontier. He never traveled across the Atlantic or the Pacific Oceans, and an 1833 missionary journey to Toronto, Canada, proved to be the extent of his international experience. The town of Salem provided a second opportunity for Smith to encounter the Asian world when he returned to the maritime town in 1836, twenty-five years after first visiting as a boy on crutches. This time he was accompanied by several ecclesiastical associates with whom he apparently hoped to discover buried treasure to help pay off church debts (see Doctrine and Covenants 111). Smith and his associates tarried in Salem for about three weeks that summer. They visited the newly constructed East India Marine Hall, an imposing columned edifice which by then housed several thousand objects from the "Orient." One historian suggests that "the objects that were collected and exhibited by this society helped define the early American vision of Eastern cultures."[15] Latter-day Saints Sidney Rigdon and Oliver Cowdery signed the museum's guest ledger on August 6, 1836, and Smith left his signature two days later.[16]

Any interactions Smith had with Asian culture, then, were superficial, and early Latter-day Saint interests clearly centered not on Asia but on the past, present, and future of the Americas—the land they believed to be the

---

13. Tweed and Prothero, *Asian Religions in America*, 51.

14. See Mark L. Staker and Donald L. Enders, "Joseph Smith Sr.'s China Adventure," 79–105.

15. Daniel Finamore, "Displaying the Sea and Defining America: Early Exhibitions at the Salem East India Marine Society," 40–51.

16. David R. Proper, "Joseph Smith and Salem," 94. See also Donald Q. Cannon, "Joseph Smith in Salem (D&C 111)," 432–36.

promised land recorded in the Book of Mormon, the gathering place for church members, and the building location of the New Jerusalem. During the 1830s and 1840s, Smith sent missionaries throughout North America and later to Europe to spread the Latter-day Saint message. It would not be until after his murder and the pioneer exodus to what became Utah Territory that Latter-day Saints would actually meet any Asians at home or abroad.

Not surprisingly, many of the earliest meetings between the two groups were the result of missionary work in the Pacific Basin frontier.[17] Smith's successor, President Brigham Young, and other church leaders discussed sending missionaries to East Asia soon after gold was discovered in California, and in 1851 they established the Pacific Mission, under the leadership of Elder Parley P. Pratt. Brigham Young did send missionaries to China and other Asian nations in 1852, as chronicled in Chapter 1, but Latter-day Saint encounters with Japan would have to wait. For one thing, the nation was closed to the commercial, diplomatic, and religious overtures of the West until 1854, when Commodore Matthew Perry and his gunboats forced Japan's Tokugawa government to normalize political and trade relations with the United States.[18]

To most Americans, Perry's diplomatic opening of Japan was another confirmation of their country's growing power. But the watershed event suggested something different to the Latter-day Saints. In September 1854 the church's *Millennial Star* periodical featured an article on the recent opening of Japan, rehearsing the exploits of Perry's naval expedition and suggesting what the new opportunities in Japan would mean for the United States from a political, economic, and social perspective. However, it also pointed to new missionary opportunities in East Asia. "While the gospel is being preached in every quarter of the globe," the author wrote, "there has been but little opportunity to plant it on the eastern coasts of Asia. This treaty with Japan, and the revolution in China, will probably open the way for it to be preached in those two great empires."[19] Church

17. See Laurie F. Maffly-Kipp and Reid L. Neilson, *Proclamation to the People: Nineteenth-Century Mormonism and the Pacific Basin Frontier*; and Laurie F. Maffly-Kipp, "Looking West: Mormonism and the Pacific World," 41–63.

18. Marius B. Jansen, *The Making of Modern Japan*, 257–93; and Kenneth B. Pyle, *The Making of Modern Japan*, 57–60.

19. "Opening of Japan," *Millennial Star* 16, no. 35 (September 2, 1854): 552.

leaders looked forward to the time when their faith tradition would spread to the Japanese and Chinese.[20]

The first interpersonal meeting between the Latter-day Saints and Japanese likely occurred in 1858 when William Wood, a twenty-one-year-old Latter-day Saint and member of the British Navy, took shore leave on Japanese soil. "I discerned a remarkable spirit of reform in them; more so than in any people I had met," he recalled of the Japanese. "I felt a desire to preach the Gospel to them."[21] Wood later emigrated to Utah, but he never returned to Japan. "I have thought it possible that I was the first Mormon to visit Japan, and this increased my desire to present the Gospel to them," he reminisced. "Years after, when I had gathered to Zion . . . this feeling increased in my mind so much that in my prayers I often mentioned it. However, it was some years before the door for the Gospel was opened by Apostle Grant to the Japanese people [in 1901], and I had become an old man."[22] Wood does in fact appear to be the first Latter-day Saint to encounter the Japanese, and others would follow.

Another informal meeting of Latter-day Saints and Japanese occurred decades later when church leaders again sent missionaries to South Asia. William Willes, George Booth, Henry F. McCune, and Milson Pratt boarded the *City of New York* in San Francisco bound for Japan en route to India. While at sea, Willes broke up an argument between a drunken crew member and an English-speaking Japanese Christian named Ishiye. Thereafter, Ishiye showed interest in the missionaries and listened to their message.[23] He informed the missionaries about evangelism prospects in Japan and explained that all religious teachers were under the protection, and constraints, of the Japanese government. The Japanese Christian also offered to have "a favorable mention made" of the church in Japanese newspapers and invited the missionaries to return to Japan as his guests the following year.[24] When their ship stopped over in Yokohama, the missionaries disembarked and visited with several expatriates living in Japan. They

20. Wilford Woodruff, Journal, November 18, 1856, and March 22, 1857, Church History Library.

21. Kate B. Carter, *Our Pioneer Heritage*, 13:264. See also William G. Hartley, "Adventures of a Young British Seaman, 1852–1862," 38–47.

22. Carter, *Our Pioneer Heritage*, 13:264.

23. William Willes, Journal, June 17, 1884, reprinted in Charleen Cutler, *Life of William Willes: From His Own Personal Journals and Writings*, 124.

24. William Willes, "Tidings from Japan and China," *Juvenile Instructor* 19, no. 19 (October 1, 1884): 291–92; and Willes, Journal, July 1, 1884.

learned that while Japan was open to Christianity, it was yet "very much hampered with restrictions that are galling to free Americans." Westerners were free to move about the handful of foreign settlement ports, but they could only travel throughout the interior of Japan when accompanied by Japanese guides.[25] The Latter-day Saints left Yokohama days later for India and did not pass through Japan again when they journeyed home to Utah months later.

There were also several interpersonal meetings between the Latter-day Saints and East Asians in the American West. The Iwakura Mission, a delegation made up of high-level Japanese officials, passed through Utah on their way east to Washington, DC, in 1872.[26] Fierce snowstorms blocked the mountain passes from rail travel and stranded the delegation in Salt Lake City for nineteen days. Seeking to make the best of the situation, the Japanese commission visited the newly completed tortoise shell–shaped Tabernacle, explored a local museum, and admired the stone foundations of the Salt Lake Temple. They also called on members of the Utah Territorial Legislature, the Utah Supreme Court, and church president Brigham Young. Moreover, they observed the territorial military, learned about the local educational system, and attended receptions and banquets prepared by their Utah hosts. Several delegates even went to Latter-day Saint religious services and recorded a short overview of the church in the delegation's official records.[27] Likewise, Salt Lake City residents made their own observations of their East Asian visitors. Church leaders including Salt Lake stake president Angus M. Cannon, First Presidency member George Q. Cannon, and church president Lorenzo Snow were particularly impressed by the Japanese stranded in their midst.[28]

This spontaneous encounter had far-reaching effects on the future of the church in East Asia. Cannon believed that the Iwakura Mission's visit to Utah was providential. "It is perhaps not hazarding too much to say that the visit of the Japanese Embassy to Salt Lake, and the principal cities of the United States, is the fore-runner of measures which may, at some

25. Willes, "Tidings from Japan and China," 292.

26. See Wendy Butler, "The Iwakura Mission and its Stay in Salt Lake City," 26–47.

27. See Kume Kunitake, *The Iwakura Embassy, 1871–1873: A True Account of the Ambassador Extraordinary and Plenipotentiary's Journal of Observation Through the United States of America and Europe*, 1:133–41, for a Japanese account of the unexpected stay in Utah.

28. "Opening of a Mission in Japan," *Deseret Evening News*, April 6, 1901.

During the presidential administration of Lorenzo Snow, Latter-day Saint leaders increased their attention toward Japan as a potential missionary field. Courtesy Utah State Historical Society.

future day, be the cause of some of the youth who read this article being sent as missionaries to Japan," he editorialized.[29] Snow acknowledged that the Japanese delegation had left a lasting impression on his mind and that their visit acted as a catalyst for the eventual opening of the Japan Mission in 1901. "This is how the thought [of the Japan Mission] originated with me," he later explained to reporters. "When I was president of the Legislative council, a party of distinguished officials of the Japanese government visited Salt Lake enroute to Washington. . . . They expressed a great deal of interest in Utah and the manner in which it has been settled by the Mormons. Our talk was altogether very pleasant and they expressed considerable wonderment as to why we had not sent missionaries to Japan."[30] Nevertheless, it would be decades before Latter-day Saint leaders sent missionaries to Japan.

That same decade, Chen Lanbin, China's first ambassador to Washington, DC, also passed through Utah and recorded meeting the Latter-day Saints. "The religion here is different from that practiced in other states of the Flowery Flag country. According to Western custom, a man cannot marry two women, but this religion permits the taking of concubines," he noted of plural marriage. The remainder of Chen's account focuses on the history of Utah and the Latter-day Saints' conflicts with the federal government.[31] Contacts like these demonstrate that East Asians were as curious about the Latter-day Saints as the Saints were about them.

The Latter-day Saints also "met" East Asians through literary means. Before his death, George Q. Cannon used his apostolic influence and editorship of the *Juvenile Instructor* to educate the Latter-day Saints on

29. George Q. Cannon, "Editorial Thoughts," *Juvenile Instructor* 7, no. 4 (February 17, 1872): 28.

30. "Opening of a Mission in Japan."

31. R. David Arkush and Leo O. Lee, *Land Without Ghosts: Chinese Impressions of America From the Mid-Nineteenth Century to the Present*, 51.

the Chinese and Japanese. In the last decades of the nineteenth century, his church-sponsored magazine featured dozens of articles on East Asia and its cultures. Almost without exception, articles presented a favorable view of East Asians.[32] Besides presenting aspects of East Asian cultures, the *Juvenile Instructor* articles were also peppered with references to future church missionary opportunities in Japan. "It is not too much to expect that Western customs and the Christian religion will in a few years gain such a foothold in Japan that the folly of idol worship will be entirely unknown amongst its highly intelligent people," one article read. Another read, "It is probable that the next few years will effect a still greater improvement in that country, as quite a number of young men from Japan are being educated in the United States, who, of course, will carry home with them American ideals of living. . . . It is possible they will modify their laws so as to admit of the gospel being preached there, as it will certainly be at some future time."[33]

George Q. Cannon was an advocate for opening a mission in Japan during the last three decades of the nineteenth century. Courtesy Utah State Historical Society.

In his own articles, Cannon could not resist plugging Japan, over China, as the most promising Latter-day Saint mission field in East Asia.

32. Unfortunately, the authorship of most of the articles is unclear, as no names or sources are given. Cannon likely reproduced interesting articles he encountered in national periodicals without making proper attribution, a common practice in nineteenth-century journalism.

33. "A Japanese Idol," *Juvenile Instructor* 8, no. 10 (May 10, 1873): 73–74; "A Country Scene in Japan," *Juvenile Instructor* 8, no. 22 (October 25, 1873): 169–70; "Festival of the Idol Tengou in Japan," *Juvenile Instructor* 9, no. 5 (February 28, 1874): 49; "Japanese Peasant in Winter Costume," *Juvenile Instructor* 9, no. 7 (March 28, 1874): 81; "Japanese Amusements," *Juvenile Instructor* 10, no. 17 (August 21, 1875): 193–94; "Japanese Customs," *Juvenile Instructor* 11, no. 2 (January 15, 1876): 18–20; "A Japanese Shoe Store," *Juvenile Instructor* 13, no. 12 (June 15, 1878): 133–34; "Japanese Children," *Juvenile Instructor* 13, no. 21 (November 1, 1878): 245; "Japanese Temple," *Juvenile Instructor* 11, no. 11 (June 1, 1876): 127–28.

"We firmly believe that Japan will yet be successfully visited by the Elders of our Church, and that from that race thousands of obedient souls will yet be gathered to swell the multitudes of those who shall be called to Zion," he asserted. Contemporary events in Japan seemed to bolster his sentiments. By the mid-1880s, the East Asian balance of national power was shifting from China to Japan, a sea change that warranted further comment. "Of all the Asiatic nations perhaps Japan is making the greatest strides at the present time in the way of education and an adoption of the inventions and discoveries of modern times. The people of this empire are unquestionably more progressive than their neighbors the Chinese, and the interest that is now being taken in that people by civilized nations is very great."[34] Cannon and other church leaders became convinced that Japan held the key to the eventual evangelization of East Asia, including the Chinese.

East Asians Migrate to the American West

Thomas A. Tweed and Stephen Prothero's other theme, *migration*, helps historians understand the social and religious encounters between East Asians and Americans in the United States, including those known as the overseas Chinese. Since the middle of the nineteenth century, when Chinese workers sailed by ship to the "Gold Mountain" of California and the mines in the American West, East Asian immigrants have added their own swatches and threads to the patchwork of American religious history. As Pacific borderlands scholar Laurie F. Maffly-Kipp argues, the story of America's religious past is generally told from a westward orientation, thereby diminishing the contributions and struggles of Asians and Pacific Islanders who immigrated to America from the Pacific Basin.[35] The traditional narrative also obscures the contact and exchanges between Americans and immigrant groups.[36]

When Americans of the eighteenth and nineteenth century were first introduced to China, they felt threatened, according to historian Robert McClellan. Here was a country that had been around for thousands of years, compared to the relative youth of the United States. Protestant leader Josiah Strong argued that America's destiny stretched beyond the

34. Vidi, "A Progressive People," *Juvenile Instructor* 28, no. 19 (October 1, 1893): 597.

35. Maffly-Kipp, "Eastward Ho!," 128–30.

36. Tweed and Prothero, *Asian Religions in America*, 8–10.

borders of North America to the Pacific Basin, including China. American Protestants rationalized that China needed to be spiritually saved and morally uplifted by their Christian nation. Not surprisingly, Americans described the Chinese as inferior to the Anglo-Saxon race. They could not imagine China as a great civilization, because that undercut the United States' role in their redemption.[37]

Beginning in the mid-1800s, hundreds, then thousands, and then tens of thousands of Chinese workers emigrated to Hawaii and the American West, the majority from China's Guangdong Province. America offered new hope for Chinese people beset by natural disasters and financial woes in their homeland. Most immigrants were male laborers, either single men or married men who left their families back in China, and they planned to return to China flush with money. American business managers viewed the men's lack of family and social attachments as a boon, since they could be easily displaced. These employers did not hesitate to put the Chinese in poor work environments and exploit them economically. Until the early 1880s, Chinese labor was abundant and little valued. White workers, however, became increasingly concerned over the massive influx of East Asian workers who threatened their jobs. Labor organizations pressured Congress to rebuff Chinese immigrants seeking citizenship rights, resulting in the 1870 Naturalization Act, which made Asian immigrants ineligible for US citizenship. The Chinese remained second-class citizens for many decades thereafter. The federal government passed additional legislation in 1875 and 1882, first impeding the immigration of Chinese women and then completely barring the immigration of any additional Chinese laborers. The 1882 Exclusion Act in particular had an immediate impact on Chinese immigration. In the year before the law took effect, over 39,000 Chinese immigrated to America; two years later the number had dropped to less than three hundred. Due to worsening social conditions, many Chinese returned to China, which in turn opened the door for increased Japanese immigration.[38]

---

37. Robert McClellan, *The Heathen Chinee: A Study of American Attitudes Toward China, 1890–1905*. See also Roger Daniels, *Asian America: Chinese and Japanese in the United States Since 1850*, 29–66.

38. Bill Ong Hing, *Making and Remaking Asian America Through Immigration Policy, 1850–1990*, 44–47. See also Daniels, *Asian America*, 9–28; and Bruce B. Lawrence, *New Faiths, Old Fears: Muslims and other Asian Immigrants in American Religious Life*.

Although Japan emerged from international isolation in the middle of the nineteenth century, its citizens were not free to travel about the globe until 1885, when the Meiji government relaxed its emigration laws. Given the recent scarcity of Chinese immigrants, American business leaders welcomed the sudden influx of Japanese laborers. The population of Japanese immigrants in Hawaii and California swelled as a result. The majority initially worked on sugar plantations in Hawaii. Those that continued east to California worked mainly in the agricultural industry, arriving after the completion of the railroads and the heyday of mining. These immigrants also opened small businesses. For a time, the Japanese were even allowed to own their own land in the United States. Nearly 27,000 Japanese immigrants made their way to America in the 1890s, including many women, who were not yet barred from immigrating as Chinese women were. The Japanese migrants were a small number when compared to the Chinese migrant population, which amounted to well over 100,000 people in the nineteenth century. It would not be until 1908 that the US government would begin to curtail Japanese immigration, as it had the Chinese immigration decades earlier.[39]

The Chinese and Japanese immigrant experiences in America were similar in many ways. Both peoples hailed from East Asia, the majority coming from lower-class backgrounds. The two immigrant groups had a skewed population of men to women. Both immigrant groups were exploited as cheap labor in America after slavery had ended; as "non-whites," the Chinese and Japanese were not initially given the protection of the US Constitution. In the American West especially, all East Asians endured politically charged anti-Chinese and anti-Japanese movements. They were linked together in white Americans' minds as a threatening, invasive force.

But the experiences of Chinese and Japanese immigrants also differed in important respects. The Chinese were originally brought to America as part of the "coolie" system of labor, wherein they were indentured workers, essentially slaves. In contrast, the Japanese who immigrated independently decades later did so freely. Immigrants from China arrived in America in the wake of the 1848 discovery of gold in California; the majority were employed in the building of the western railroads. Immigrants from Japan, on the other hand, began arriving *en masse* after the railroads were largely completed. The Chinese were excluded from immigration several decades

39. Hing, *Making and Remaking Asian America*, 53–59. See also Daniels, *Asian America*, 100–54; and Tsurutani Hisashi, *American-Bound: The Japanese and the Opening of the American West*, 13–35.

before the Japanese were. The East Asian groups overlapped, but they had distinct eras of influence and majority status among Asian Americans.[40]

The influx of Asian immigrants to the United States also brought the attention of religious organizations. Protestant leaders and laity in the American West were eager to evangelize the East Asian immigrants moving into their midst. Some "home missionaries" (proselytizing domestically rather than abroad) viewed the influx of Asians in California as a providential means of taking Christianity across the Pacific Rim, and they anticipated that East Asian American converts would return to their native countries with their newfound faith. In that way, antebellum California and its immigrants seemed a likely Christian springboard to Asia.[41] During the second half of the nineteenth century, Presbyterian, Congregational, Baptist, and Methodist home missionaries and clergy worked with the Chinese in the San Francisco Bay Area. Like other American Protestants, these California Christian workers believed it was their duty as both Christians *and* Americans to spiritually strengthen and socially support the peoples of Asia. They organized schools, provided medical care and social services to the Chinese immigrants, and defended them from anti-Asian sentiment.[42]

In his study of Protestant reactions to Chinese immigrants living in the Pacific Northwest during the nineteenth century, historian Daniel Liestman likewise points out the Protestant clergy's concern for East Asian immigrants in America. In contrast to much of American society, which disparaged the Chinese and later the Japanese, Protestant groups in Washington and Oregon sought to aid the Asian newcomers. Like their counterparts in California, these men and women hoped that their Chinese and Japanese communicants would ultimately spread Christianity among their friends and family across the ocean. After the Civil War, American Protestants expended much energy on both foreign and home missions. A number of Protestant denominations opened home missions specifically for the Chinese beginning in the mid-1870s. One of the most successful programs was operated by the Portland Baptist Mission, and others were sponsored by the Episcopalian, United Brethren, Methodist, Christian Alliance, and Christian (Campbellite) churches, as Liestman documents. These orga-

40. Daniels, *Asian America*; and Gary Y. Okihiro, *Margins and Mainstreams: Asians in American History and Culture.*

41. Laurie F. Maffly-Kipp, *Religion and Society in Frontier California*, 48.

42. Wesley Stephen Woo, "Protestant Work among the Chinese in the San Francisco Bay Area, 1850–1920 (California)," 30–153.

nizations taught English classes, operated Sunday schools, and organized Chinese church services in order to both Christianize and Americanize their charges. As anti-Chinese feelings increased in the Pacific Northwest, many Protestant leaders and missionaries acted as much-needed advocates for the Chinese. At the same time, however, other Protestant clergy spoke out against the growing Asian population, which they believed was hurting the morals of their cities and undermining job opportunities for their fellow whites. By the late nineteenth century, with the Chinese population shrinking, some Protestants shifted their attention to the Japanese, or simply combined their outreach initiatives to both communities. In time, however, their efforts produced minimal results, and most Protestants lost interest in evangelizing East Asians domestically.[43]

East Asian Encounters with Latter-day Saints in California and Hawaii

In the century following Captain James Cook's European "discovery" of the Sandwich Islands in 1778, the population of native Hawaiians plummeted due to disease and low fertility rates among the islanders. Moreover, intermarriage between foreigners and Hawaiian women was on the rise, producing ethnically mixed offspring. As Pacific historians Russell Clement and Sheng-Luen Tsai document, this "drastic decline in the native Hawaiian population had far-reaching effects on the economy as well, specifically causing plantation owners to look for foreign sources for labor. One of these foreign sources was Asia."[44] The majority of Chinese and Japanese immigrants arrived in Hawaii between 1852 and 1924, with the Chinese coming in larger numbers first, most from southeast China's Kwangtung Province. These early Chinese peasants were seeking better economic opportunities abroad, especially during the devastating Opium War (1839–1842) and the Taiping Rebellion (1850s) in China. During the 1870s and 1880s, the number of Chinese immigrants swelled dramatically in Hawaii. By 1884 there were 18,254 Chinese living in Hawaii, making up 23 percent of the islands' population.[45]

43. Daniel Liestman, "'To Win Redeemed Souls from Heathen Darkness': Protestant Response to the Chinese of the Pacific Northwest in the Late Nineteenth Century," 179–201.

44. Russell T. Clement and Sheng-Luen Tsai, "East Wind to Hawai'i: Contributions and History of Chinese and Japanese Mormons in Hawaii," 90.

45. Clement and Tsai, "East Wind to Hawai'i," 90–91.

Joseph Smith and Latter-day Saint leaders in Nauvoo, Illinois, assigned Addison Pratt and several missionary companions to the Sandwich Islands in 1843, but they ended up evangelizing in French Polynesia instead. It would not be until December 1850 that ten missionaries from Utah and California arrived in Hawaii and established the church there. By 1854, there were about four thousand Hawaiian Latter-day Saints scattered across all of the main islands. That same year the missionaries established a gathering place on Lanai, which they later abandoned.[46] The first Chinese Latter-day Saints were immigrant laborers living in Hilo, Hawaii, who converted to the church in 1854, when Chinese migration was just beginning in the islands.[47]

Alexander Badlam, an early convert who participated in much of early Latter-day Saint history in Ohio, Missouri, and Illinois, took an interest in the salvation of the Chinese. In February 1849, he immigrated from Boston, Massachusetts, where he had been living with family members, to San Francisco, where his infamous brother-in-law, Samuel Brannan, was living and prospering during the California Gold Rush. Over the next several years he corresponded with Latter-day Saint apostles in Utah, reminding them of his loyalty to the church and its leadership. Badlam eventually moved temporarily to Utah before returning to California in 1852. While passing through San Bernardino, the Latter-day Saint colony in southern California, and while in San Francisco, he met and spent time with the three missionaries church president Brigham Young had assigned to evangelize in Hong Kong.[48]

In September 1853, Badlam, who was then living in Sacramento, California, wrote a letter to Young at church headquarters in Utah. He told the church leader about his efforts to learn Chinese to be able to evangelize immigrants from China. That October, Young responded by letter to Badlam in Sacramento, expressing his pleasure that he was learning Chinese while living in California. "I was much pleased to learn that you had turned your attention to the Chinese language," Young began. "My counsel to you is to continue to use such time as you can spare and such skill as the spirit of the Lord gives you until you become proficient in the Chinese language. And I would also suggest that you associate with the Chinese as much as possible, to assist you in learning, and to become acquainted with

---

46. R. Lanier Britsch, "Hawaii," in *Encyclopedia of Latter-day Saint History*, 474–75.

47. R. Lanier Britsch, *Moramona: The Mormons in Hawaii*, 90.

48. Will Bagley, *"Cities of the Wicked": Alexander Badlam Reports on Mormon Prospects in California and China in the 1850s*, 5–10.

their habits, and mode of thinking." In Young's mind, Badlam could begin to evangelize the Chinese in California, instead of traveling to China like James Lewis, Hosea Stout, and Chapman Duncan had unsuccessfully earlier that year. "This method will give you the opportunity to profit by your knowledge as you progress, and through faith & obedience, I feel you will be able to perform a good mission without leaving California, and e'er long be able to ordain Natives, and send them home to preach the Gospel in China."[49] Apparently, Badlam took Young's counsel seriously and continued to study Chinese. In February 1854, Young sent him another letter of encouragement: "I hope you will not spare any reasonable efforts until you are sufficiently acquainted with the Chinese language to be able to preach in it."[50] Badlam would continue to study Chinese in the years to come and report his linguistic progress to church leaders, including apostles Wilford Woodruff and George A. Smith.[51]

In January 1855, Badlam wrote to Elder George A. Smith about his ongoing experiences in California with the immigrant Chinese. "For the present I expect that Sacramento will be the field of my operations and the study of the Chinese, my principle [*sic*] object," he began his letter. "In a former letter, I have given you some idea of the Chinese. Since writing to you on that subject I have had the pleasure of extending my acquaintance with that people and the more I learn about them, the more highly I esteem them, and wish to learn of them." Badlam then described the efforts of Presbyterian missionaries among the Chinese in neighboring San Francisco.[52] Later that spring, he sent Smith "a few gleanings of Chinese history," which he had transcribed from a book by Walter Henry Medhurst, a former Christian missionary in China who was now viewed by some as an expert on the Chinese.[53] Through these and other means, Latter-day Saint leaders were able to learn more about China as a mission field.

---

49. Brigham Young to Alexander Badlam, October 31, 1853, Church History Library.

50. Brigham Young to Alexander Badlam, February 28, 1854, Church History Library.

51. Bagley, *"Cities of the Wicked"*; and Alexander Badlam to Wilford Woodruff, February 9, 1856, The Wilford Woodruff Papers.

52. Alexander Badlam to George A. Smith, January 12, 1855, Church History Library, as transcribed in Bagley, *"Cities of the Wicked"*, 12–13.

53. Alexander Badlam to George A. Smith, May 28, 1855, Church History Library, as transcribed in Bagley, *"Cities of the Wicked"*, 14–21.

President Brigham Young and his fellow apostles were encouraged by Badlam's updates and additional reports of a handful of Chinese immigrants embracing the church in California and the Sandwich Islands. In March 1857, he wrote to his nephew John R. Young, who was proselyting in Hawaii, expressing hope that the gospel might go forth among all people, including the Chinese, and reflecting nineteenth-century (Latter-day Saint, Protestant, American) attitudes of Asian religions:

> The millions of China's population, that now worship, they know not what, have yet to learn of the living & true God, and tho they have turned a deaf ear to them when we sent unto them [in 1853], they may yet listen to the truth, when proclaimed to them by some of their own nation. I am glad that you have baptized some of them, and pray that the number, intelligence and faith of all such may be increased.[54]

Brigham Young remained optimistic that someday the Chinese would embrace his church's message.

Despite such optimism for spreading their religion abroad, including among the Chinese, however, Latter-day Saint evangelism worldwide was disrupted in 1857 when the US government sent 2,500 troops to Utah to take control of the territory by force. Young recalled men of all ages from their missionary responsibilities around the world to help fortify the territory from federal assault. The missionaries teaching the Chinese in Hawaii and California packed their belongings and returned to Utah. Tensions cooled, and the feared Utah War never came to outright battle, yet as historian Will Bagley suggests, church leaders' eagerness to preach their message in places like Asia, even as the Latter-day Saints struggled to survive in the American West, shows that the church had a "vision that encompassed the entire world." He further points out a troubling irony in the church president's global mindset: "As Brigham Young was adopting exclusionary policies against African peoples that would saddle the religion with a dubious legacy of discrimination for more than a century, [Alexander] Badlam recommended a policy of acceptance of Asians that ran counter to popular prejudices, especially in California."[55]

Once the Utah War was resolved with US government officials, church leaders resumed global evangelism, including in Hawaii. In 1865, the church purchased six thousand acres at Laie, on the north shore of Oahu, for a new gathering place, including what would become a sugar

54. Brigham Young to John R. Young, March 1, 1857, Perry Special Collections.
55. Bagley, *"Cities of the Wicked"*, 4.

plantation and the mission's headquarters until 1921.[56] Although a few Chinese immigrants joined the church in Hawaii during the second half of the nineteenth century, these conversions were "uncommon," according to Clement and Tsai. "While the Chinese and Japanese population in Hawaii dramatically increased in the latter nineteenth century, Latter-day Saint missionaries continued to labor almost exclusively among the native Hawaiian population until well into the twentieth century, when acculturation and intermarriage confused and blurred the issue."[57]

Most of the contacts and exchanges between the Latter-day Saints and Chinese in Hawaii occurred in and around the church's sugar plantation in Laie, Oahu. A growing number of Chinese immigrants worked at the neighboring plantations at Kahuku, where the church's sugar cane was processed. Moreover, church leaders in Laie leased some of their plantation lands to Chinese workers looking to cultivate their own crops. They reported in their letters to church headquarters in Utah the cordial relations with these hardworking Chinese farmers. While they were grateful for these business opportunities with the immigrant Chinese, church leaders "were reluctant to hire Chinese laborers at the Church-owned plantation and mill for fear the Chinese would weaken the morale of the islanders. Moreover, no attempts to convert the local Chinese are mentioned" in mission records "even though some must have become close business associates." Clement and Tsai suggest that the Chinese immigrants' "language and traditions of ancestor worship were completely foreign to American-raised, Utah-trained, nineteenth-century missionaries. Early Chinese planters were most likely tradition-bound foreigners who were neither interested in nor ready to accept Christianity. Contact between Mormons and Asians was maintained, however, at the plantation and at the mission's day school."[58]

Church members and missionaries in Hawaii also encountered a growing number of Japanese immigrants during the final decade of the nineteenth century. Two of these Japanese men, Tomizo Katsunuma and Tokujiro Sato, have "legitimate claim" to being the first Japanese Latter-day Saints, scholar Shinji Takagi notes.[59] Katsunuma, a well-educated veterinarian, emigrated to Hawaii and then spent time in Utah before

56. Britsch, "Hawaii," 475.

57. Clement and Tsai, "East Wind to Hawai'i," 92.

58. Clement and Tsai, "East Wind to Hawai'i," 93–94.

59. As both Katsunuma and Sato were Asian American immigrants, I have used the westernized spelling and order of their names.

joining with the Latter-day Saints, while Sato emigrated to Hawaii and labored in various industries.[60] During the first decades of the twentieth century, additional Chinese and Japanese men and women embraced Latter-day Saint teachings and established a fledgling East Asian Latter-day Saint presence in the mid-Pacific.

Clement and Tsai summarize the interpersonal and cultural challenges facing these early Chinese and Japanese Latter-day Saints in Hawaii, the "handful of Asians who were converted from the 1870s to around 1920," as follows: "These pioneer Asian Saints must be regarded as novelties in the nineteenth- and early-twentieth-century mission dominated by Hawaiians and haloes [whites]. Since the early missionaries found success among the Hawaiian population, there were few, if any, attempts to spread the gospel to foreign labor immigrants, even those working on leased land in Laie. Church officials seemed most concerned with establishing Laie as a gathering place for Hawaiian Saints." According to these historians, "the uneducated, illiterate early Asian immigrants undoubtedly seemed as foreign and remote to nineteenth-century Mormons as they did to all nineteenth-century Hawaiians."[61]

The East Asian Experience in Utah

Chinese and Japanese workers did not limit their destinations to Hawaii and California, and hundreds of these immigrants made Utah their home during the nineteenth century.[62] (Several Koreans also worked in Utah mines during the 1890s, but little is known of their backgrounds. The Korean migration to Utah would not begin in earnest until the first decade of the twentieth century.[63] Moreover, Latter-day Saints would not have meaningful encounters with the Koreans abroad until after World War II.[64]) These migrations resulted in regular interactions between East Asian and white residents of Utah, and contact with the predominant population

60. Shinji Takagi, "Tomizo and Tokujiro: The First Japanese Mormons," 73–106.

61. Clement and Tsai, "East Wind to Hawai'i," 100–101.

62. Pamela S. Perlich, *Utah Minorities: The Story Told by 150 Years of Census Data*, 1–19.

63. Lee, "Korean," in John H. Yang, *Asian Americans in Utah: A Living History*, 145–77.

64. Dong Sull Choi, "History of the Church of Jesus Christ of Latter-day Saints in Korea, 1950–1985," 80–92; and Palmer, *Korean Saints*.

of Latter-day Saints was inevitable.[65] By the late nineteenth century, the majority of Latter-day Saints lived in North America due to the church's earlier policy of gathering to the "American Zion," with most church members living in Utah, the stronghold of Latter-day Saint country.[66]

Chinese immigrants first arrived in Utah as laborers helping to build the Central Pacific Railroad that linked Sacramento, California, with Promontory, Utah, in the years following the Civil War. When the transcontinental railroad was completed in 1869, former railroad construction workers settled in northern Utah, most in Box Elder County, and continued to work in the railroad industry. In pioneer Utah, most Chinese railroad workers formed close-knit communities near their places of employment and apart from white residents. At one point in the late nineteenth century, Corinne, Utah, was home to about three hundred Chinese immigrants. Ogden, which was Utah's quintessential railroad town as the connection point for several railroad lines, had over a hundred Chinese residents by 1890. Most of these East Asian immigrants congregated in a growing Chinatown noted for its unique structures and Chinese businesses. The mining towns of Park City, Pleasant Valley, and Silver Reef also benefited from the contributions of hundreds of Chinese workers. By 1890, there was a total of 806 Chinese in Utah. By the turn of the twentieth century, Salt Lake City claimed the most Chinese residents of any city in Utah, most of them living in downtown's Plum Alley.[67]

The nineteenth-century Euro-American response to the Chinese in Utah was wide-ranging. As in other parts of the West during postbellum America, the Chinese faced increasing hostility in Utah, especially in mining areas where they were seen as an economic threat to lower-class white workers. Nevertheless, the Utah Chinese did not face the same level of discrimination that they did in other western states. Some Utah newspapers even defended the Chinese immigrants during the period of anti-Asian

65. From 1850 to 1960, at least 98 percent of Utahns were white. By 1990 this figure had dropped only slightly, to 94 percent. "Hispanic" was not a separate category until the 1970 census. *Deseret Morning News 2004 Church Almanac*, 234; Perlich, *Utah Minorities*, 1–19.

66. Jan Shipps, *Sojourner in the Promised Land: Forty Years Among the Mormons*, 258–60.

67. Don C. Conley, "The Pioneer Chinese of Utah," 85–86; Perlich, *Utah Minorities*, 13; Daniel Liestman, "Utah's Chinatowns: The Development and Decline of Extinct Ethnic Enclaves," 269–89; Conley, "The Pioneer Chinese of Utah," 251–77.

sentiment. Many Utahns viewed the Chinese as benign curiosities to be tolerated and sometimes even celebrated, especially during their holiday festivals. "Most white residents of Utah tended to view the Chinese as a faceless, if not nameless, seemingly indistinguishable group of people who tended to cluster in predominantly white communities," historian Daniel Liestman describes.[68] As the Chinese population expanded, however, some Utah residents viewed the mysterious Chinatowns as "dens of iniquity." They were concerned with the gambling, prostitution, violence, and opium smoking that had become, or at least were believed to be, commonplace in these Chinese enclaves. Nativist white labor groups also complained that their members were losing jobs to the Asian immigrants. With mining on the decline, many Chinese switched to service industries, including laundries, restaurants, and grocery stores. Some also worked in the medical field, introducing traditional Chinese healing practices to Utah.[69]

Although the Chinese and white inhabitants of nineteenth-century Utah lived in essentially separate spheres, members of various Utah Christian denominations attempted to evangelize the Chinese. Several Protestant churches sought to build relationships with their East Asian neighbors through English conversation classes in hopes of eventually introducing Christianity to their students. Lena Wakefield, a representative of the American Home Missionary Society in Salt Lake City, began teaching an English class in 1881. By 1895 the Congregational Church's education outreach enjoyed the attendance of over a hundred Chinese students in Utah. Utah Methodists also focused on the Chinese for conversion and in time held services specifically for their growing Chinese communicants. Baptists in Ogden set up a Chinese Sunday school in the 1890s. For some reason, Latter-day Saints were skeptical of the Protestant evangelism of the Chinese immigrants in their midst. They were unconvinced that Christian educational efforts would result in lasting conversions. Ironically, the normally missionary-minded Latter-day Saints did next to nothing to fellowship and evangelize the Chinese in Utah. The Chinese likewise showed little interest in Utah's predominant faith and continued to worship in the handful of "joss houses" (Chinese temples and shrines) located in northern Utah.[70]

68. Liestman, "Utah's Chinatowns," 269.

69. Liestman, "Utah's Chinatowns," 269–80. See also Michael Lansing, "Race, Space, and Chinese Life in Late-Nineteenth-Century Salt Lake City," 219–38.

70. Liestman, "Utah's Chinatowns," 281–82; Lansing, "Race, Space, and Chinese Life," 236–37.

In their study of Chinese-white relationships in the late nineteenth and early twentieth centuries in Utah, scholars Melissa Wei-Inouye and Joseph Soderborg argue that "Chinese Americans in Utah lived amidst formal and informal structures of racism that constrained their opportunities for socialization, marriage and family, property ownership, and even just being present in a space." However, these same historians point out that "racism and isolation were not the only reality of the lives of Chinese in Utah. They demonstrated extraordinary resilience both in their presence as fixtures within the community and in their determination to pursue their own personal goals." Their Chinese (Ju) and white (Soderborg) ancestors enjoyed a "symbiotic relationship" during this era as they shared their harvested produce and religious principles with one another over time.[71]

Nevertheless, Wei-Inouye and Soderborg make the case that "the specter of racial integration" among the Chinese and whites partially accounted for lack of evangelism by Latter-day Saints of East Asian immigrants in Utah. "For a White missionary, it was one thing to convert Māori in New Zealand or Hawaiians in Hawaii, but another thing entirely to practice religion with them in integrated congregations in one's own neighborhood," they explain. "In marked contrast with their policy toward White European, Australian, and New Zealand converts, Church leaders encouraged non-White converts from New Zealand and the Pacific Islands to remain in their homelands instead of emigrating to Utah." They further point out that when Pacific Islanders began to emigrate to Utah in the late nineteenth century so that they could enjoy temple ordinances, "Latter-day Saint leaders arranged for them to be segregated in their own settlement in Skull Valley over sixty miles from the White Latter-day Saint population in Salt Lake City."[72]

When Japanese immigration swelled in the United States in the late nineteenth century, hundreds of Japanese immigrants made their way to Utah, where they were employed by the railroads and the agricultural community. Japanese labor agents such as Yozo Hashimoto and Edward Daigoro helped recruit additional Japanese to the Intermountain West.[73] By the end of the nineteenth century, there were over four hundred Japanese immigrants living in Latter-day Saint country. This figure

71. Melissa Wei-Inouye and Joseph Soderborg, "We Had a Symbiotic Relationship," 78.

72. Wei-Inouye and Soderborg, 75.

73. See Wendy Butler, "Strategies, Conditions, and Meaning of Early Japanese Labor in Salt Lake City, Utah, 1890–1920."

would jump to over two thousand within a decade.[74] During the early years of the twentieth century, the Japanese would take the place of the Chinese who emigrated out of Utah amid federal anti-Chinese legislation. By 1940 there were 2,210 Japanese to only 228 Chinese living in Utah.[75] Compared to available Chinese immigrant history, scholars have written little on the nineteenth-century Japanese migration to Utah. The fact that the Japanese did not congregate in high-profile ethnic enclaves like the Chinese or face the same type of anti-immigration persecution (until the 1920s) may explain this gap in scholarship.[76]

There are some indicators as to how the Latter-day Saints interacted with the Japanese immigrants living in predominantly Latter-day Saint communities in the West.[77] Drawing on church records, oral histories, and a few written reminiscences, historian Eric Walz was surprised to learn that there was little effort to evangelize the first- and second-generation Japanese living among the Latter-day Saints in the late nineteenth and early twentieth centuries, although the church would eventually expend tremendous resources to run a mission in overseas Japan. Walz suggests several reasons for this neglect of the Japanese immigrant community. Most Latter-day Saints, particularly those involved in agricultural enterprises, viewed the Japanese as a highly desired labor pool, rather than as prospective converts. There were in fact several Japanese conversions to the gospel when individual Latter-day Saints looked beyond the laborer stereotype. But it was not until the rise of the second-generation Japanese that the two groups met on more equal terms, especially through church programs for children and teenagers.[78] During World War II, when more than 10,000 Japanese Americans were incarcerated at the Topaz relocation center in central Utah, the Latter-day Saints exhibited somewhat greater

74. Helen Z. Papanikolas and Kasai, "Japanese Life in Utah," 333–39; Robert A. Wilson and Bill Hosokawa, *East to America: A History of the Japanese in the United States*, 76–93; Nancy J. Taniguchi, "Japanese Immigrants in Utah," 281–83.

75. Perlich, *Utah Minorities*, 8, 13–14.

76. For a history of twentieth-century race relations between the residents of Utah and the Japanese, see Elmer R. Smith, "The 'Japanese' in Utah," 129–44; and "The 'Japanese' in Utah: Part II," 208–30.

77. To study twentieth-century race relations between the Latter-day Saints and Japanese in Canada see David B. Iwaasa, "The Mormons and their Japanese Neighbors," 7–22.

78. Eric Walz, "Japanese Immigrants and the Mormons," 1–11. See also Wendy Butler, "Eyes Only for the Orient: Early Twentieth-Century Mormon Neglect of Salt Lake City Japanese."

tolerance to these Japanese Americans in their midst than most other American religious groups.[79]

Meeting and Migration

Interpersonal and literary meetings between the Latter-day Saints and East Asians were important sources of information for church leaders evaluating future Asian missionary opportunities. Evangelistic encounters abroad helped the isolated Latter-day Saints learn something about the Asian world and its peoples. But they never achieved the level of knowledge sought by American Protestants, who were the leading interpreters of Asian cultures and religions in America. Latter-day Saint missionaries and travelers did not crisscross the globe during the nineteenth century as investigators of other peoples and faiths. Judging from missionary diaries and extant correspondence, few missionaries showed real interest in Asian cultures and belief systems during this era.

Moreover, early Latter-day Saint missionary opportunities to observe Asian cultures and religions firsthand ended prematurely in the 1850s. The China Mission closed after months of struggle in 1853, and the East Indian mission was a losing battle that same decade before it was shuttered.[80] In retrospect, the early 1850s may be considered the heyday of the nineteenth-century church and its missionary program throughout the Pacific world, and its flourishing and demise were intimately linked to events back home in Utah Territory when Young recalled all missionaries from both domestic and foreign mission fields to return to Utah and defend Zion against a potential conflict with the US government.[81] In subsequent years, American missionaries returned to many of their churches in former Pacific outposts, but no Latter-day Saint missionaries

---

79. Leonard J. Arrington, "Utah's Ambiguous Reception: The Relocated Japanese Americans," 92–97; Leonard J. Arrington, *The Price of Prejudice: The Japanese-American Relocation Center in Utah during World War II*; and Sandra C. Taylor, "Leaving the Concentration Camps: Japanese American Resettlement in Utah and the Intermountain West," 169–94.

80. R. Lanier Britsch, "Church Beginnings in China"; and R. Lanier Britsch, "The East India Mission of 1851–56: Crossing the Boundaries of Culture, Religion, and Law," 150–76.

81. Richard E. Bennett, "Utah War," in *Encyclopedia of Latter-day Saint History*, 1282–84. See also Britsch, *Moramona,* 46–49; and Marjorie Newton, *Southern Cross Saints: The Mormons in Australia*, 33.

were stationed in Asia, South America, or much of Polynesia between 1856 and 1901.[82]

Given the apparent limitations of interpersonal meetings abroad, literary meetings took on added importance. It was difficult to find in-depth materials on Asia in pioneer Utah libraries,[83] so church periodicals, including the *Juvenile Instructor*, educated the generation of Latter-day Saints who would be responsible for taking the gospel to Japan. As noted above, the rise of Japan politically, economically, and militarily led Latter-day Saint leaders to conclude that the Japanese, rather than the Chinese, were the more progressive people and the nation most likely to give Latter-day Saint missionaries the best reception. These impressions were confirmed on at least two occasions when high-ranking Japanese officials assured church leaders that their petitions to evangelize in Japan would be permitted. Later events proved them prescient.

East Asian migration to Hawaii and the American West during the second half of the nineteenth century reminded Latter-day Saint leaders that there were many peoples, especially in East Asia, that they had overlooked while prioritizing their missionary efforts on the Atlantic world. Nevertheless, the church's leadership continued to concentrate on North American and Western European missionary fields. "It was a strange dichotomy that Mormon leaders sent missionaries all the way to Hong Kong in 1853 if they then later ignored the Chinese population which gathered on their doorstep," observes one historian of Chinese in pioneer Utah. "Plum Alley was only a few blocks from Mormon Temple Square."[84] Similarly, Wei-Inouye and Soderborg point out that "the missionary-minded Latter-day Saints, who had sent evangelists to Hong Kong in 1853, to New Zealand in the 1880s, and who had even built a temple in Laie, Hawaii, in 1919, to accommodate the spiritual needs of a burgeoning community of Hawaiian members, appear to have made almost no sustained efforts to proselytize to the non-Christian Chinese in their midst in Utah."[85] The same goes for the Utah Japanese.

---

82. Gordon Irving, *Numerical Strength and Geographical Distribution of the LDS Missionary Force, 1830–1974*, 11.

83. See Reid L. Neilson, "A Mormon and a Buddhist Debate Plural Marriage: The Letters of Elder Alma O. Taylor and the Reverend Nishijima Kakuryo, 1901," 98–99.

84. Conley, "The Pioneer Chinese of Utah," 114. See also Shi Xu, "Images of the Chinese in the Rocky Mountain Region: 1855–1882," 289.

85. Wei-Inouye and Soderborg, "'We Had a Symbiotic Relationship,'" 73–74.

CHAPTER THREE

Opening the Japan Mission and Exploring China

Nearly five decades passed after the closing of the short-lived China Mission in 1852–1853 before the First Presidency of The Church of Jesus Christ of Latter-day Saints again assigned missionaries to East Asia. Unlike their Christian counterparts who began evangelizing in Japan immediately following the Asian empire's official "opening" to the outside world in 1853, American Latter-day Saints waited until 1901 to commence missionary work among the Japanese. Moreover, as described in Chapter 2, church leaders had made little attempt to evangelize the East Asians living in their midst in the American West. While social, linguistic, and political realities all seemingly factored into this course of action, so did unique Latter-day Saint theological conceptions of race and lineage. It would take a dramatic drop-off in missionary success in the North American and Western European mission fields, coupled with a renewed sense of millenarian urgency, to persuade church leaders to finally look to the East instead of the West.

Latter-day Saints have long understood the world and its ethnic groups through the Bible and Book of Mormon scriptural narratives. Most Euro-American members believed themselves to be direct descendants of one of the scattered twelve tribes of ancient Israel in the Old Testament, and they understood that in the latter days, the scattered tribes would once again be gathered. Additionally, they drew upon broader Euro-American Christian ideas of the nineteenth century that different races descended from different scriptural figures. Under this interpretation, the light-skinned seed of Ephraim, who was the son of Joseph and one of the tribes of Israel, enjoyed a privileged role at the top of the Latter-day Saint ethnic grading in the nineteenth century. By contrast, the dark-skinned descendants of Ham, one of Noah's sons, were understood to be cursed and therefore unworthy to hold the priesthood and enjoy temple blessings. As sociologist Armand L. Mauss describes it, Native Americans were near the top of this order, since they were seen as part of an ancient Israelite diaspora in the New World. Also high on the list were the offspring of Judah, another of Israel's sons, or the Jews. Then there were the descendants of the other Israelite clans, who had been spread and "lost" across the globe and likewise were to receive the promised blessings of the Abrahamic covenant at the end of days. Beneath the favored Israelites but above the condemned Hamites stood the "Gentiles," who could enjoy the full blessings of the Abrahamic covenant by accepting the church's message and ordinances.[1] Conspicuously missing from this ethnic hierarchy were the peoples of East Asia.

Historian Norman Douglas makes the case that Latter-day Saint leaders prioritized the allocation of the human and financial missionary capital according to this ethnic ladder that evolved as their elders and sisters evangelized across the world, especially throughout the Pacific Basin frontier. As we have seen, the first missionaries called to teach the gospel in the Sandwich Islands, China, India, and New Zealand in the 1850s initially understood their missions to be focused on the Euro-Americans living in these lands, not the native Pacific Islanders or Asians, until they were met with disappointment.[2]

Latter-day Saints became increasingly curious but remained ambivalent about the relationship between the house of Israel and the peoples of Asia. For example, George Jarvis, a Latter-day Saint serving in the British navy off the East Asian coasts in the late nineteenth century, tried to evangelize in Japan while at port in Yokohama. Despite a lack of success, he became interested in the lineage of the Japanese. Decades later in 1902, while serving in the Latter-day Saint position of patriarch in the St. George Utah Stake, Jarvis laid his hands on the head of his son Erastus, who had just been assigned to preach in the Japan Mission, and invoked a blessing that he would be able to "learn the origin of the Japanese people," in reference to their scriptural lineage. George Jarvis also told his son that he believed that Hagoth, a Book of Mormon seafarer, might have landed on the Japanese coast, and he described to Erastus an "Israelitish altar" on a bluff overlooking the Yokohama harbor.[3]

As early as 1887, some Latter-day Saints were interested to learn about the possibility of Israelite blood coursing through the veins of the Japanese. In an unsigned letter reproduced in the *Millennial Star* church periodical,

---

1. Armand L. Mauss, *All Abraham's Children: Changing Mormon Conceptions of Race and Lineage*, 2–3; and W. Paul Reeve, *Religion of a Different Color: Race and the Mormon Struggle for Whiteness.*

2. Norman Douglas, "The Sons of Lehi and the Seed of Cain: Racial Myths in Mormon Scripture and their Relevance to the Pacific Islands," 100. See also Norman Douglas, "'Unto the Islands of the Sea': The Erratic Beginnings of Mormon Missions in Polynesia, 1844–1900," 249–51.

3. G. Stanford Jarvis, "The Far East: Footprints and Fulfillments," 1–2.

a non–Latter-day Saint traveler related his experiences meeting Nicholas McLeod, a Scottish expatriate working in Asia, while both men were living in Japan. During the late 1870s, McLeod self-published several books in Japan that theorized that the Japanese people were actually Israelites.[4] Like McLeod, the writer believed the Japanese that had immigrated to the isles of East Asia were the literal descendants of biblical Jacob—the "lost tribes" of Israel. A *Millennial Star* editor added a footnote to this recital that suggested that the Book of Mormon might hold the key to understanding the great diaspora of Israel throughout the Pacific Basin frontier, including Asia: "It is probable that these people were drifted to the islands of the Pacific Ocean and inhabited them. It was doubtless in this manner that the Sandwich Islands were peopled, as also other islands and even Japan, as there is a great similarity between the American Indians, Sandwich Islanders, the Maori in New Zealand and the Japanese."[5]

Years later, a *Deseret News* editorial with the identical title "Are They of Israel?" followed the same line of reasoning regarding the settlement of East Asia. "It is well known that scholars are at a loss to account satisfactorily for the ancient history of Japan. That some of the descendants of Jacob should have found their way to Japan, after the breaking up of the Assyrian empire, is not improbable," the author noted. "Israelites have been found in China, preserving much of the old tradition and religion, and it is by no means incredible that some of that race should have crossed over to the Japanese islands, and there become a factor in the development of the country and the nation. Israel was scattered throughout the world, in order to act as a leaven, preparing all the nations of the earth for the last dispensation."[6]

---

4. Nicholas McLeod, *Epitome of the Ancient History of Japan*; Nicholas McLeod, *Illustrations to the Epitome of the Ancient History of Japan*; Nicholas McLeod, *Album and Guide Book of Japan, from Satsuporo [sic] in the North to Kagoshima in the South, with historical and statistical notes*; and Nicholas McLeod, *Korea and the Ten Lost Tribes of Isreal [sic], with Korean, Japanese and Isrealitish [sic] illustrations*. See Joseph Rogala, *Collector's Guide to Books on Japan in English*, 142.

5. "Are They of Israel?" *Millennial Star* 49, no. 3 (January 17, 1887): 33–36.

6. "Are They of Israel?" *Millennial Star* 58, no. 31 (August 2, 1906): 479–80. In ensuing years, several researchers have written on the possibility of Israelite blood being spread throughout Asia, including China and Japan. C. H. Kang and Ethel R. Nelson, *The Discovery of Genesis: How the Truths of Genesis were Found Hidden in the Chinese Language*; Joseph Eidelberg, *The Biblical Hebrew Origin of the Japanese People*; and Sidney Shapiro, *Jews in Old China: Studies by Chinese Scholars*.

Following the death of Wilford Woodruff, Lorenzo Snow was sustained as the church's fifth president in September 1898. His short administration (1898–1901) was marked by the church's improving financial position and heightened international outreach. At the time Snow began his presidency, the church owed an overwhelming $2.3 million to creditors. This debt was the result of the US government's seizure and mismanagement of church property following the passage of the anti-polygamy Edmunds-Tucker Act of 1887, as well as the church's debt-financed public work projects in the 1890s. Seeking a solution to the church's dire financial straits, an inspired Snow reemphasized the paying of tithes. As a result, the financial crisis concluded by the beginning of the new century, and church leaders began thinking about new opportunities.[7]

Under President Snow's direction, the church entered the twentieth century with 283,765 members, 967 wards and branches, 43 stakes, and 4 temples. In addition, nearly a thousand men and women were evangelizing in more than a dozen mission fields.[8] However, most of these members, congregations, and edifices were in North America and were not representative of the world's population. As we have seen, up to this point Latter-day Saint missionary work and resources were mainly focused on the nations of North America and Western Europe, while in the minds of church members, the countries of Asia languished in spiritual darkness.

Disturbed by this trend, Snow determined to shift the church's attention to the nations of East Asia, South America, and Eastern Europe. Due to a resurgence of millennialism, church leaders believed that Christ's Second Coming was near and felt that they needed to fulfill the Great Commission, in which Jesus asked his followers to spread his message, in lands theretofore untouched by Latter-day Saint missionaries.[9] It had been fifty years since the church had sent missionaries on an evangelical errand to Asia, the world's most populous continent. In Snow's mind, the central responsibility of apostles in the Quorum of the Twelve Apostles was "to warn the nations of the earth and prepare the world for the coming of the

7. Maureen Ursenbach Beecher and Paul Thomas Smith, "Snow, Lorenzo," 3:1369–70. See also Thomas G. Alexander, *Mormonism in Transition: A History of the Latter-day Saints, 1890–1930*, 3–6.

8. *Our Heritage: A Brief History of The Church of Jesus Christ of Latter-day Saints*, 104; Gordon Irving, *Numerical Strength and Geographical Distribution of the LDS Missionary Force, 1830–1974*, 14–15.

9. Rudger Clawson, Diary, June 26, 1901, in *A Ministry of Meetings*; "A Farewell Reception," *Improvement Era* 4, no. 10 (August 1901): 796.

Savior," not to overly busy themselves with local administrative duties, which were the responsibilities of stake presidents and bishops.[10] Snow believed that his fellow apostles needed to refocus their energies outward, not inward, to fulfill their errand to the world, just as their predecessors had done for much of the nineteenth century.

Snow was not a lone voice in the First Presidency pointing out the church's slowing missionary enterprise at the start of the twentieth century; his counselor George Q. Cannon was likewise concerned. He believed church leaders were "expending means and time with deficient [conversion] results" in the British Isles and other parts of Europe as they entered the new century.[11] Rather than converting thousands of Europeans each year, missionaries were now barely gleaning hundreds of new members. Moreover, changing political, economic, and social circumstances in Western Europe made what was still a largely American church less appealing to would-be European converts. These new missionary realities also encouraged Cannon and others to advocate the opening of new missionary fields in countries where the "believing blood of Israel" might yet be uncovered.[12] Cannon expressed his millenarian vision of twentieth-century evangelism in the October 1900 general conference: "Oriental lands now untouched by the Elders of the Church have to be penetrated and the honest souls sought out." Cannon viewed Japan as the toehold needed for the Latter-day Saint expansion into East Asia. "If the time has come for Elders to go to Japan, let Japan be penetrated," he stated. "After a while perhaps an opening may be made in Korea, and in Manchuria, and in China."[13]

Opening the Japan Mission

Japan loomed large on the horizon of new Latter-day Saint missionary possibilities in 1900. Rather than orchestrating the evangelism of hundreds of Chinese and Japanese immigrants living within miles of their offices in Salt Lake City, however, the First Presidency determined to take the gospel directly to East Asia. As chronicled in Chapter 2, a series of nineteenth-

---

10. Joseph F. Smith, "The Last Days of President Snow," *Juvenile Instructor* 36, no. 22 (November 15, 1901): 689–90; and B. H. Roberts, *Comprehensive History of The Church of Jesus Christ of Latter-day Saints*, 6:375.

11. George Q. Cannon, Journal, July 12, 1900, Church History Library.

12. Mauss, *All Abraham's Children*, 32–34.

13. George Q. Cannon, in *Seventy-First Semi-Annual Conference* (1900), 63–64, 66–68. See also Cannon, Journal, September 6, 1900.

century encounters with East Asians both at home and abroad convinced church authorities that Japan, not China, should be the church's Eastern priority. Accordingly, on February 14, 1901, during a weekly meeting of the Council of the First Presidency and Quorum of the Twelve Apostles, President George Q. Cannon announced the establishment of the Japan Mission and called Elder Heber J. Grant as its president.[14] Over the next several months, Grant selected three missionary companions: Horace S. Ensign, Louis A. Kelsch, and Alma O. Taylor. The Latter-day Saint errand to the East Asian world had recommenced.

Many Latter-day Saints in Utah were delighted when the First Presidency publicized the creation of the Japanese mission field. Historian Leonard J. Arrington describes the thrill in Utah over the Japan Mission as "somewhat analogous to excitement over early space flights"[15] sixty years later. The *Deseret Evening News* reported that the announcement of the Japan Mission had "aroused no little interest" in church circles.[16] In the months leading up to the departure of the elders to Japan, Latter-day Saints and other Salt Lake City citizens feted the elders on several occasions. Although missionaries were generally sent off with some sort of farewell party, the opening of a new mission in East Asia by an apostle garnered more excitement and caused more celebration than usual. The First Presidency even sponsored a benefit concert for the Japan Mission in the Salt Lake Tabernacle.[17] Nearly a dozen Salt Lake City Japanese residents hosted another farewell party at the 21st Ward chapel, where Japanese and American flags hung side by side. "The evening's entertainment concluded with general hand shaking and expressions of good will on the part of the Japanese to the Mormon Elders who were about to leave for the Orient," one reporter described.[18]

Despite the excitement in Utah over sending missionaries to Japan, there was disagreement among Latter-day Saints regarding the propriety of evangelizing East Asians. In the weeks leading up to the April 1901 general conference, some church members expressed concern about the

---

14. Heber J. Grant, Journal, February 14 and June 26, 1901, Church History Library; Rudger Clawson, Diary, February 14, 1901.

15. Leonard J. Arrington, "Utah's Ambiguous Reception: The Relocated Japanese Americans," 92.

16. "Opening of a Mission in Japan," *Deseret Evening News*, April 6, 1901.

17. Clawson, Diary, April 25, 1901; "The Japanese Mission Benefit," *Deseret Evening News*, May 30, 1901.

18. "American and Japanese Flags," *Deseret Evening News*, June 19, 1901.

The first Latter-day Saint missionaries called to Japan in summer 1901 in Salt Lake City. Standing (*left to right*): Horace S. Ensign, Alma O. Taylor. Seated (*left to right*): Heber J. Grant, Louis A. Kelsch. Courtesy Church History Library, The Church of Jesus Christ of Latter-day Saints.

church's prospects among the Japanese. Despite articles like "Are They of Israel?," most church members saw the Japanese as perhaps beyond the reach of the "believing blood" of the house of Israel.[19] "We know not what is in store for this Church in the Empire of Japan," First Presidency counselor Rudger Clawson admitted.[20] Elder John W. Taylor tried to dismantle the ingrained Latter-day Saint belief that only the obvious descendants of the house of Israel would be receptive to the gospel. "Some of you have heard that Elder Grant is going to Japan, and you begin to query in your minds, Is this nation of the house of Israel? Is it a proper thing for Elder Grant to go to Japan?" Taylor declared that "there is no nation on the face of the earth but will hear the everlasting Gospel; . . . Then our minds may be set at rest in regard to Elder Grant going to Japan."[21]

At the next general conference in October 1901, a full two months after Grant and his companions landed in Japan, church authorities felt it

19. For positive appraisals during April 1901 general conference, see Reed Smoot, in *Seventy-First Annual Conference* (1901), 6; and Matthias F. Cowley, in *Seventy-First Annual Conference*, 16.

20. Rudger Clawson, in *Seventy-First Annual Conference*, 8.

21. John W. Taylor, in *Seventy-First Annual Conference*, 29.

necessary to continue addressing these theological concerns. "People have asked the question whether or not Brother Grant would be successful in Japan, and whether the Gospel would gather people from other nations," Elder Matthias F. Cowley related. "Such a question need not be asked, for it was answered this morning in the revelation read by Apostle Smoot, where it says in relation to Zion, 'And there shall come unto her out of every nation under the heaven.' We need, therefore, have no concern whatever about that."[22] It would be up to the Japanese people to demonstrate their receptivity to the restored gospel, and thereby assert their biblical birthright to the promised blessings of the house of Israel in the last days.

Grant and his three missionary companions had departed on July 24, 1901. They had purposefully scheduled their departure to coincide with Pioneer Day, a religious and civic holiday in Utah commemorating the vanguard company of Latter-day Saint pioneers entering the Salt Lake Valley in 1847,[23] and they were prepared to do some trailblazing of their own in Japan. The youngest member of the evangelism quartet, Alma O. Taylor, expressed hopeful enthusiasm as he contemplated his pending separation from his loved ones in Utah. "This being the day of starting on my mission to Japan, it is one of excitement and work," he reflected in his journal. "With most people, the thoughts of leaving relatives and friends for so long a time as I may be gone on this mission, would be very sad but with me this contemplation of the labor lying before me is so pleasant that I say good-bye to all with joy."[24]

The missionaries traveled north by train to Ogden, Utah, where they caught a rail connection to Vancouver, British Columbia. After making their way to the harbor, the four men boarded the *Empress of India*, a 6,000-ton steamship operated by the Canadian Pacific Railway Company.[25] After two weeks at sea, the missionaries finally caught sight of the Japanese coastline on August 12. They were dazzled by the new sights and sounds they encountered. Taylor captured several observations in his journal that

---

22. Matthias T. Cowley, in *Seventy-Second Semi-Annual Conference* (1901), 18. See also Brigham Young, in *Seventy-Second Semi-Annual Conference*, 40.

23. See R. Mark Melville, "Twenty-Fourth of July: An Overview of Utah's State Holiday, 1849–2022," 69–114.

24. Alma O. Taylor, Journal, July 24, 1901, Perry Special Collections.

25. Mowbray Tate, *Transpacific Steam: The Story of Steam Navigation from the Pacific Coast of North America to the Far East and the Antipodes*, 141–51; and Shinji Takagi, "Mormons in the Press: Reactions to the 1901 Opening of the Japan Mission," 141.

first day. From the veranda of his hotel, the young missionary looked out over the bay and was entranced by his surroundings. "Seeing also the apparel and manners of the people, I indeed felt 'A Stranger in a strange land.'"[26] Despite any apprehension, however, Taylor and his fellow missionaries were excited to be on Japanese soil and were eager to evangelize. On September 1, 1901, Grant offered an apostolic blessing on the nation of Japan and the Japanese people, as described in Chapter 4. In the missionaries' minds, the Japan Mission was now officially open for Latter-day Saint evangelism.

Alma O. Taylor in Tokyo, Japan, ca. 1906. Photograph by S. Yeghi. Courtesy Church History Library, The Church of Jesus Christ of Latter-day Saints.

During their first few months in Japan, however, the four elders enjoyed little missionary success. Nevertheless, they looked for physical traits and religious practices that might signal that at least some of the Japanese were related to Native Americans—and thereby descendants of the Book of Mormon peoples, who were promised great spiritual blessings in the latter days according to their scriptures. By the beginning of the twentieth century, sociologist Armand L. Mauss explains, "the varied missionary outreach of the church began to produce evidence of the blood of Israel in other parts of the world, where the gospel was starting to be well received. These include in Latin America, southern and eastern Europe, Russia, Asia, New Zealand, and various Pacific islands." He continues: "These and other LDS mission leaders and missionaries thus became advocates, as it were, for extending literal Israelite identity to a great variety of peoples, some quite exotic by comparison with Anglo-Ephraimites of Utah. In the process, 'believing blood' came to be found almost everywhere the missionaries went."[27] The original Latter-day Saint missionaries in Japan were likewise hopeful that the blood of Israel, which suggested pending belief, might be coursing through the Japanese populace they were there to convert to their Christian gospel.

26. Taylor, Journal, August 12, 1901.
27. Mauss, *All Abraham's Children*, 33–34.

Nevertheless, the dozens of Latter-day Saints who evangelized in Japan during those early years continued to see themselves as strangers in a strange land, just as had the early missionaries in Hong Kong.[28] Over the next decade, Latter-day Saint missionaries would labor to fulfill the church's missionary errand to the Japanese. Despite the earlier transpacific encounters with the Chinese and Japanese, which led to the First Presidency's announcement of the Japan Mission in 1901, these same mappings, meetings, and migrations still did not lead church leaders to reformulate their evangelical outlook or practices for an Asian audience.

The Euro-American Latter-day Saint missionary model in Japan at the turn of the twentieth century differed in important ways from the American Protestant missionary approach. First, the Latter-day Saints focused on preaching Christ rather than exporting Western culture to the Japanese, regardless of the latter's benefits. Unlike the Protestants who operated schools, hospitals, and churches in Japan, the Latter-day Saints tracted, held preaching meetings, engaged in intra-Christian debates, and contacted prospective converts on the streets.

Second, Latter-day Saint missionaries called to Japan, especially by the late nineteenth century, came from quite homogeneous backgrounds. The majority were living in Utah when they received their mission calls, and most had no formal schooling beyond secondary education. American Protestants, on the other hand, hailed from across the Northeast and Midwest, representing numerous denominations. While Latter-day Saint women did not formally evangelize until 1898, Protestant females constituted a major force within the foreign missionary enterprise. But the only females from Utah who represented the church in Japan were wives or daughters of married male missionaries.

Third, the Latter-day Saint elders were typically sent on their missions to Japan with little, if any, missionary training. While some attended theological classes before departing, most learned how to be missionaries once they arrived in their fields, in intensive on-the-job training. In contrast, most Protestant men and women enjoyed the benefits of higher education before arriving in East Asia; nearly all received formal missionary training through their mission boards before leaving America.

Fourth, Latter-day Saint missionaries were short-timers in their Japanese fields of labor, usually staying about two years before returning to their prior vocations. These amateurs and their families eventually had

28. Hosea Stout to Brigham Young, May 16, 1853, Brigham Young Office Files, Church History Library.

to pay much of the cost of their voluntary missionary service. On the contrary, their Protestant counterparts often committed the balance of their lives to further the cause of Christ in Japan. These professionals were financed through mission board fundraising activities back in America.

Fifth, the vast majority of Latter-day Saints labored in the United States, Canada, Great Britain, and Scandinavia, all Christian nations—not in East Asia. Conversely, American Protestants served the peoples of the Levant, South Asia, Africa, and East Asia, who knew little, if anything, of Christ.[29]

So, while the Latter-day Saint Euro-American missionary model continued to be well suited for the evangelism of Christians in the North Atlantic world, it remained too provincial to missionize in East Asia, where the inhabitants spoke Japanese, Chinese, and Korean, and where the people practiced Buddhism, Shinto, and Daoism. Believing they could merely impose and translate their religion in non-Christian Asia, the missionaries floundered. The Latter-day Saints anticipated business as usual in the East. By the opening of the Japan Mission in 1901, they seemed to have forgotten the hard lessons learned in China, India, Siam, and Burma during the 1850s.

The Progressive Era in Utah and the Chinese Abroad

Church leaders in Utah had launched Latter-day Saint evangelism in Japan during the Progressive Era in the United States, a time of great reform designed to improve society. "Progressives were concerned with reform in American politics, economic life, and social institutions, and generally believed that both national and local governments must broaden the scope of their activities to bring about needed reform. In the social realm, reformers looked with dismay at the evils of crowded cities which seemed to foster poverty, crime, ill health, and general lack of opportunity for the underprivileged," historians James B. Allen and Glen M. Leonard describe. "The Church, too, was concerned with the social ills of the early twentieth century, though it did not necessarily urge its members to become involved with the active reform groups that were attracting national followings."[30]

Nevertheless, by the early twentieth century, as the church was emerging from financial difficulties, leaders desired to act on the church's

---

29. See Reid L. Neilson, *Early Mormon Missionary Activities in Japan, 1901–1924*, 35–58, 83–119.

30. James B. Allen and Glen M. Leonard, *The Story of the Latter-day Saints*, 455–56.

homegrown humanitarian impulse. Latter-day Saints wanted to bless those beyond their cultural region in the American West and those outside their theological worldview. For example, the female-led Relief Society repeatedly turned their gaze outward, including to the Chinese who were starving during the famine of 1907. The church held its 77th Annual General Conference on Temple Square in Salt Lake City, Utah, the first weekend of April 1907. During the Relief Society session of conference, the organization's leadership presented a resolution to ship dozens of tons of flour to China to alleviate suffering there, just as they had done for the suffering citizens of San Francisco a year earlier.[31] The proposal was approved unanimously by the sisters in attendance and then shared with the First Presidency for church-wide consideration.[32] During the Sunday morning session of general conference, John R. Winder of the First Presidency read the following resolution from the Relief Society sisters:

> Whereas, The president of the United States has called national attention to the existence of the sore distress in China on account of famine, and
>
> Whereas, The Lord has greatly blessed the Saints and all the interests of the Church, and,
>
> Whereas, our Relief Societies have stored up grain against a time of need; now therefore, I move that the Trustee-in-Trust be, and is hereby authorized to appropriate and donate toward the relief of the poor in famine stricken China 20 tons of flour.[33]

Next, Elder Brigham H. Roberts of the First Council of the Seventy stood and endorsed the Relief Society's generous offer of wheat for the starving Chinese. "I desire to second the resolution offered by President Winder to this conference; and in doing so I desire to call attention to the fact that we are connected with an institution founded of God for the benefit of the whole world, and that it is an institution of world-wide sympathies," he began. "No calamity can fall upon any of our Father's children but what our hearts go out in sympathy to them. I trust also that this movement, which I believe will be unanimously endorsed by this conference, may bear witness to the wisdom that exists in our methods of collecting means for charitable

---

31. See "Earthquake and Fire," *Woman's Exponent* 34, no. 10 (May 1906): 68.

32. "General Conference of the Relief Society," *Woman's Exponent* 35, no. 9 (May 1907): 71; and Jessie L. Embry, "Relief Society Grain Storage Program, 1876–1940," 25.

33. John R. Winder, "Famine in China," in *Seventy-Seventh Annual Conference*, 59. See also "Church Sends Flour to China," *Deseret Evening News*, April 8, 1907.

and religious purposes."[34] Following Roberts's remarks, the congregation of women and men who were gathered in the Tabernacle voted to adopt the Relief Society's resolution to share the church's grain and flour with the famine-stricken citizens of China.[35]

During that same general conference weekend, Assistant Church Historian Andrew Jenson spoke during an overflow meeting in the Assembly Hall. He offered a status report to conference attendees on how the church was doing in preaching to "all the world." The report was optimistic but candid; church membership remained tilted toward North America, and to have "the globe fully covered by our missionary operations," Jenson reported, more resources were needed in Asia, Central and South America, and Africa.[36] He briefly recounted the unsuccessful Hong Kong mission of 1853, then noted, from a Euro-American perspective, "The Chinese, however, have become more enlightened since that time, and we have reason to expect that a successful missionary field will be opened in that land in the near future."[37] Jenson acknowledged that the church and its membership had done little evangelism in the Near East, Middle East, and Far East. "In Asia, we have done limited work in Turkey (in Asia) including Palestine and Asia Minor, and also in parts of India, and we have visited China and Siam; but we have done nothing in Asiatic Russia [north Asia], Afghanistan, Baluchistan [Pakistan], Persia [Iran], Thibet, Arabia and Korea."[38] Desiring to share the gospel message globally, Jenson concluded with a plea for religious liberty to open the doors to all nations.

Later in the summer of 1907, Latter-day Saint Frank J. Hewlett, the former president of the Salt Lake City Council, published a lengthy article in the church's *Improvement Era*, sharing his experiences and impressions during a recent business trip to East Asia. Like other Americans, Hewlett was optimistic that China was finally beginning to follow the modernizing example of rival Japan in East Asia, which was taking its place economically, militarily, socially, and religiously alongside Western powers. He harbored

34. Brigham H. Roberts, in *Seventy-Seventh Annual Conference*, 59.

35. Unfortunately, by the time the Relief Society's valuable flour arrived in China, it was no longer needed and was sold for $5,800, which was eventually returned to the Relief Society's coffers. Embry, "Relief Society Grain Storage Program," 25.

36. Reid L. Neilson and Scott Marianno, *A Voice in the Wilderness: The 1888-1930 General Conference Sermons of Mormon Historian Andrew Jenson*, 71–72.

37. Jenson, in *Seventy-Seventh Annual Conference*, 103.

38. Jenson, in *Seventy-Seventh Annual Conference*, 104.

high hopes that the gospel could be preached among the Chinese. "China has also been awakened from her lethargy in regard to Christianity. The persecution of Christian missionaries has ceased almost entirely, and they can go about their work unmolested," he shared with his Latter-day Saint readers. Hewlett further related that when he was recently in Shanghai, he observed Protestant missionaries gathered for an evangelistic conference. He described the wealth of the American Protestant missionary boards and their ability to "easily raise" hundreds of thousands of dollars for their evangelistic activities and facilities in China. As a successful Utah entrepreneur, he concluded his article with boosterism for economic and spiritual opportunities in East Asia.[39] During the Progressive Era, individuals like Frank Hewlett and Andrew Jenson in Utah were anxious to seize opportunities to help uplift surrounding society, including in East Asia.

Alma O. Taylor's Fact-Finding Mission to China

Alma O. Taylor, who arrived in Yokohama with Elder Heber J. Grant in 1901, devoted himself to the Japan Mission with remarkable fervor and religiosity. Over the next eight and half years, he learned both the spoken and written Japanese language, assisted in the translation of missionary tracts and church hymns, organized Sunday School classes, performed priesthood ordinances, and opened new proselytizing areas throughout Japan, all the while finding, teaching, converting, and strengthening many of the early Japanese Saints. After being selected to translate the Book of Mormon into Japanese, he spent years on the project. And in 1908, he became the president of the Japan Mission, succeeding Horace S. Ensign, who had in turn replaced Heber J. Grant in that role in 1903. Remarkably, Taylor accomplished all this while he was still unmarried and in his early twenties.

Nevertheless, after serving as a missionary for nearly a decade in Japan, Taylor was ready to return to Utah. Before leaving East Asia, however, he hoped to survey neighboring countries as potential mission fields the church had not yet entered. Accordingly, he wrote the First Presidency with a proposal: "I would like to visit China and Korea for the purpose of getting an idea of the conditions there. From all the reports I hear, these two countries afford opportunities for missionary work, equal with, if not superior to, those in Japan." Taylor continued, "Of course, this is entirely out of my jurisdiction and my conscience somewhat censures me for

39. Frank J. Hewlett, "New China and Japan," 815–16, 19.

being so presumptive as to even propose such a move, but again I have the feeling that my closeness to these two countries is a partial excuse, at least, for entertaining the desire to visit them."[40] It appears, then, that Taylor believed that either China or Korea might yield more converts than Japan, where converts numbered only thirty-five during his long tenure there.[41]

Like Frank J. Hewlett back in Utah, Taylor was intrigued by the evangelistic possibilities of continental East Asia as he concluded his missionary service in Japan. Like other mission presidents who preceded and succeeded him in Tokyo, he was aware of and frustrated by the meager number of missionaries that church leaders had historically assigned to Asia, the world's largest and most populous continent. As documented in Chapter 1, the church at the time had allocated less than 1 percent of its available missionary force to all of Asia. Calls from church leaders like George Q. Cannon, urging a reallocation of Latter-day Saint missionaries from Western Europe and North America to East Asia and other regions unevangelized by Latter-day Saints in 1900, went largely unheeded. Other than opening the fledgling Japan Mission that same year, there was little reprioritization of missionary resources throughout the first half of the twentieth century.

What were the prospects for the Latter-day Saints in China in 1910? To begin with, Roman Catholic missionaries had spread their faith in China since the Middle Ages, facing repression, persecution, and martyrdom. Protestants entered in 1807 and built upon the existing Chinese Christian foundation. Both Christian groups benefited from the foreign treaties of 1844 and 1860, which enhanced China as a viable mission field. For instance, by 1890, there were about half a million baptized Catholics, led by 639 foreign missionary priests and 369 Chinese priests, and by the end of the century, there were about 1,500 Protestant missionaries, located in about five hundred evangelism stations scattered throughout China.[42]

Between the years 1895 and 1900, however, some militant Chinese groups came to violently resist increasing foreign intervention in China. Finally, the Peking-based Chinese government issued an imperial edict ordering all foreigners out of China or threatening them with death. "Boxer" was the name given to members of Chinese secret society who

40. Alma O. Taylor to First Presidency, February 9, 1909, Japan Mission, "Letterpress Copybooks, 1901–1923," Church History Library, 378.

41. Murray L. Nichols, "History of the Japan Mission of The Church of Jesus Christ of Latter-day Saints, 1901–1924," 133.

42. Stephen Neill, *A History of Christian Missions*, 286.

believed that their rituals of boxing and calisthenics would protect them from enemy gunfire. This militant group grew in popularity in northern China as the Chinese suffered terribly due to economic challenges and humiliating concessions forced upon them by Western nations. The "Boxer Rebellion," which resulted in the deaths of Chinese Christians and Westerners, was extinguished within three months by a foreign fighting force, but not before several Catholic and Protestant missionaries were murdered and some twenty to thirty thousand Chinese Christians massacred. The victorious foreign powers heaped tremendous sanctions against the Chinese government and its subjects. Humbled by defeat, the Chinese sought to strengthen their nation by embracing Western education, ideals, and even foreign Christianity. Ironically, given the preceding slaughter, both the Roman Catholics and Protestants benefited from this new era of openness in the Chinese realm in the early twentieth century.[43]

Because the Latter-day Saint missionaries had few, if any, relationships with their Protestant counterparts in Japan, it was unlikely that Taylor was aware of the tremendous contemporary success of Christian evangelists in mainland China when he made his initial proposal to the First Presidency. Noted mission studies scholar Daniel H. Bays has identified the period between 1902 and 1927, which overlapped with the early Latter-day Saint Japan Mission (1901–1924), as the "golden age" of Christian missionary work in China. "This period of about a quarter-century was the high point of the foreign missionary age in China (though not of the overall Christian movement). China seemed to be modernizing and Christianizing at the same time," he documents in his study of Christianity among the Chinese. Thousands of foreign missionaries gathered in the nation, reaching more than eight thousand by the 1920s, and Chinese Protestants grew in numbers from about 100,000 in 1900 to 500,000 in the 1920s.[44] Informed of these statistics or not, the Latter-day Saints were seemingly missing out on this remarkable evangelistic window that had recently opened—and would soon close—in China.

Taylor's proposal to tour China on behalf of the church was well received at headquarters in Utah, and First Presidency members Joseph F. Smith, John R. Winder, and Anthon H. Lund readily consented to Taylor's request. On March 3, 1909, his proposal letter was read during the weekly meeting of the First Presidency and Quorum of the Twelve Apostles. John Henry Smith motioned that Taylor be given permission to

43. Neill, *A History of Christian Missions*, 346–47.
44. Daniel H. Bays, *A New History of Christianity in China*, 92, 94.

visit China and Korea, and Heber J. Grant, Taylor's former mission president in Japan, further suggested that fellow Japan missionary Frederick A. Caine accompany Taylor on his journey. Days later the First Presidency responded to Taylor: "We have pleasure in saying that the unanimous sentiment of the Council was that you may consider yourself at liberty to act on the suggestion after your release, and that you do not go alone, but that you take Elder Fred Caine with you, in the understanding of course that the Church is to bear your expenses."[45]

The First Presidency likely had several reasons for supporting Taylor's proposal. To begin with, of all the elders the church could send to investigate conditions for the gospel in East Asia, Taylor seems to have been the best prepared: no other American Latter-day Saint had lived as a missionary in Asia as long. While China and Japan differed in many respects, they did share a similar Asian heritage, Buddhist theology, character writing system, and Confucian mentality, which Taylor understood as well as any American Latter-day Saint. Moreover, Taylor had proven himself extremely capable and loyal to the church. For years, the First Presidency had trusted Taylor's decisions and conclusions while he served as mission president. He had completed his translation of the Book of Mormon into Japanese and had successfully arranged for its printing and sale—a complex and arduous task. Furthermore, Taylor had volunteered to investigate China, which negated the expense of sending another missionary there in the future. Finally, the First Presidency was increasingly concerned with China's temporal and spiritual condition, as demonstrated by their willingness to ship flour to China for its famine victims years earlier.

Taylor finally received notice of his release from the Japan Mission on December 18, 1909. "Whenever the question of your release has been referred to in our Councils," the letter began, "we have had in our minds associated with it the accomplishment of the important work undertaken by you, namely, the translation and publication of the Book of Mormon in Japanese; and now since success has so signally crowned your labors . . . we have great pleasure indeed in tendering to you the release which we feel you so well deserve." It continued, "In thus releasing you, after having spent so long a time on a foreign mission, we feel to say that your labors as a missionary and presiding officer have met with our hearty approval and entire satisfaction." They also included a bank draft of ¥2,000 to pay for

45. John R. Winder and Anthon H. Lund to Alma Owen Taylor, March 9, 1909, Japan Mission, "Incoming Letters, 1901–1921," Church History Library.

Taylor and Caine's upcoming travel expenses to Korea and China.[46] Over the following weeks, Taylor busied himself with the transfer of mission records and affairs to his successor, Elbert D. Thomas. He also participated in the baptism and confirmation of a recent convert and finalized Christmas preparations.

Taylor was released as president of the Japan Mission on January 1, 1910. Three days earlier, he had written the First Presidency about his final travel plans: "Elder Caine and I . . . shall be in Korea and China perhaps 45 days so until a brief visit at Hawaii we do not expect to reach Zion till April."[47] While he initially planned to investigate both Korea and China, a reading of his daily diary entries makes it clear that China was his main area of ecclesiastical concern. For the next several weeks, Taylor and Caine traveled together through both countries. After fourteen days in Korea, the two elders spent forty-nine days in China, both north and south of the Yangtze River. They traveled about 4,385 miles by "land and water in and about China," visiting thirty cities along the way.[48] While most of these cities were on the main rail lines or shipping lanes, these were the places most accessible to Westerners and therefore the most likely candidates for future Latter-day Saint missionary activities.

Throughout his entire journey, Taylor kept a detailed travel log in his journal specifying miles traveled, persons visited, money paid, places lodged, sites seen, and interviews held. As a result, he was well prepared to share his experiences and observations when he returned to Utah. After carefully reviewing Taylor's detailed journal and formal report, one comes to appreciate the way he thoroughly investigated and relied on a variety of sources to form his conclusions: personal experience and observations, extensive interviews with foreigners, and outside reading.

At the same time, Taylor's writings relied on the sources he drew upon—and consequently shared their limitations and biases, with conclusions that often stereotyped the Chinese in unflattering terms. Unaware

46. First Presidency to Alma O. Taylor, November 23, 1909, Japan Mission, "Letterpress Copybooks, 1901–1923," Church History Library, 486; and Taylor, Journal, December 18, 1910.

47. Alma O. Taylor to First Presidency, December 27, 1909, Japan Mission Letterpress Copybooks, Church History Library, 3:489.

48. In northern China, Taylor and Caine traveled exclusively by train, eventually logging an impressive 1,463 miles on the Chinese rail system. In the south, they traveled primarily by steamer along the Yangtze and the coast of China. Alma O. Taylor, "Report of Our Visit to China," 1–5.

of a world outside the cities' vices and eager to Christianize and reform, English speakers characterized the Chinese in broad, sweeping brushstrokes. That such stereotypes found their way into Taylor's report is no surprise. The combination of observation, interview, and reading made Taylor's resulting report to the First Presidency representative of contemporary attitudes of the Western community in China. There appears to be no evidence that other Christian missionaries purposely colored his view of China to discourage the Latter-day Saints from entering.

To begin with, Taylor relied on his own personal experiences and observations. As planned, he and Caine departed from Tokyo by train on January 10 and traveled south to the Japanese port city of Shimonoseki and there boarded a steamer for Korea. The duo next traveled north up the Korean peninsula by train, passing through Seoul and Pyongyang and eventually reaching Mukden, Manchuria. From Mukden, they continued southwest to Tianjin and finally arrived in the capital city of Peking. Leaving Peking, they endured the 750-mile train ride south to Hankow, where they boarded an eastbound steamer on the Yangtze River. By canal and train, the men eventually reached Shanghai; there, they were forced to wait eight days for a steamer to transport them along the southern coast of China to Hong Kong—a delay that Taylor recorded as "the first hitch in our travels so far."[49] Aboard the steamer, they visited Fuzhou, Amoy, and Swatow before reaching Hong Kong. Canton was next on their itinerary. Departing Canton, Taylor and Caine boarded a steamer returning to Japan, passing through Hong Kong and Shanghai on the way. All together, they spent seventeen days both north and south of the Yangtze River.

During this time, what were Taylor's impressions of China's transportation system, established religions, and boarding conditions? Taylor frequently detailed the travel conditions and lamented his long train rides in northern China, eventually expressing great joy in his diary after disembarking at the last train station. In contrast, he enjoyed the steamer ride along the coast of the South China Sea despite the incessant rolling and rocking of their vessel. One night Taylor smugly noted, "Elder Caine soon lost his supper. I felt very fine."[50] The coastal scenery was magnificent. Taylor excitedly penned, "At last we have found a spot in China were the scenery looks fresh and beautiful! Our disgust with the poverty of scenic landscape in north and central China is partially forgotten when we behold the magnificence of the scenery from the mouth of the Min up to the

49. Taylor, Journal, February 22, 1910.

50. Taylor, Journal, February 17, 1910.

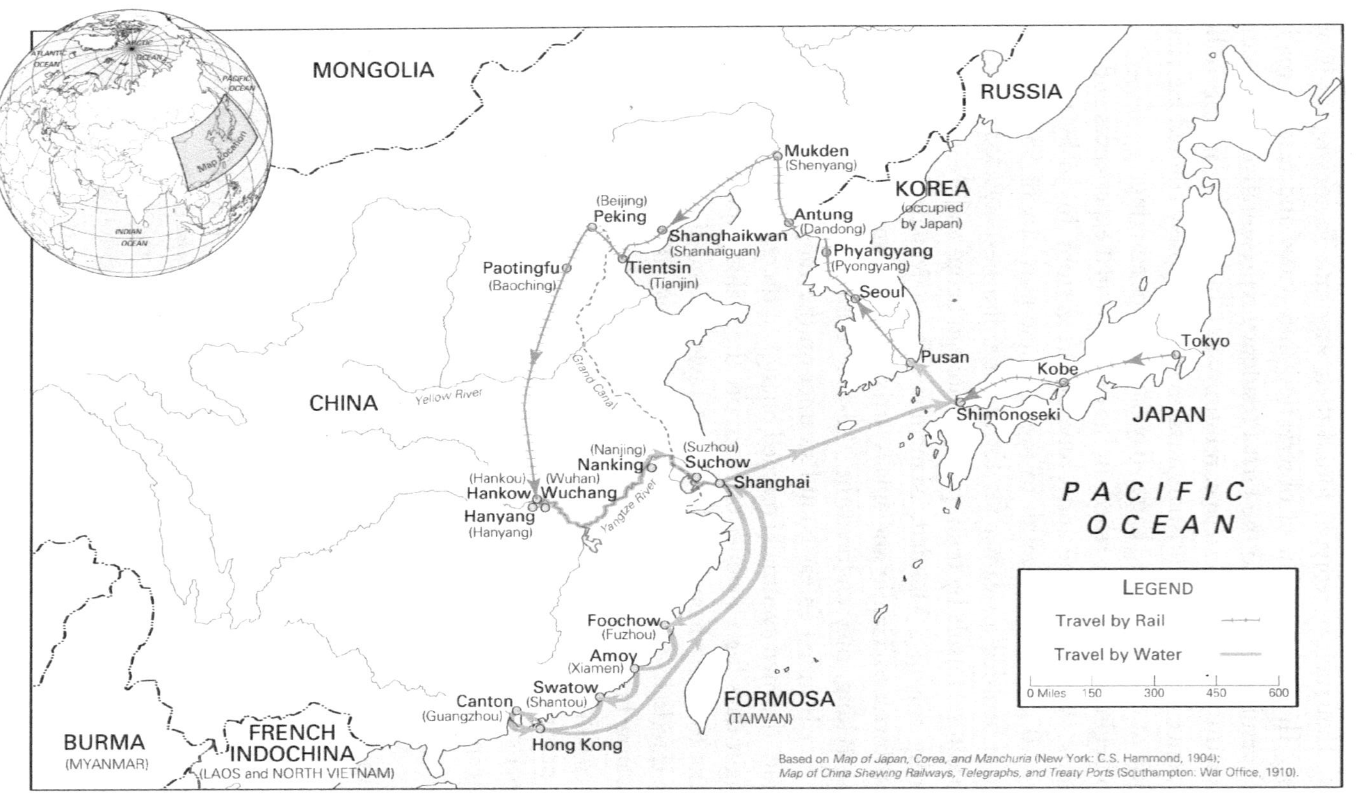

Alma O. Taylor's Fact-Finding Journey to Korea and China, 1910

Taylor left Tokyo for Korea on January 10, 1910, and returned to Shimonoseki, Japan, on March 18, 1910.

city of Foochow [Fuzhou]."[51] The duo's most amusing form of transportation must have been riding donkeys in Suchow, the "Venice of China." Taylor wrote, "We . . . entered the city on donkeys. This was real fun. Our donkeys rushed rapidly through the narrow, thronged streets while our knees kept poking the people in the ribs. The donkey boys ran ahead to clear the way and the bells on the donkey's necks rang merrily. Here we saw large attractive Chinese stores, and numerous water canals and bridges."[52]

Taylor had mixed emotions regarding established religions in China, both Christian and Buddhist. One Sabbath morning, he and Caine attended the American (Episcopal) Church Mission Chinese services. "It was Christian idolatry without Spirit," he observed. "The audience was composed mostly of young people. . . . The singing and Psalm reading were excruciatingly out of tune. Not more than 120 were present."[53] That afternoon, they attended the London Mission's Chinese services. More favorably impressed, Taylor noted, "Here we saw a larger audience, people of more mature years, and more humility in dress and spirit. . . . An English gentleman had charge of the service and did the speaking. This is the first Chinese sermon by a foreigner we have heard in China. There was quite a cordiality manifested by the people for each other."[54]

Interestingly, Taylor was most impressed by the aesthetic qualities of a Peking Catholic Church. "The magnificence of this building in comparison to the plainness of the Protestant churches is striking," admitted Taylor. Nevertheless, the Latter-day Saint viewpoint of a Christianity that had become corrupt meant that he saw the religious practices in a less favorable light: "As we entered the auditorium of the Church and saw the ornaments, tapestries, images, pictures etc. with a silent worshipper here and there, the power and mystic influence of Catholicism was easily felt. Certain it is that an idolatrous people have not far to go and nothing to lose by becoming Catholics."[55]

Later, in Shanghai, he determined to observe the Chinese in their native worship by visiting a Buddhist temple. Taylor was underwhelmed as evidenced in his diary: "We soon reached the city temple, a dark, dirty and conclusive witness to the utter degradation of operating Buddhism. The buildings were filled with smoke from the candles which burned by

51. Taylor, "Report of our Visit to China," 4.
52. Taylor, Journal, February 17, 1910.
53. Taylor, Journal, February 13, 1910.
54. Taylor, Journal, February 13, 1910.
55. Taylor, Journal, February 7, 1910.

the hundreds from the paper money which was being burned in deceitful homage to the dingy gods which sit or stand almost buried in soot and dust, smoke and from the incense which the people lighted with almost reckless waste."[56] Clearly, Taylor felt that the Latter-day Saints had something to offer other Christians and Buddhists in China.

Taylor was generally underwhelmed with the Chinese boarding conditions, as well. Ever the good sport, he humorously recorded his eating and living conditions. One night in Baoding, he stayed at a Chinese inn and ordered dinner. Disgusted by the meal, Taylor recalled, "In a short time two bowls of greased rice and twenty-one eggs were served! The eggs were cooked in three ways, boiled fried and poached. The greasy rice gagged me so I also lost my appetite."[57] The evening's sleeping arrangements were even worse. Taylor exclaimed, "The beds! Nothing in my experience will describe them unless I go to the old American country morgue in the undertaker's back yard and choose the slab for the comparison. Nothing but plainish boards on top of wooden pedestals. Here we were supposed to spread our blankets and sleep well! Our blankets being too few we applied for more and got four quilts hard and greasy. But we had come to see, to taste and to feel so we laughed and rejoiced over the experience. We piled our clothing on top and I slept very comfortably but Elder Caine said he didn't look half as much like a corpse as he felt like one, being cold and 'stiff' all night."[58]

The next morning, the two men eagerly departed after a fitful night of sleep. They fared no better that evening. "We again found lodging in a Chinese inn," complained Taylor. "They had a room fixed up for foreigners. But oh what a room! It was much more crude than any house in the western wilds of America." Other disgusted foreigners had covered the plaster walls with witty messages to vent their own frustrations. A classic read, "Chicken hot, chicken cold, chicken young, chicken old, chicken tender, chicken tough, of chicken sure, I've had enough."[59] That night Taylor noted, tongue in cheek, "The feather pillow provided was not tempting as there was too much fear that while the chickens might be dead the vermin in the feathers may not be, so I wrapped up a book in my towel and slept restlessly through the night."[60] For better or worse, Taylor was experiencing 1910 China firsthand.

---

56. Taylor, Journal, February 12, 1910.
57. Taylor, Journal, February 8, 1910.
58. Taylor, Journal, February 8, 1910.
59. Taylor, Journal, February 10, 1910.
60. Taylor, Journal, February 10, 1910.

Taylor's second major source of information on China was gleaned through extensive conversations with foreigners. Unable to speak Chinese, he instead attempted to interview each Western missionary and English-speaking resident he met. He typically received an audience in each new city through introductions from previous contacts in the close-knit foreign community in China. This method enabled him to meet with nearly sixty foreign missionaries, several of whom were regarded as experts on China by their peers. Taylor held interviews at chapels and mission compounds, English schools, Western universities, Christian hospitals and humanitarian centers, government offices, US consulates, newspaper offices, Western printing companies, Catholic missions, business offices, Chinese cultural centers, temples, government agencies, and even ruins.

Sometimes, Taylor withheld his religious affiliation until questioned by his interviewees due to the lampooning the church suffered at the hands of the worldwide press. However, when the subject of the church surfaced, he boldly defended his faith tradition. For example, he spent some time with a staunch Methodist couple as they steamed down the Yangtze River. During the middle of their pleasant conversation, the following incident occurred: "The fact that we are 'Mormons' didn't leak out until we were seated around the table. The old gentleman's inquisitiveness brought it out. Some of the people on learning our religion, seemed to lose for a moment their equilibrium. The old man, however, continued his questions, which got on to principle in hot succession and occasionally it was hard for him to maintain his gentlemanly attitude."[61] For the most part, though, Taylor was well received by his Christian and Western counterparts.

Lastly, Taylor formed his conclusions by reading voraciously during his entire China trip. He then compared his reading with what he was experiencing. Taylor visited bookshops in many of the cities he toured. In Shanghai, for example, he went to a bookstore called Kelly and Walsh and purchased several books on China, Buddhism, and Confucianism. That night he recorded, "Returned to the hotel, read about China, ate supper, wrote my journal and retired."[62]

One book of great significance to Taylor was Arthur H. Smith's *Chinese Characteristics* (1890).[63] One historian claims that it was "the most widely read and influential American work on China of its generation. Written in the late 1880s, it was still among the five most read books on China

61. Taylor, Journal, February 16, 1910.
62. Taylor, Journal, February 13, 1910.
63. Arthur H. Smith, *Chinese Characteristics*.

among foreigners living in China as late as the 1920s. . . . Smith's contemporaries read it as a wise and pungent handbook."[64] Taylor quoted Smith and various other authors in his final report to the First Presidency. He also perused the pages of S. H. Chester's *Lights and Shadows of Mission Work in the Far East* (1899), Chang Chih-Tung's *China's Only Hope* (1900), and some writings by Reverend J. Macgowan, likely gleaned from his *Christ or Confucius, Which?* (1889) or *History of China* (1906).[65] From a modern perspective, many of these books were biased against the Chinese, but they were the reality of the times and represented pervading Western thought.

Return to Utah and Report to the First Presidency

The two Latter-day Saint travelers arrived in Tokyo in mid-March 1910 and were welcomed by the missionaries and Japanese Saints. That evening Alma O. Taylor recorded, "It was a happy meeting. I was happy beyond words. . . . Everything and everybody at headquarters was in fine shape." Then he opened a letter from home that dramatically changed his mood: his brother Edward Theodore had died, as had his brother Samuel's little girl, and his mother and little boy were sick. Of this news he wrote, "Calamities always come together and often as an aftermath of joys."[66] The following day he attended his church meetings with a heavy heart. "The privilege to attend the sacrament meeting and worship with the saints was one which came as a drink to a man dying of thirst in the desert," he wrote. That same day, "in the public preaching meeting held in the evening, I was called upon to speak. I felt quite out of practice." Already Taylor was transitioning from Japanese missionary to American lay church member.[67] Finally on March 30, 1910, Taylor and Frederick A. Caine said their final goodbyes and departed for the United States via the Pacific Ocean.

On April 26, Taylor finally returned home to his family in Salt Lake City after an absence of eight years and eight months. Reunited with his

---

64. Charles W. Hayford, "Chinese and American Characteristics: Arthur H. Smith and His China Book," 154.

65. S. H. Chester, *Lights and Shadows of Mission Work in the Far East: Being the Record of Observations Made during a Visit to the Southern Presbyterian Missions in Japan, China, and Korea in the Year 1897*; Chang Chih-Tung, *China's Only Hope*; John Macgowan, *Christ or Confucius, Which? or, The Story of the Amoy Mission*; John Macgowan, *Imperial History of China: Being a History of the Empire as Compiled by the Chinese Historians.*

66. Taylor, Journal, March 19, 1910.

67. Taylor, Journal, March 20, 1910.

father, mother, sisters, and brothers, he naturally felt disoriented. "It was a strange home into which I was received," he wrote, "one that has been built since I went to Japan. . . . Dear old father has aged and weakened considerably. . . . Mother also shows the marks of the passing years. . . . I felt almost like being in an unknown world."[68] The evening of his arrival, Taylor and Caine reported on their missions to the First Presidency and received President Joseph F. Smith's blessing. That first evening, Taylor emphasized in his journal, he slept in a Western-style bed.[69] The next morning, Taylor and Caine met again with church leaders. During the ensuing three-hour interview, they "explain[ed] the manners, customs and life" of the Chinese and were in turn "asked a great many questions" by the First Presidency.[70] The two elders reported on their lengthy service in Japan and on their fact-finding mission to Korea and China. They continued presenting their report over the next several days.

In addition to his verbal report, Taylor submitted a written account with Caine's assistance. He drafted a lengthy manuscript entitled "Report of Our Visit to China."[71] The report highlighted their itinerary along with the political, military, educational, social, religious, and moral climate in China. It concluded with their own analysis of the events. After traveling nearly five thousand miles throughout China over nearly three months, Taylor reversed his earlier hopes and concluded that China was not ready for the gospel:

> China is in an uncertain, transitional state. The probability of revolution is not past. The program for the establishment of a constitution and a parliament is drawn up. Will the constitution grant religious liberty, and the laws and officials protect every man in his worship? Or will it make a state religion of Confucianism and put a ban on all others? . . .
>
> It appears to us that the Latter-day Saints will not be neglecting their duty to the world if they postpone the opening of a mission in China until the present chaotic, transitory state changes sufficiently to assure the world that China really intends and wants to give her foreign friends protection and a fair chance.[72]

Taylor's conclusions were rooted in the political and socioeconomic instability he and Caine encountered while in China. Several other

---

68. Taylor, Journal, April 26, 1910.
69. Taylor, Journal, April 26, 1910.
70. Taylor, Journal, April 27–30, 1910.
71. See Alma O. Taylor, "Report of Our Visit to China," 1910, Appendix B, herein.
72. Taylor, "Report of Our Visit to China," 31–32.

Joseph F. Smith and his counselors, ca. 1910: Anthon H. Lund (*left*) and John Henry Smith (*right*). After reviewing Alma O. Taylor's report, the First Presidency decided not to open a mission to China. Courtesy Church History Library, The Church of Jesus Christ of Latter-day Saints.

factors unique to the church probably influenced his reasoning. Unlike other Christian churches, The Church of Jesus Christ of Latter-day Saints lacked an established physical and human infrastructure in China. Large financial resources would be needed to permanently establish this infrastructure in China in 1910. This was money the corporate church, only recently out of debt, did not have. Taylor must have been aware of the church's previous failure in Hong Kong in 1853 and that it was partially due to this lack of infrastructure. Furthermore, he had only recently completed an arduous mission to Japan. He was aware of how difficult it was for Indo-European English speakers to learn Asian languages. Although his experience in the Japan Mission had proven that language was not an impenetrable barrier, Latter-day Saint missionaries in Japan were few. Opening China would tax the resources of Taylor's former mission, which still had a limited infrastructure itself.

Alma O. Taylor was a unique individual, well suited to performing missionary work in Japan and to surveying China for the preaching of the gospel. He was an informed observer, drawing on a variety of personal and external sources while in China, and his findings were indicative of contemporary Western attitudes toward China. In fact, his conclusions were bolstered when the ruling Chinese Qing Dynasty was overthrown in 1911, and China was again thrown into political disarray. To the Roman Catholics and Protestants, this revolution was but another storm to be weathered; to Latter-day Saint church leaders it was vindication of Taylor's conclusions. A small missionary force in China would have been overwhelmed. Taylor's report had far-reaching effects on the future expansion of Latter-day Saint missionary work into the Chinese realm. With China still in "an uncertain, transitional state," church leaders looked elsewhere to share the gospel. While we can never know for sure all the factors at play in a decision not to open a new mission, Taylor's report provided a factual basis for the church's postponement of missionary work in China in 1910.

CHAPTER FOUR

Unlocking the Doors to All Nations

Following Alma O. Taylor's fact-finding mission through China on behalf of the First Presidency in 1910, it would be another decade before leaders of The Church of Jesus Christ of Latter-day Saints sent another representative there to assess conditions for potential evangelism. In the meantime, the small number of elders and sisters called to Japan labored to fulfill the Great Commission as the church's lone representatives in all of Asia—the world's most populous continent. Nevertheless, after about twenty years of missionary work in Japan, church leaders and missionaries had little to show for their efforts. During the first two decades of the twentieth century, the church did not operate a single congregation in all East Asia, except for the handful of fledgling mission units in Japan.[1]

Elder Heber J. Grant, who offered the dedicatory prayer over Japan, became church president in November 1918. Of more than fifty men who had served in the Quorum of the Twelve Apostles since its organization in 1835, only Grant (1901–1903) and Elder Parley P. Pratt (1851) had served as a missionary or leader beyond North America or Europe. Up to the end of the Great War (World War I), no other members of the First Presidency or Quorum of the Twelve Apostles had ever personally ministered on the continents of South America, Africa, Asia, or Australia/Oceania (except for the Hawaiian Islands), despite the presence of missions and congregations in many of those areas. Both the growth and challenges in these regions encouraged Grant and other church leaders to adopt a more global mindset.

In late 1920, the First Presidency called Elder David O. McKay on an around-the-world tour assignment, including fact-finding initiatives in East Asia. The prophet had further invited the apostle to consider offering a dedicatory prayer over China. "Before we left home, President Grant suggested that when we were in China, if we felt so impressed, to set the land apart for the preaching of the Gospel. As Peking [Beijing] is really the heart of China, we had concluded that this would be an appropriate place

---

1. For more on the challenges of the first twenty years in Japan, see Reid L. Neilson, *Early Mormon Missionary Activities in Japan, 1901–1924*, 83–145.

to perform this sacred and far-reaching duty," McKay noted of this special assignment from the church president.[2]

When the First Presidency assigned McKay to embark on an ecclesiastical world tour and to open and prepare the land of China for missionary work, the leaders understood the call as being supported by ancient and modern scriptural passages and historical precedent. The church is organized with the First Presidency, the president of the church and his two counselors, at the top. The First Presidency directs the Quorum of the Twelve Apostles, modeled after the apostles of the New Testament. The Doctrine and Covenants, one of the faith's books of scripture, explains that the apostles "are called to go into all the world to preach [Jesus Christ's] gospel unto every creature."[3] The Quorum of the Twelve Apostles directs the Quorums of the Seventy, who are based on a New Testament passage (Luke 10:1) that mentions Jesus appointing "other seventy also." Together these three priesthood quorums preside over the entire church and its membership. In Latter-day Saint theology, the church's apostolic leaders are said to hold "keys," which represent authority given from God, as the New Testament (Matt. 16:19) records Jesus telling Peter he would give him "the keys of the kingdom of heaven." The following sections examine the Latter-day Saint understanding of the apostolic duty to evangelize around the globe and the tradition of "dedicating" lands for the preaching of the gospel.

Apostolic Dedicatory Prayers

Over two centuries, the Latter-day Saints have developed their own religious rites, some of which closely resemble the practices of their fellow Christians and others that depart from these familiar rituals. One of the more understudied and least understood Latter-day Saint rites is the dedicating of countries, which is connected to the apostolic duty to preach the gospel in all the world.

As explained by Jonathan A. Stapley, a scholar of Latter-day Saint rituals, the system of rites enacted by a church constitutes its liturgy. "While the term often refers to a specific formal ritual like the Roman Catholic Mass," he writes, "church liturgy is also used to celebrate major life events—birth, coming of age, marriage, death." The most readily apparent site of Latter-day Saint rites is the temple, but "Mormon liturgy . . . constitutes a much

---

2. David O. McKay, Diary, January 9, 1921, Marriott Special Collections.
3. Doctrine and Covenants 18:28.

larger and more complex set of rituals and ritualized acts of worship than specific rites of initiation, instruction, and sealing that are localized within the temple walls."[4]

In general, Latter-day Saints do not think of their religion as ritualistic. Instead, they are more familiar and comfortable with the term *ordinance* to describe their religious rites performed by priesthood authority. Religion scholar Victor L. Ludlow explains, "There are two general types of ordinances: those essential to our salvation in God's kingdom, and those that edify and strengthen us during mortality." Ordinances of salvation include baptism, confirmation (receiving the gift of the Holy Ghost), male priesthood ordination, temple endowment, and temple celestial marriage. Edifying ordinances, meanwhile, "are given through the power of the priesthood to comfort, console, and encourage" church members as they go through the challenges of life and fulfill ecclesiastical responsibilities, according to Ludlow. Ordinances for edification include the sacrament of the Lord's supper, naming and blessing of infants, blessings of comfort and counsel, administering to the sick, consecrating olive oil for the blessing of the sick, and dedicating homes, chapels, temples, lands, countries, and graves.[5]

The concept of a religious act of dedication or consecration is not unique to the Latter-day Saint tradition. Two years before Joseph Smith organized the church in 1830, American lexicographer Noah Webster, in his *American Dictionary of the English Language* (1828), defined "dedicate" as follows: "To set apart and consecrate to a divine Being, or to a sacred purpose; to devote to a sacred use, by a solemn act, or by religious ceremonies; as, to *dedicate* vessels, treasures, a temple, an altar, or a church, to God or to a religious use." As an example, Webster referenced the "vessels of silver, of gold, and of brass, which king David did *dedicate* to the Lord" in 2 Samuel 8 in the Old Testament.[6] Similarly, Latter-day Saints believe in formally dedicating or consecrating physical objects for righteous purposes by priesthood authority.[7]

From the earliest days of the church, apostles have also dedicated specific temple sites and structures by special ordinance, transforming them spiritually into the House of the Lord, by authority of their

---

4. Jonathan A. Stapley, *Power of Godliness: Mormon Liturgy and Cosmology*, 1–2.

5. Victor L. Ludlow, *Principles and Practices of the Restored Gospel*, 346–56, italics in original. See also Immo Luschin, "Ordinances," 3:1032–33.

6. Noah Webster, "Dedicated," *American Dictionary of the English Language* (1828).

7. Tad Callister, "Dedications," 1:367.

apostolic priesthood keys. Latter-day Saint temple dedicatory prayers are well known and extensively documented in both devotional literature and scholarly studies.[8] The first Latter-day Saint temple was completed in 1836 in Kirtland, Ohio, and was ceremonially inaugurated with a dedicatory prayer. Joseph Smith and several church associates prepared the text of the prayer by inspiration the day before the ordinance was performed, March 27, 1836, setting a pattern for future dedications.[9] By 2025, Latter-day Saint apostles had formally dedicated over 200 temples around the world, with dozens also rededicated following extensive remodeling or expansion. Apostolic temple dedications (including the initial consecration of temple sites) are publicly celebrated, attended, and documented. The church and affiliate organizations have subsequently published transcripts of all temple dedicatory prayers in print and online, making them readily accessible to interested Latter-days and curious individuals.[10]

In contrast, apostolic country dedications are not nearly as well known or studied,[11] even though the prayers were routinely published in church

---

8. See, for example, D. Arthur Haycock, "Temples: LDS Temple Dedications," 4:1455–56; N. B. Lundwall, *Temples of the Most High*; Samuel Brown, "A Sacred Code: Mormon Temple Dedication Prayers, 1836–2000," 173–96; and Jared M. Halverson, "Global Gatherings: Temple Dedications and the Spread of Sacred Space."

9. See Historical Introduction to "Minutes and Prayer of Dedication, 27 March 1836 [D&C 109]," in Brent M. Rogers et al., *Documents, Volume 5: October 1835–January 1838*, 188–91.

10. See "Temples," The Church of Jesus Christ of Latter-day Saints; and "Statistics: Temple Dimensions," Temples of The Church of Jesus Christ of Latter-day Saints.

"Between 1999 and 2002, the dedicatory services of a few newly constructed temples in significant historic sites, including Palmyra, New York; Winter Quarters, Nebraska; and Nauvoo, Illinois, were broadcast over a secure satellite system, allowing members of the Church in remote locations to participate. This established a pattern of broadcasting temple dedications to local stake centers so that all worthy members in the temple district and sometimes the broader area can participate." Church History Topics, "Temple Dedications and Dedicatory Prayers."

11. Although I will be using the terms country, nation, state, land, and territory interchangeably when referring to the priesthood ordinance of dedicatory prayers, each geopolitical word carries nuanced definitions.

Generally, Latter-day Saint apostles dedicate specific countries, but on occasion they have dedicated entire continents and regions. For example, Elder Melvin J. Ballard dedicated the South American continent for missionary work. See

The House of the Lord, later known as the Kirtland Temple, was begun in 1833, and dedicated by Joseph Smith on March 26, 1836. Courtesy Church History Library, The Church of Jesus Christ of Latter-day Saints.

periodicals for the first century of Latter-day Saint history. These dedications, like temple dedications, are ordinances for edification, not salvation. As explained by Victor L. Ludlow, Latter-day Saints believe these formal dedications of lands, performed by apostolic keys, "help God's children find truth and spirituality as they call upon the powers of heaven for enlightenment. They help the missionary work in such places and lands to go forward, often in miraculous ways."[12]

The dedication of a nation, normally performed by an apostle, is always conducted under the direction of the First Presidency and by virtue of

---

Melvin J. Ballard, "Dedicating the Lands of South America to the Preaching of the Gospel," *Improvement Era* 29, no. 6 (April 1926): 575–77, which includes an account of the dedicatory service and the complete apostolic prayer in Buenos Aires, Argentina, in December 1925. Moreover, Elder Spencer W. Kimball similarly offered a dedicatory prayer over all Central America for missionary work in 1952. See "Elder Spencer W. Kimball Dedicates Land of Central America," *Church News*, 5, 6, 13.

12. Ludlow, *Principles and Practices*, 346–56.

shared apostolic priesthood keys. Joseph Smith emphasized this apostolic responsibility on three separate occasions. In February 1835, within weeks of the Quorum of the Twelve Apostles being constituted, the prophet taught that global evangelization, including the "unlocking" of a nation's doors by priesthood keys, was the special responsibility of the apostleship:

> What importance is there attached to the calling of these twelve Apostles, different from the other callings, or officers of the Church? . . . They are to hold the keys of this ministry, to unlock the door of the kingdom of heaven unto all nations, and to preach the gospel to every creature. This is the power, authority, and virtue of their Apostleship.[13]

During the dedicatory services of the Kirtland Temple, Smith reemphasized this priesthood responsibility and the primacy of priesthood keys:

> I then called upon the quorums and congregations of saints to acknowledge the 12 Apostles who were present as Prophets and Seers and special witnesses to all the nations of the earth, holding the keys of the kingdom, to unlock it or cause it to be done among them; and uphold them by their prayers, which they assented to by rising.[14]

Smith's language of "keys" and "unlock" would be echoed in future country dedications. Apostles were to unlock the entrances to all nations through their priesthood keys and a specific priesthood ordinance known as a country dedicatory prayer.

A week after the dedication of the Kirtland Temple, on April 3, 1836, Joseph Smith experienced one of his most profound spiritual visions. According to the Latter-day Saint prophet, Jesus Christ appeared to Smith and his fellow priesthood leader Oliver Cowdery within the temple and accepted the sacred structure. Three ancient prophets—Moses, Elias, and Elijah—then appeared to both men and bestowed additional priesthood keys, according to Doctrine and Covenants 110:11–16. These keys included "the gathering of Israel from the four parts of the Earth" and the priesthood authority to bind or "seal" families in life and death.[15]

These additional priesthood keys, together with all of the previously conferred keys, constitute the apostolic keys used to administer ordinances in the church. Smith and Cowdery, the church's earliest apostles (D&C 20:12), asserted divine authority from "diverse angels" who declared to them "their dispensation, their rights, their keys, their honors, their

13. Joseph Smith, History, 1838–1856, vol. B-1, The Joseph Smith Papers, 576–77.
14. "Journal, 1835–1836," The Joseph Smith Papers, 175–76.
15. "Journal, 1835–1836," The Joseph Smith Papers, 193.

majesty and glory, and the power of their priesthood; giving line upon line, precept upon precept; here a little, and there a little" (D&C 128:21). In subsequent years, these restored priesthood keys would empower members of the Quorum of the Twelve Apostles to dedicate countries for the preaching of the gospel, according to Smith's revelations (D&C 107:35; 112:16; 124:18).

Nineteenth-Century Country Dedicatory Prayers

The ordinance of dedicating a country for the preaching of the gospel and the gathering of Israel dates back to the official Latter-day Saint dedication of the Holy Land—the geographical area situated between the Mediterranean Sea and the Jordan River—by apostle Orson Hyde in 1841.[16] A year earlier, Hyde dreamed that he had undertaken a missionary assignment to the European and Near Eastern capitals of London, Amsterdam, Constantinople, and Jerusalem. Encouraged by this night vision, he volunteered to serve a mission to the Jews. Joseph Smith thereafter appointed Hyde to represent the church to the leaders of the Jews in foreign countries. From Nauvoo, Illinois, Hyde traced the very path of his earlier dream across Europe and then traveled south to Jerusalem, where he arrived in the fall of 1841.[17]

On Sunday, October 24, Hyde went onto the Mount of Olives to dedicate the land. He did not bring a prepared prayer text that morning; instead, he drafted the prayer as he overlooked Jerusalem that day. He prayed that the land might be the gathering place for scattered Israel, that it would eventually be home to a temple, and that the inhabitants would soften their hearts. As he closed his prayer, he implored, "Give us, therefore, strength according to our day, and help us to bear a faithful testimony of Jesus and his gospel, and to finish with fidelity and honour

---

16. See Orson Hyde, *A Voice from Jerusalem, or a Sketch of the Travels and Ministry of Orson Hyde, Missionary of The Church of Jesus Christ of Latter-day Saints, to Germany, Constantinople, and Jerusalem*, 28–32. Historians have been unable to find evidence that Elder Heber C. Kimball or his fellow apostles offered a dedicatory prayer over England or Great Britain in 1837–41. David J. Whittaker to Reid L. Neilson, email, November 2, 2022. Whittaker was one of the coauthors of the definitive *Men With a Mission, 1837–1841: The Quorum of the Twelve Apostles in the British Isles.*

17. Church History Topics, "Dedication of the Holy Land."

Orson Hyde dedicates the Holy Land on October 24, 1841, by Clark Kelley Price. Courtesy Church History Library, The Church of Jesus Christ of Latter-day Saints.

the work which thou hast given us to do, and then give us a place in thy glorious kingdom."[18]

Since the time of Hyde's prayer in Jerusalem in 1841, latter-day apostles have pronounced dedicatory prayers for the gathering of scattered Israel in many countries beyond the Near East. But Hyde's dedication of the Holy Land was "different from later dedications of countries for Latter-day Saint missionary work," historians note. Hyde believed "that this dedication would set in motion the gathering of God's ancient covenant people, the Jews, and would be a work that the Jewish people themselves would then carry out."[19] For Latter-day Saints, the purpose of Hyde's prayer (and subsequent rededications of the Holy Land) was unique to that region, including to help bring about the literal return of the Jews to their ancestral lands. However, in every country or region dedication, the same apostolic priesthood keys were exercised.

18. Blair G. Van Dyke and LaMar C. Berrett, "In the Footsteps of Orson Hyde: Subsequent Dedications of the Holy Land," 60–61; Hyde, *A Voice from Jerusalem*, 28–32.

19. Church History Topics, "Dedication of the Holy Land."

Just as Joseph Smith's prepared dedicatory prayer text for the Kirtland Temple in 1836 provided a pattern for all later temple dedicatory prayers, Hyde's prayer of dedication over the Holy Land in 1841 provided a pattern for subsequent country dedicatory prayers. To begin with, a member of the Quorum of the Twelve Apostles would be assigned to dedicate a specific land by the First Presidency.[20] So commissioned, the apostle would then travel to the designated country, normally to its capital city, and there find a peaceful, reverential location such as a wooded park, mountainside, or hilltop with a view of the surrounding area. Before offering the dedicatory prayer, the apostle and his companions might sing a hymn, share a scripture, or bear a testimony, and then offer an invocation asking for the Lord's Spirit to be present.

The dedicatory ordinance is generally structured as follows: the apostle addresses Father in Heaven, states that the dedicatory prayer is being offered by the authority of the Melchizedek Priesthood and by virtue of his apostolic keys, invokes relevant scriptural phrases such as "turn the key" or "open the door" for the preaching of the gospel, pronounces additional promises and blessings upon the nation and peoples at hand, and then closes in the name of Jesus Christ. This has been the basic outline of the ordinance of a nation dedicatory prayer since 1841.

Three years after Hyde's journey to the Holy Land, Joseph Smith and his brother Hyrum were murdered in Carthage, Illinois, which set in motion the Latter-day Saint exodus from their gathering place in neighboring Nauvoo. By July 1847, the vanguard company of Latter-day Saint pioneers had entered the Salt Lake Valley under the direction of Brigham Young, then the president of the Quorum of the Twelve Apostles. Despite their geographic isolation and accompanying poverty, within two years Young called several of his fellow apostles to open missionary work in non-English-speaking European nations. During the October 1849 general conference in Salt Lake City, the First Presidency assigned Elder Lorenzo Snow to Italy, Elder Erastus Snow to Denmark, and Elder John Taylor to France. Their fellow apostle Franklin D. Richards was called to preside over the European Mission in Great Britain. Following the congregation's sustaining vote, Young remarked,

20. Between 1850 and 1921, several dedicatory prayers were offered by non-apostle missionaries, including prayers for the Sandwich (Hawaiian) Islands in December 1850, Cape of Good Hope (South Africa) in May 1853, Australia in April 1854, Canada in October 1886, and Greece in October 1905. I have not included these prayers in this study of apostolic dedications.

When the Twelve are abroad in any nation, they dictate the affairs of the Church there, the same as I do here. The inquiry may be made, can Lorenzo Snow dictate any where but in Italy? Yes—The Twelve dictate in all the world, and send Elders where they please, and as they deem wisdom. We have appointed Lorenzo and Erastus Snow, to certain missions, have they any right to go anywhere else? Yes; I wish they would open the door to every nation on the earth.[21]

By the following summer, all four apostles, along with several missionary companions, had begun evangelizing on the European continent and had offered country dedicatory prayers. Erastus Snow offered his dedicatory prayer in Copenhagen on June 14, 1850. "After being shown an upper room, we bowed together and offered up thanksgiving to God, and dedicated ourselves to His Service upon this land, and implored His protection and blessings upon our labours," Snow wrote to Richards in the British Mission.[22] Unfortunately, no record of Snow's dedicatory prayer is extant.

About two weeks later, John Taylor and three fellow missionaries traveled to the port city of Boulogne-Sur-Mer on the coast of northern France. On June 26, they went to the seashore in the evening to be "separated from the world," and then the apostle performed the ordinance or dedicatory prayer for the country of France. After expressing gratitude for their safe passage from the Salt Lake Valley to the European continent and for William Howells, who had preceded them as a missionary among the French, Taylor pleaded with God for divine assistance:

And, Holy Father, we ask Thee, in the name of Jesus Christ, to give unto us wisdom to lay before this people the principles of eternal truth; for we have come to unlock the door of salvation to this mighty nation, and we ask thee, O Lord, to aid us in our enterprise, and O glory to thy name, do honor to ourselves, and lead many to a knowledge of the truth; that thousands in this land may rejoice in the fullness of the blessings of the Gospel of peace.[23]

Later that summer, Lorenzo Snow gathered with his small band of missionaries in LaTour to dedicate Italy for the preaching of the gospel. On September 19, the apostle prayed, believing that "a portion of the House of Israel" had been hidden in Italy and hoping that the ensign, or

21. "Minutes of the [October 1849] General Conference, Held at the Great Salt Lake City," *Millennial Star* 12, no. 9 (May 1, 1850): 133.

22. Erastus Snow to Franklin D. Richards, June 19, 1850, as quoted in "Letter to President F. D. Richards," *Millennial Star* 12, no. 15 (August 1, 1850): 237.

23. John Taylor to Editor, July 21, 1850, reprinted as "Letters to the Editor," *Millennial Star* 12, no. 17 (September 1, 1850): 269.

banner, of the kingdom of God might "once more [be] established among men."[24] He later wrote to Orson Pratt: "In most countries the opening of the door of the kingdom of God, has been attended with much trouble and anxiety. Not a little of this has fallen to our share." He then described their first baptism in Italy and concluded, "Upon the whole, we have reason to rejoice, though surrounded by numerous difficulties. Our way is gradually opening, and every step we are taking, is blest of the Lord."[25]

Having dedicated Italy for the preaching of the gospel, Snow assigned one of his missionary companions, T. B. H. Stenhouse, to begin preaching in Switzerland.[26] By the beginning of December 1850, Stenhouse had crossed the Alps and was proselytizing in Geneva, and Snow joined him in February 1851. As intended, Snow pronounced a dedicatory prayer over Switzerland, and Stenhouse expressed gratitude for Snow's priesthood influence on that land: "Since Elder Snow visited and left his blessing on the place, investigation has increased day by day. His writings are spreading among all classes. I may say, with confidence, there is not a minister, Protestant, Catholic or Methodist of any shade or colour in Geneva, but is more or less acquainted with 'Mormonism' and Lorenzo Snow."[27]

About the same time apostles Erastus Snow, John Taylor, and Lorenzo Snow were opening the nations of Europe for the preaching of the gospel, Brigham Young assigned Parley P. Pratt to "open the door and proclaim the Gospel in the Pacific Islands, in Lower California [Baja California in northwestern Mexico] and in South America." Two years earlier the church president had suggested to Pratt that he begin his missionary labors in Chile on the Pacific coast. Pratt was accompanied first to California and then to Chile by one of his plural wives, Phoebe Soper, and a missionary named Rufus C. Allen.[28] While visiting San Francisco, Pratt wrote

---

24. Lorenzo Snow to Orson Pratt, November 4, 1850, reprinted as "Organization of the Church in Italy," in *Millennial Star* 12, no. 24 (December 15, 1850): 373.

25. Lorenzo Snow to Orson Pratt, November 4, 1850.

26. Lorenzo Snow to Orson Hyde, January 25, 1851, reprinted in Lorenzo Snow, *The Italian Mission*, 24.

27. T. B. H. Stenhouse to Franklin D. Richards, May 17, 1851, reprinted as "Letter from Elder T. B. H. Stenhouse," *Millennial Star* 13, no. 12 (June 15, 1851): 187. Historians have been unable to locate Lorenzo Snow's apostolic dedicatory prayer for Switzerland.

28. A. Delbert Palmer and Mark L. Grover, "Hoping to Establish a Presence: Parley P, Pratt's 1851 Mission to Chile," 116–19.

to Addison Pratt, who was then serving as a missionary in the Society [Tahitian] Islands, relating his current apostolic responsibilities. "My long contemplated mission to the Pacific has at length become a reality," Pratt shared with his fellow evangelist. "I hold the presidency of all the islands and coasts of the Pacific, under the direction of the First Presidency of the Church—to open the door to every nation and tongue, as fast as the way is prepared and the Lord directs, for the preaching of the gospel of salvation." The apostle anticipated evangelizing in Chile and neighboring Peru, with John Murdock soon heading to do missionary work in the then-British colonies of New Zealand, Van Diemen's Land (Tasmania), and New Holland (Australia).[29]

Pratt and his companions sailed to Valparaiso aboard the *Henry Kelsey* and arrived on November 8, 1851. The following January they moved to the "less expensive area" of Quillota, located about twenty miles north, to learn the Spanish language. There they remained for five weeks before they returned to the port city of Valparaiso and sailed back to San Francisco on March 2, 1852. For a variety of reasons, Pratt decided not to dedicate Chile. He wrote a letter to Young while onboard the *Dracut,* explaining their return to America and his thoughts for the future: "We staid till all our means were exhausted and sought and prayed diligently for our way to open; but we could neither speak the language sufficiently to preach the Gospel nor find any way to earn our living, so we found it necessary to return to California while we still study the language on board."[30] After describing social, political, and religious conditions as he understood them in other parts of Latin America, Pratt suggested a path forward in the years ahead. He recommended that "the Book of Mormon and some cheap publications should be translated into Spanish and printed." Language barriers were an obstacle to the apostles' goals, but Pratt continued, "If the Twelve Apostles will divide the European languages between them, and each become thoroughly versed in one," then they could "translate the fulness of the Gospel and turn the keys of the same."[31] Tragically, Pratt was murdered in 1857, and evangelization in that South American country would not recommence for another century.

---

29. Parley P. Pratt to Addison Pratt, July 26, 1851, reprinted in Parley P. Pratt, *Autobiography*, 429.

30. Parley P. Pratt to Brigham Young, March 13, 1852, reprinted in Parley P. Pratt, *Autobiography*, 443–44.

31. Pratt to Young, March 13, 1852, 448–49.

Three decades after Pratt attempted to establish the church in Latin America, church leaders intensified their missionary efforts in Mexico as part of their efforts to convert Indigenous peoples, whom they viewed as descendants of the ancient Lamanite civilization found in the Book of Mormon. In 1881 Wilford Woodruff related that he and his fellow members of the Quorum of the Twelve Apostles "have been commanded of the Lord to now turn our attention to the Lamanites and preach the Gospel to them, which we are now endeavoring to do."[32] A few apostles oversaw evangelizing among the Indigenous tribes in the western United States, while apostle Moses Thatcher focused on the peoples in Mexico.[33]

On April 6, 1881, the fifty-first anniversary of the organization of the church, Thatcher led several of his fellow American missionaries and local Mexican members from Mexico City to climb the neighboring Popocatepetl volcano. That morning on the mountainside they gathered for a mission conference. Thatcher wrote in his journal of the experience: "Here crowding close up to the frozen snow under the rocky cliff I read a few selections from the Book of Mormon, referring to the promises made to the remnants of Israel on this Continent, and to the Covenants made with their forefathers."[34] By virtue of his apostolic keys, Thatcher then performed the ordinance of a nation dedicatory prayer on the snowy volcanic slope. According to his understanding, the native peoples of Mexico descended from the Lamanites, who in turn descended from Jacob's son Joseph in the Old Testament: "I dedicated the land to Peace that the seed of Jacob through the loins of Joseph might learn the truth and rejoice in the gospel of their salvation. I dedicated the Mountain upon which we were praying that it might become a holy place of worship when the sons of Joseph should hereafter upon it, seek the Lord; that they might knock and have the door open, ask and receive."[35] Within a few months, Thatcher was released from his stewardship over the church in Mexico and he returned to Salt Lake City. Evangelism began to move steadily forward in Mexico in the 1880s following his departure. Thatcher's 1881 prayer on the mountainside of Mexico's Popocatepetl would be the Quorum of the Twelve Apostles' final nineteenth-century country dedicatory prayer outside of the Holy Land.

---

32. Wilford Woodruff to a "Brother Johnson," December 7, 1881, reprinted in F. LaMond Tullis, *Mormons in Mexico: The Dynamics of Faith and Culture*, 41.

33. Tullis, *Mormons in Mexico*, 41.

34. Moses Thatcher, Journal, April 6, 1881, Perry Special Collections.

35. Thatcher, Journal, April 6, 1881.

Early Twentieth-Century Country Dedicatory Prayers

Until the end of the nineteenth century, Latter-day Saint evangelism continued to be focused mainly on the nations of North America and Western Europe, with a few exceptions in Latin America and the Pacific islands, as described in Chapter 3. Nevertheless, when church president Lorenzo Snow's counselor in the First Presidency, George Q. Cannon, discussed the state of missionary work at the October 1900 general conference, he cast a wider net. "Every land and every nationality will have to contribute of its strength and numbers, in greater or less degree, to fulfill the words of God concerning the building up of Zion. Oriental lands now untouched by the Elders of the Church have to be penetrated and the honest souls sought out," Cannon preached in the Salt Lake Tabernacle. "My feeling is that we should withdraw our efforts to a great extent from the countries where we have been spending so much time and means with so little fruits. Let the Gospel be sent to lands afar off, where tyranny reigns; and when the Gospel goes there, God will soften the hearts of the rulers, and greater freedom will follow." Continuing his discourse, Cannon expressed his hopes for evangelism in East Asia: "If the time has come for Elders to go to Japan, let Japan be penetrated. After a while perhaps an opening may be made in Korea, and in Manchuria, and in China, and these lands be penetrated by the Elders with this message of salvation as soldiers of Christ."[36] Latter-day Saint leaders were taking more notice of Asian missionary prospects by the beginning of the twentieth century.

The following year, President Snow assigned Elder Heber J. Grant to commence evangelism in East Asia. On Sunday, September 1, 1901, two weeks after arriving in Japan, Grant and his three missionary companions left their hotel in Yokohama's foreigner district and walked for about twenty minutes until they located a grove of trees that offered them privacy on a hillside known as "The Bluff," overlooking the Yokohama harbor. They looked forward to spending some time together outside of their lodging. Wearing light-colored summer suits to help them endure the blazing heat and humidity, the four men sat down in a circle and opened their prayer meeting by singing a favorite Latter-day Saint hymn, "We Thank Thee, O God, for a Prophet." Then they knelt, and Grant and Louis A. Kelsch both offered opening prayers on this momentous occasion. Horace S. Ensign and Alma O. Taylor each offered their own prayers in turn, petitioning God for strength and wisdom to fulfill their missionary charge, and for

36. George Q. Cannon, in *Seventy-First Semi-Annual Conference* (1900), 63–68.

Grant to be inspired in his apostolic opening of Japan for the preaching of the gospel. They continued kneeling in a circle as Grant, acting as both apostle and mission president, performed the ritual of offering a country dedicatory prayer.[37] This would be the only such prayer that Grant would offer during his six decades of apostolic service, including his later time as church president.

Grant's apostolic appeal was different from other Christian prayers offered on behalf of the nation of Japan. Grant expressed thanks that they had arrived in Japan safely after crossing the Pacific and asked that their sins might be forgiven. Grant next dedicated the nation of Japan for the preaching of the gospel, the gathering of Israel, and the "establishment of righteousness upon the earth." Invoking the name of Jesus Christ and the authority of his priesthood, he rebuked Satan and commanded him to release his hold over the minds of the Japanese and give up any efforts to thwart the rise of the church in Japan. He also praised God that the Japanese had been preserved from the "power of the Great and Abominable Church"—which, given Latter-day Saint thought at the time, was likely a reference to the Catholic Church—and expressed his opinion that God had blessed the Japanese "with sufficient knowledge to see the shallowness of the man-made Christianity which was sought to be introduced among them." He also prayed that the Lord might soften the hearts of the Japanese people so they might accept the gospel message. Interestingly, Grant further prayed that the "Three Nephites," disciples in the Book of Mormon who were promised they would live until the Second Coming, like John the Beloved according to the New Testament, would visit the missionaries in Japan and assist them in their evangelism.

Louis A. Kelsch, one of Grant's fellow missionaries, brought with him a copy of the text of Elder Orson Hyde's 1841 dedicatory prayer over the Holy Land. Prior to Grant beginning his own dedicatory prayer over Japan, Kelsch presented him the text of Hyde's apostolic blessing unsolicited, hoping to provide Grant with some inspiration. "He handed it to me just before I offered the prayer of dedication, and as I had never read it and was a little at a loss as to how to proceed, I read a few words of the prayer and then handed it back to Brother Kelsch," Granted noted in his diary. "I did not want any other prayer to influence me but hoped and prayed that our prayers would be answered that I might be inspired to bless the land and the people as the Lord wanted it done and that I would keep my mind

37. Alma O. Taylor, Journal, September 1, 1901, Perry Special Collections.

free."[38] Following Grant's dedicatory prayer, the four missionaries sang a closing hymn and then the apostle read aloud the text of Hyde's prayer.[39] Grant noted that evening in his personal record that "the prayer at the top of the Mount of Olives offered by Bro. Hyde is a grand prayer and I shall make a copy of it for my journal."[40] Six decades after Hyde offered his apostolic prayer on the Mount of Olives overlooking the Old City of Jerusalem, Grant offered his own petition on "the Bluff" in Yokohama overlooking the modernizing Tokyo Harbor.

To Elder Francis M. Lyman, his mentor and fellow apostle who was then presiding over the European Mission, Grant described that sacred prayer ordinance. "We went out into the woods yesterday, it being Fast day, and found a quiet spot and each of us prayed, and we sang a number of songs, and I then earnestly prayed to the Lord to open up the way in this land, and in the authority of the Priesthood which He has given me, and in the name of His Son Jesus Christ, dedicated the land and the people to the opening up of the Gospel of our Lord," Grant wrote with feeling. "I had good liberty in dedicating this land to a reception of the truths of the Gospel, and I feel that a great work is to be done here." Grant also shared with Lyman his thoughts on additional prospects for the church in the region: "From what I can learn here of the people of China, it will be a very much harder thing to get a foothold there than it will in this land" of Japan.[41] Indeed, it would not be until after the devastation of World War II that Latter-day Saint missionary work would formally begin in most East Asian nations.

When President Lorenzo Snow assigned Elder Francis M. Lyman to preside over the well-established European Mission (1901, about the same time he invited Grant to open the Japan Mission), he encouraged Lyman to likewise look for opportunities to open the gospel door to countries unevangelized by Latter-day Saints. "It will now become your duty to take charge, as President of the Mission, of all interests connected therewith," Snow wrote to Lyman in his appointment letter. "To see that the Gospel is preached, as far as possible, through the nations where the Elders now labor, and, as the Lord shall open the way, to seize any new opportunities which may present themselves for the introduction of the Gospel to

38. Heber J. Grant, Diary, September 1, 1901, Church History Library.

39. Taylor, Journal, September 1, 1901.

40. Grant, Diary, September 1, 1901.

41. Heber J. Grant to Francis M. Lyman, September 2, 1901, reprinted as "Letter from Apostle Grant," *Millennial Star* 63, no. 40 (October 3, 1901): 654.

regions where it has not yet been preached."[42] Over the next two years, Lyman would dedicate four new nations. In the church's first century, no other latter-day apostle would come close to "turning the key" to dedicate as many countries as Francis Lyman.

About six months after arriving in England to oversee the European Mission, Lyman passed through Belgium after touring the German and Swiss Missions in January 1902. The apostle and his traveling companion, President Sylvester Q. Cannon of the Netherlands-Belgium Mission, arrived in Liege, Belgium, early on the morning of January 15. That evening, Lyman and Cannon knelt together, and Lyman offered "a glorious prayer and blessing in the nature of a dedication of that land and its inhabitants for the increased spread of the Gospel and the seeking out of the honest in heart," Cannon wrote in an article for European church members in the faith's periodical the *Millennial Star*. "President Lyman's visit has been, and will be, we feel sure, a great blessing for the progress of the work of truth in these nations."[43] Belgium was the site of Lyman's first nation dedicatory prayer ever, but it would not be the energetic apostle's last.

In early spring 1902, Lyman set off from Liverpool, England, on a three-month tour of the Turkish Mission and the Holy Land, both of which fell within the boundaries of his European Mission. He was accompanied again by President Cannon, and they were later joined by President Albert Herman of the Turkish Mission. While in Palestine, Lyman felt inspired to bless the region several more times.[44] The editors of the *Millennial Star* published Cannon's report of the traveling apostle's most recent prayers in the Holy Land. "Wherever inspiration suggested, prayers were offered by an Apostle holding the keys of authority and blessing for the prosperity of the land and people, and everything done seasonably," Cannon related.[45] The two men also traveled across the lands of other ancient kingdoms, including the Egyptian, Babylonian,

42. Lorenzo Snow to Francis M. Lyman, n.d., reprinted as "Apostle Francis M. Lyman's Address," *Millennial Star* 63, no. 23 (June 6, 1901): 369.

43. Sylvester Q. Cannon, "President Lyman's Tour," *Millennial Star* 64, no. 4 (January 23, 1902): 62–63.

44. Van Dyke and Berrett, "In the Footsteps of Orson Hyde," 78–84.

45. Sylvester Q. Cannon, "President Lyman's Tour," *Millennial Star* 64, no. 18 (May 1, 1902): 278; and Sylvester Q. Cannon, "Renewal of the Prayer Dedicating the Land of Palestine to the Gathering of the House of Judah," *Millennial Star* 64, no. 14 (April 3, 1902): 209–13. See also "Gathering of the Jews," *Millennial Star* 64, no. 14 (April 3, 1902): 216–17.

Assyrian, Turkish, Greek, Roman, and Byzantine Empires. "In every country visited[,] a good understanding of the history as well as of the present conditions, manners, and customs, has been obtained. Besides the prayers on the Mount of Olives and Mount Carmel, Apostle Lyman has been inspired to bless the lands and peoples of Egypt, Greece, and Italy for the spread of the Gospel," Cannon noted.[46]

As president of the European Mission, Lyman took his responsibilities seriously and desired to open even more doors for evangelism using his apostolic keys. Five years earlier, he had introduced a travel proposal during an April 1896 meeting of the Quorum of the Twelve Apostles: each year, send at least one apostle to visit each of the church's non–North American missions. As one attendee noted, Lyman "favored a trip around the world at least once a year by one of the Apostles. He felt the Apostles should be in a position from personal knowledge through visiting our missions to be able to report their condition correctly to the Presidency of the Church."[47] However, church leaders did not act on Lyman's proposal at that time.

While presiding in England, Lyman proposed to the church's First Presidency that he be allowed to travel around the world to visit all the church's missions upon his anticipated release from the European Mission. He hoped to offer dedicatory prayers over unevangelized nations while he traveled: "My mind has been drawn to the fact that there are many countries on this side of the world that have not been visited and blessed by any of the Apostles. I have felt disposed to offer my services at the close of my labors here to go home by way of India, China, Japan, Philippines, Australia, New Zealand, Samoa and the Sandwich Islands." Lyman assured the First Presidency he was up for the task. He imagined the trip would last about four months and cost roughly $1,000.[48] President Joseph F. Smith

---

46. Sylvester Q. Cannon, "President Lyman's Tour," *Millennial Star* 64, no. 19 (May 8, 1902): 304. See also "President Lyman's Return," *Millennial Star* 64, no. 19 (May 8, 1902): 296–97. A close reading of Sylvester Q. Cannon's daily diary of tour of the Turkish Mission clarifies that Lyman did not offer any apostolic nation dedicatory prayers while in Egypt, Greece, or Italy. See Cannon, Diary, January–May 1902.

47. Anthon H. Lund, Diary, April 1, 1896, Church History Library.

48. Francis M. Lyman to Joseph F. Smith and Counselors, December 19, 1902, Church History Library. See also Kahlile B. Mehr, *Mormon Missionaries Enter Eastern Europe*, 28.

and his counselors, however, denied the request and suggested that Lyman instead focus on his current European assignment.[49]

Still enthusiastic, Lyman shared his millenarian hopes with Elder Matthias Cowley before leaving on his anticipated tour of Scandinavia in the summer of 1903: "If I take the pulse of those people and turn the key for the introduction and preaching of the Gospel I shall feel that we have another foothold in an important and extensive section of the whole world where we must yet preach the Gospel of the Kingdom as a witness before the end shall come."[50] Joseph J. Cannon, his new traveling companion and a correspondent for the *Millennial Star*, explained the importance of this latest apostolic tour: "There are many missions that may be given an Elder of Israel. The one that President Lyman is now filling may be characterized as a mission of prayer, though naturally prayer is not the only matter that has occupied his time and attention."[51]

The first leg of their Scandinavian tour took the two church leaders to Norway, where Lyman dedicated a new chapel before passing through Stockholm, Sweden, en route to neighboring Finland.[52] They arrived in Abo (Turku), the former capital city of Finland, on August 4, 1903, and found a small hilltop to dedicate Finland for the preaching of the gospel. "This is the highest ground for miles around, and from it a splendid view could be had of the country," Cannon described to his *Millennial Star* readers.[53] From that scenic vantage point, the apostle offered a dedicatory prayer: "President Lyman besought the Lord in behalf of Finland and its people. He prayed that this sturdy race might never be crushed or subjected to tyranny, but that the people might ever have liberty to worship the Lord. He prayed for the government that the officers might be just and merciful, that they might feel kindly toward the people and toward the servants of the Lord when they come to preach the Gospel," Cannon noted. "He asked that the Spirit of the Lord might be poured out upon

---

49. Francis M. Lyman to Joseph F. Smith and Counselors, February 27, 1903, Church History Library.

50. Francis M. Lyman to Matthias Cowley, June 29, 1903, as quoted in Mehr, *Mormon Missionaries Enter Eastern Europe*, 28.

51. Joseph J. Cannon, "Prayer of Dedication Offered at Abo, Finland," *Millennial Star* 65, no. 33 (August 13, 1903): 517.

52. "Dedication Service of the Christiania Meeting-House," *Millennial Star* 65, no. 31 (July 30, 1903): 481–84. See also Zachary R. Jones, "Conversion amid Conflict: Mormon Proselytizing in Russian Finland, 1861–1914," 38–39.

53. Cannon, "Prayer of Dedication Offered at Abo, Finland," 518.

the people that they might hunger for the truth, and with the authority of the Priesthood he turned the key and opened the door for the preaching of the Gospel in Finland, and dedicated the land for this work."[54]

Lyman and Cannon next traveled by train to St. Petersburg, the Russian Empire's capital city. When they arrived at their hotel there, they were rejoined by two missionaries who were then serving in Germany. That afternoon the four men made their way to St. Petersburg's Summer Garden, on the left bank of the Neva River just past the Field of Mars, where they found a secluded location for the dedicatory prayer over Russia. "It was a fervent petition for the Lord to open this great land that His servants may preach the Gospel here. He dedicated it for this purpose, and turned the key that salvation and truth might be brought in," Cannon noted in his periodical account.[55] After touring St. Petersburg for three days, Lyman and Cannon continued further east into the Russian Empire to Moscow. On Sunday morning, August 9, they made their way to Alexander Garden, which was located along the northwest wall of the Kremlin, to offer an additional dedicatory prayer over the sprawling Eurasian nation. Of Lyman's prayer, Cannon wrote, "He besought the Lord to break the bondage of priestcraft that afflicted the people, and prayed that image worship might be overcome by the spread of truth in the land. He prayed that the hearts of the sincere and honest might be turned to seek for the truth, and petitioned the Lord to send servants full of wisdom and faith to declare the Gospel to the Russians in their own language."[56]

From Moscow, Lyman and Cannon headed thirty hours by train west to Warsaw, the capital city of neighboring Poland, then under the control of the Russian Empire. Unlike in St. Petersburg and Moscow, where the Russian Orthodox Church was the dominant Christian faith, Poland was inhabited by Roman Catholics and a sizable population of Jews. The two Latter-day Saints went to Lazienki Park, Warsaw's largest commons and botanical garden, and found a secluded grove of mature trees for their prayer. As he had done in the other places, Lyman prayed that the people of Poland would accept the Latter-day Saint message. "He prayed that all forms of anarchy, lawlessness and disorder might disappear, that Poland

---

54. Cannon, "Prayer of Dedication Offered at Abo, Finland," 518–19.

55. Joseph J. Cannon, "Praying in St. Petersburg for the Land of Russia," *Millennial Star* 65, no. 34 (August 20, 1903): 531–32.

56. Joseph J. Cannon, "The Visit to Moscow, the City of Churches," *Millennial Star* 65, no. 35 (August 27, 1903): 548.

and the whole of Russia might have peace, and that people and rulers might be prepared for a better state of things," Cannon noted.[57]

Having dedicated several nations under the control of the Russian monarchy, the two men finally "were permitted to leave Russian domain" at a border crossing, and they continued to Berlin, Germany, and then to Rotterdam, Holland.[58] These apostolic petitions over Finland, Russia (twice), and Poland would be the final dedicatory prayers of Lyman's apostolic ministry. He was released from presiding over the European Mission in November 1903 and moved back to Utah, where he assumed the presidency of the Quorum of the Twelve Apostles.

Unlocking the Doors to All Nations

During the six decades between Elder Orson Hyde's dedicatory prayer of the Holy Land in 1841 and Elder Francis M. Lyman's prayer over Poland in 1903, members of the Quorum of the Twelve Apostles offered a total of nineteen prayers to formally dedicate nine nations in Europe and the neighboring Near East, one country in Latin America (Mexico), and one nation in all of Asia and Oceania (Japan)—as well as the dedication and seven separate rededications of the Holy Land. Lyman was responsible for offering eight of the nineteen total prayers. Following Francis M. Lyman's 1903 prayer in Poland, Latter-day Saint apostles would not offer any more country dedicatory prayers until China in 1921.

Offering prayers over different nations has long been an important part of the work of Latter-day Saint apostles, and it continues to be so today. During the church's first century (1830–1930), church leaders regularly published accounts of these experiences and the texts of these dedicatory prayers in church periodicals and newspapers. The pace of country dedications accelerated when air travel become prevalent after World War II, and the practice has continued to remain a significant duty of the faith's modern apostles. For instance, Elder Russell M. Nelson visited 134 countries and helped dedicate 31 of them between 1984 and 2018, when he became president of the church.[59] Reflecting on the significance

57. Joseph J. Cannon, "Religious Conditions in Russia. Prayer for the People of Poland," *Millennial Star* 65, no. 36 (September 3, 1903): 565–66.

58. Cannon, "Religious Conditions in Russia," 566.

59. Aubrey Eyre, "President Nelson's 36 Years of Influencing World Leaders and Sharing the Gospel throughout the Globe," *Church News*, September 11, 2019. See also Sarah Jane Weaver, "President Russell M. Nelson's Prophetic

of country dedications to Latter-day Saints, Nelson said, "When you dedicate a country, it is like unlocking a door," enabling God to work in that land through missionaries, humanitarian efforts, and other means.[60] Nelson believed deeply that these apostolic rituals have a real spiritual impact on countries and peoples. On special occasions, Latter-day Saints gather at these locations across the globe to remember the prayers offered on their homelands by the church's senior leadership—whether the prayers happened well over a century ago or only a few years ago.

Ministry: 5 Years of Historic Leadership, Revelation, and Invitations," *Church News*, January 7, 2023.

60. Sheri Dew, *Insights from a Prophet's Life: Russell M. Nelson*, 261–63.

CHAPTER FIVE

David O. McKay and the 1921 Dedication of the Chinese Realm

By the end of 1920, the membership of The Church of Jesus Christ of Latter-day Saints was still largely confined to America's Intermountain West, but that was changing. Across the globe there were 525,987 members of record, worshipping in 1,527 wards and branches within the church's overarching missions.[1] Latter-day Saints lived in eighty-three stakes, with more than half of them in Utah and all of them in the western United States and adjoining settlements in Canada and Mexico. Moreover, there were twenty-four proselyting posts around the world: ten in North America, six in the Pacific, six in Europe, and one each in Asia (Japan) and Africa (South Africa). The church had only five temples, four in Utah and one in Hawaii, with another under construction in Canada.

The US intermountain region and its concentration of Latter-day Saints still reflected the pioneer settlements from the colonizing generations. For nearly a century, church members from various global climes had been encouraged to gather with other Latter-day Saints in the central governing locus of the church. The migration created a cultural corridor in western North America, stretching north to south from Canada to Mexico. Though the number of church members outside North America had grown steadily until 1920, the political, economic, and religious affairs in the corridor governed the attention of church leaders. By 1920, the church had spread across both the Atlantic and Pacific Oceans, spilling onto the European, Asian, and African continents and into the isles of the Pacific. Latter-day Saint leaders were becoming aware of the need to address the increasingly complex project of spreading church policies, teachings, and personnel around the globe.

To begin remedying the church's limited global outreach, the First Presidency announced in October 1920 that Elder David O. McKay and stake president Hugh J. Cannon would embark "on one of the most unique missions yet instituted by the Church." The two men were tentatively assigned to visit the church's missions in Japan, China, Hawaii, New Zealand, Australia, Samoa, Tonga, Tahiti, and possibly South Africa. A *Deseret News* reporter explained, "The journey will take in some rather

1. *Deseret News 2013 Church Almanac*, 212.

intricate water routings, as journeys to some of the South Sea Islands will undoubtedly have to be taken on the little native steamship lines rather than the better known lines of travel." It was also possible that their trip would extend beyond the Pacific and African regions, allowing McKay to tour the European missions before returning home.[2]

Arranging transportation, bookings, accommodation, and meetings would postpone McKay and Cannon's departure for several weeks. Several days after the initial announcement, a more detailed itinerary was shared with the public, accompanied by the explanation that both men would not only study "conditions in the L.D.S. colonies in each of the [Pacific] island groups, with regard to physical needs, missionaries, meeting places and spiritual affairs," but also engage in the "study of the customs and needs of the people in general at each place visited" to better know how to minister to them.[3]

McKay and Cannon began their yearlong circumnavigation of the globe on December 4, 1920. After departing from Utah, they traveled northwest by railroad to the deepwater ocean port of Vancouver, Canada, just across the northern US border, where their transpacific steamship awaited. Along the way, the two briefly stopped in Portland, Oregon, and in Seattle and Bellingham, Washington, to visit church leaders and missionaries serving in the Northwestern States Mission, presided over by Heber C. Iverson. After their stopover, McKay and Cannon boarded their steamship, where they spent two weeks at sea. Their journey to Japan was at times tempestuous, and McKay tried to relate his ongoing struggle with seasickness in good humor. Steamship travel was commonplace throughout their mission; that following year, McKay and Cannon calculated a total travel distance of 37,819 miles by sea—well eclipsing the pair's travel by land.

Touring Japan, Korea, and China in East Asia

With the morning sun gleaming on the hills of Yokohama, Elders David O. McKay and Hugh J. Cannon took in their initial view of the Japanese mainland on December 23, 1920. As the first apostle to visit the Japanese Mission since Heber J. Grant presided over it nearly two decades earlier, McKay was struck by the scenery, customs, and language that were so different from those of his native rural Utah. Between *jinrikisha*

2. "Two Church Workers Will Tour Missions of Pacific Islands," *Deseret News*, October 15, 1920.

3. "Plan Visit to Island Missions," *Deseret News*, October 23, 1920.

David O. McKay and Hugh J. Cannon being pulled by *jinrikisha* runners in Tokyo, Japan, December 1920. Courtesy Church History Library, The Church of Jesus Christ of Latter-day Saints.

rides and site visits, they toured the mission with President Joseph H. Stimpson. The duo spent Christmas and New Year's in Japan, visiting with church members, missionaries, and other locals. The elders and sisters in the mission struggled to convert the locals, almost none of whom were Christian. By 1920, there were only 127 baptized Japanese members, and only several dozen regularly attended church meetings.

Not surprisingly, the two Utahns experienced culture shock. By the second decade of the twentieth century, Japan had emerged internationally as a hybrid of traditional Asian and progressive European cultures through its efforts to adapt to and take advantage of the world's best technologies. "Here, too, one enters a new world," Cannon described his impressions of East Asia in his personal record. "The people, themselves so different in features and dress from the Europeans, the buildings, temples, pagodas and shrines, rikishas drawn by fleet-footed youths, heavy wagons drawn by men or oxen or small horses or by a combination of all three, all were as unusual as if the stranger were indeed arriving on a heretofore unknown planet." He continued: "But no! After running the gauntlet of custom officials he attempts to cross the street and is in grave danger of colliding with an intimate acquaintance—one might say a rattling good friend—a Ford automobile. One feels inclined to pick it up and hug it, such is the delight at seeing something so familiar."[4] The two Americans continued to be fascinated by Japan's mixture of "occidental" and "oriental" cultures, including its transportation system. Both regarded Tokyo's trains, streetcars, automobiles, and watercraft to be excellent by Euro-American standards. They even appreciated the novelty of the antiquated *jinrikishas* that transported them from the docks to the mission home.

But the First Presidency's ecclesiastical observers were less enamored with the status of the church's evangelistic results among the Japanese. On the first Sunday of 1921, McKay presided over a mission conference and asked the missionaries for details on the spiritual status of each Japanese convert. He and Cannon were disappointed by the reports. "We discovered thereby that this mission is at the very lowest possible ebb," he lamented in his diary. The next day, McKay offered several suggestions to the assembled missionaries. As an apostle and seasoned missionary, he had not traveled to Japan as a mere tourist, and he hoped to help improve the fortune of the mission. He devoted much of his official report for church leaders in Utah to suggesting potential connections between Latter-day Saint Christianity and Japanese culture.[5] After completing the initial portion of their official tour of the Japanese Mission, McKay and Cannon packed up their bags for their upcoming tour of China. They hoped to reach Peking (Beijing), its capital city, the following Saturday night so that McKay could offer the apostolic dedicatory prayer for China on the Sabbath, if he felt so inspired.[6] "As Peking is really the heart of China, we had concluded that this would be an appropriate place to perform this sacred and far-reaching duty," McKay explained in his diary.[7]

On January 6, 1921, McKay and Cannon departed from Shimonoseki, Japan, on the steamer *Koma Maru*, bound for Pusan, Korea. They next traveled northwest up the Korean peninsula and across the Yalu River to Manchuria. However, as McKay and Cannon continued their hurried journey east, they lamented the more primitive Korean transportation system. "Roads appear to consist mainly of foot paths and the transportation of the country seems to be carried on the backs of cows and oxen," Cannon recorded, no doubt recalling the superior roads in Japan. "Yonder an immense load of straw moved along the path without any visible means

4. Hugh J. Cannon, "Around-the-World Travels of David O. McKay and Hugh J. Cannon," 20–21.

5. David O. McKay, Diary, January 2, 3, and 5, 1921, Marriott Special Collections.

6. McKay, Diary, January 9, 1921.

7. McKay, Diary, January 9, 1921.

of locomotion, but somewhere under the mass was a patient cow. At the same time the driver, trudging along on foot, had a huge load on his own back."[8] The widespread poverty and famine were on display even more prominently as McKay and Cannon rode the rails through Korea and China, presenting a heartbreaking and disturbing picture to the First Presidency's representatives.[9]

The Latter-day Saint duo was nevertheless pleased when their train arrived at the Peking Train Station on Saturday evening, January 8, as hoped. Yet their impressions of the Chinese metropolis were hardly positive, in contrast with their earlier opinions of modernizing Tokyo. "The horde of ragged and revolting mendicants, grimy porters and insistent jinrikisha men, who fought noisily for possession of us, as we emerged from the station, was not such as to inspire a feeling of affectionate brotherhood," Cannon bemoaned. "However, we had gone to Peking to do the Lord's will, as nearly as we could ascertain what it was," he resolved.[10] Writing of the transportation in China's capital city, Cannon made no effort to hide his disappointment:

> Think of a city of a million inhabitants without a street car or omnibus line! The principal means of transportation—indeed the only means except for one's legs and an occasional auto or a small horse-drawn carriage at the time of this visit were the innumerable rikishas. These flit rapidly and silently through crowded streets, dexterously avoiding collisions which to the traveler appear wholly unavoidable and furnish an excellent opportunity of seeing Chinese life. A facetious American has dubbed these conveyances 'pull-man' cars. This was Peking.[11]

McKay and Cannon would have been hard-pressed to arrive in the capital city during a more challenging time period for the local Chinese population. Peking and the surrounding areas were experiencing an intense famine caused by drought and exacerbated by insufficient response from the government. According to historian Jonathan D. Spence, "At least 500,000 people died, and out of an estimated 48.8 million in those five provinces, over 19.8 were declared destitute." He continues his description of local Chinese life as follows:

> Houses were stripped of doors and beams so that wood could be sold or burnt for warmth; refugees crowded the roads and railway lines, and many

8. Cannon, "Around-the-World Travels," 33.
9. McKay, Diary, January 8, 1921.
10. Hugh J. Cannon, "The Land of China Dedicated," 115.
11. Cannon, "Around-the-World Travels," 35.

> lost limbs or were killed trying to force their way onto overcrowded trains; tens of thousands of children were sold as servants or, in the case of girls, as prostitutes and secondary wives. In one village, sixty homes out of a hundred had no food, and villagers were reduced to eating straw and leaves. Epidemics—typhus being the most dreaded and the most prevalent—decimated those already too weak to fight back.[12]

In short, McKay and Cannon toured China during one of its most economically depressed and socially trying times in modern history. The suffering they witnessed had a profound effect on their view of the Chinese nation—and no doubt influenced the apostolic prayer McKay would soon give. As he spent time observing the East Asian customs of the day, the apostle frequently made comparisons between the Korean, Chinese, and Japanese peoples, who were all modernizing at different speeds. McKay made clear his frustrations with the professional beggars he encountered throughout his journey and commented on the poverty-stricken state of the Asian countryside: he was irritated by the unscrupulous people who seemed to be taking advantage of the charitably minded passersby.

Seeking Space for a Dedicatory Prayer

Elders David O. McKay and Hugh J. Cannon spent their first night in Peking at the French-funded Grand Hôtel de Pékin, today known as the Grand Hotel Beijing, located just south of the ancient Forbidden City. Before retiring to bed, McKay and Cannon prayed to know if they should proceed with the anticipated dedication on the morrow. "[God's] inspiration rested upon his servant in charge," Cannon noted of his apostle-companion, and they tentatively determined to move forward.[13] McKay was well aware of the historic nature of his first (and only) nation dedicatory prayer, though he had never personally witnessed the actual sacred ordinance. "It had been Peter's duty and privilege to preach the Gospel first to the Gentiles. Please note that when the Lord desired the Gentiles to hear His word, He instructed the Chief of the Twelve to turn the key that opened the Gospel door to them. This is one of the special duties of the Apostleship," he later wrote.[14] McKay believed that he was about to recapitulate Peter's act of turning the key, but this time for the Gentile Chinese.

12. Jonathan D. Spence, *The Search for Modern China*, 298–99.
13. Cannon, "The Land of China Dedicated," 115.
14. David O. McKay, *Ancient Apostles*, 113.

After a sound night's sleep, McKay and Cannon awoke on Sunday, January 9, ready to complete their First Presidency assignment. There was not a cloud on the horizon, and the sun was shining brightly. They knelt and prayed together, and then prayed independently, seeking renewed confirmation of their late-night decision to offer a dedicatory prayer. Finally, McKay concluded that the time was right for an apostolic petition for the Chinese.[15] After breakfast, the two men left their hotel, bundled in winter coats and warm hats, in search of a proper dedication site. "But where, in the midst of that clamor and confusion, could a suitable spot be found?" Cannon pondered. "The city lies on a level, barren plain. There are no forests, and, as far as we knew, no groves nor even clumps of trees. We were wholly unfamiliar with the city and had met no one who could enlighten us. If we went outside the surrounding walls, there was reason to believe no secluded spot could be found nor the ever-present crowd of supplicants avoided." So, they remained for a time within the walled seclusion of the neighboring Legation Quarter, under the control of the United States and other foreign embassies, before venturing out into the bustling Chinese capital, where they felt the prayer needed to be offered.[16]

Although McKay and Cannon's personal writings do not explain the exact course they took, a careful reading of these sources provides clues to understand what happened next. From their landmark French hotel, the duo likely walked south on either the British Road or Rue Meu, both of which bifurcated the Legation Quarter, and then turned west when they reached Legation Street or Wall Street, passing by the American legation and its fluttering flag. Leaving the calm of the foreigner enclave, McKay and Cannon again changed direction, heading north toward the Imperial City, eventually passing through the Gate of Heavenly Peace, the main southern entrance of the Chinese compound. From here, their options would have been limited in 1921. To their northeast was the sacred Temple of Ancestors, then off-limits to foreign tourists and Chinese commoners. To the north was the Meridian Gate, which only Chinese royalty could use to enter the still aptly named Forbidden City. But to their northwest was the Central Park, a popular public pleasure ground since 1914, which surrounded the ancient Altar of Earth and Grain. According to one contemporary writer, the sixty-acre public garden was "even gayer with its old stone benches under the trees of what used to be Palace gardens, till they were set aside for public recreation, and its flower

15. McKay, Diary, January 9, 1921.

16. Cannon, "The Land of China Dedicated," 115.

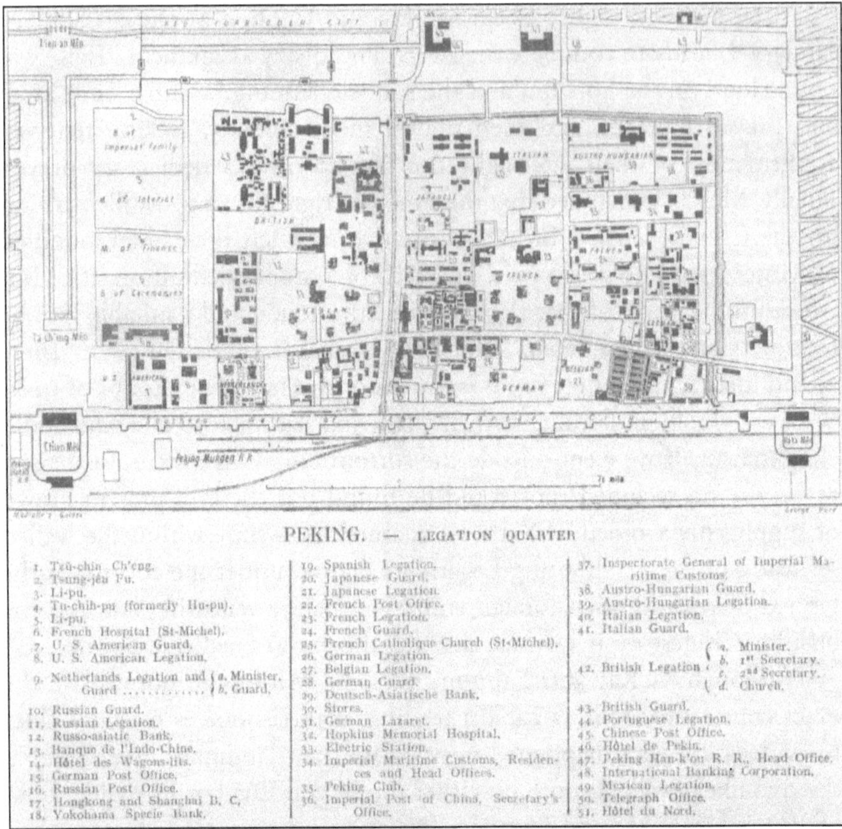

Map of the Peking (Beijing) Legation Quarter in 1912. This is the area in China's capital city where many foreign legations, or diplomatic missions, were housed between 1861 and 1959. From Claudius Madrolle, *Northern China, The Valley of the Blue River, Korea*. Hachette & Company, 1912. Courtesy of the Perry-Castañeda Library Map Collection, University of Texas at Austin Libraries.

beds enlivened by booths and restaurants, its artificial hills, its *kangs* filled with wonderful goldfish. The crowds that patronize all these attractions are extremely well dressed, decorous, intelligent."[17] Today these grounds are known to Beijing residents as Zhongshan Park, renamed in 1928 in honor of Chinese revolutionary Sun Yat-sen.

The area, not technically part of the Forbidden City, seemed appropriate as a general setting for the dedicatory prayer. "Directed, as we believe, by a Higher Power, we came to a grove of cypress trees, partially surrounded by

17. Juliet Bredon, *Peking: A Historical and Intimate Description of its Chief Places of Interest*, 123, 456.

a moat, and walked to its extreme northwest corner, then retraced our steps until reaching a tree with divided trunk which had attracted our attention when we first saw it," Cannon described. McKay felt impressed that the dedication should occur under its boughs. Two men loitered nearby but soon departed. "A reposeful peace hovered over the place which seemed already hallowed; one felt that it was almost a profanation to tread thereon with covered head and feet," Cannon recalled. "There, in the heart of a city with a million inhabitants, we were entirely alone, except for the presence of a divinely sweet and comforting Spirit."[18]

The apostle was likewise pleased with the weather conditions for such a solemn ordinance. "The sky was cloudless. The sun's bright rays tempered the winter air to pleasantness," McKay noted. "Every impression following our earnest prayers together and in secret, seemed to confirm our conclusions arrived at last evening; viz., that it seems that the time is near at hand when these teeming millions should at least be given a glimpse of the glorious Light now shining among the children of men in other and more advanced nations." By now it was around noon on Sunday. Before he offered his own dedicatory prayer, McKay invited Cannon to consecrate the location as a sacred space for "prayer and supplication."[19]

Then McKay, under the priesthood direction of President Heber J. Grant and by the authority of their shared apostolic keys, but without a prepared, written prayer text, spontaneously "dedicated and set apart the Chinese realm for the preaching of the glad tidings of great joy." The apostle recorded:

> Under the century old limbs and green leaves of this, one of God's own temples, with uncovered heads, we supplicated our Father in heaven and by the authority of the Holy Melchizedek Priesthood, and in the name of the Only Begotten of the Father, turned the key that unlocked the door for the entrance into this benighted and famine-stricken land of the authorized servants of God to preach the true and restored gospel of Jesus Christ.[20]

Dedicatory Prayer over the Chinese Realm

Born into a Latter-day Saint home and reared as an active church member, Elder David O. McKay would have prayed on multiple occasions each day over nearly five decades. By this time in his life, he had

18. Cannon, "The Land of China Dedicated," 115.
19. McKay, Diary, January 9, 1921.
20. McKay, Diary, January 9, 1921.

offered thousands of personal and public prayers. Praying in secret and before others would have been one of the most natural things in his spiritual practices. Yet this would be the first and only nation dedicatory prayer he would offer in his sixty-four years as an apostle. In his life of service in the church, this prayer in Peking was truly a unique priesthood ordinance for him.[21] McKay's 1921 dedicatory prayer over the Chinese realm marked the second East Asian land officially "unlocked" for Latter-day Saint evangelism, after Elder Heber J. Grant's dedication of Japan in 1901.

Thankfully, McKay was not alone in Peking that Sabbath morning, so there was someone to record the prayer he offered. Hugh J. Cannon, after offering his own vocal prayer consecrating the physical site for the dedicatory prayer, drafted copious notes as McKay gave the dedicatory prayer. However, more than six weeks would pass before Cannon arranged his real-time minutes into a formal prayer text in his own diary. "The following prayer has been written from notes made at the time, but which we have not had the spirit of putting together until today [February 23], when the same sweet spirit was upon us that we experienced at the time the land of China was dedicated," Cannon prefaced his record of McKay's prayer text. He continued: "Offered by David O. McKay, in company with Hugh J. Cannon, within the walls of 'The Forbidden City,' Peking, January 9, 1921, setting apart the Chinese Realm for the Preaching of the Gospel as restored in this Dispensation."[22] Cannon's resulting transcript organizes McKay's apostolic dedicatory prayer into thirteen paragraphs, which are arranged naturally into the traditional structure of Christian prayers: adoration, confession, thanksgiving, and supplication.[23]

McKay, like previous apostles who had offered nation dedicatory prayers, opens the first paragraph by expressing adoration for God. After demonstrating his devotion, McKay then makes a confession of his own fallen nature. Accordingly, he asks for divine forgiveness and for God to inspire him and his companion as they seek to fulfill their commission from the First Presidency and dedicate China for the preaching of their message. In the second through fifth paragraphs, McKay shifts the content of his prayer, giving thanks for the many blessings in his and Cannon's lives, especially the success of their journey thus far from the United States, across the Pacific, throughout Japan, and into mainland Asia. "With grateful hearts, we acknowledge thy guiding influence in our

21. McKay, Diary, January 9, 1921.

22. Hugh J. Cannon, Diary, February 23, 1921, Church History Library.

23. See Appendix C, herein, for a full transcription of McKay's dedicatory prayer.

travels to this great land of China, and particularly to this quiet, and secluded spot in the heart of this ancient and crowded city," he says.

It is not until about halfway through his prayer, beginning in the sixth paragraph, that McKay shifts to supplication. It is this portion of the prayer that demonstrates how McKay feels about China and the work he hopes to perform there. In the seventh paragraph, McKay invokes his apostolic priesthood and dedicates the surrounding lands for Latter-day Saint evangelism: "To this end, therefore, by the authority of the Holy Apostleship, I dedicate and consecrate and set apart the Chinese Realm for the preaching of the Gospel of Jesus Christ."

McKay uses the colloquial designation of the *Chinese realm* and not just *China* in his prayer. Several years earlier, Hebert H. Gowen, an Episcopal minister who was on the faculty of Oriental Studies at the University of Washington, published his popular *Outline History of China* (1913), a helpful text for understanding this distinction. Gowen's work explained that there were five main divisions of the Chinese realm: "1st, China proper (i.e. the Eighteen Provinces); 2nd, Manchuria; 3rd, Mongolia; 4th, Chinese Turkestan; 5th, Tibet."[24] Although we have no evidence that McKay had read Gowen's reference work, the book seems to illustrate the common understanding of what constituted the Chinese realm at this historical juncture.[25] Moreover, as the apostle continued his tour of the Pacific isles, he encountered several overseas Chinese who embodied the growing Chinese diaspora beyond East Asia, including in places like Samoa and the Hawaiian Islands.

One of the apostle's greatest concerns was the political instability he had heard about and witnessed during his brief time in China, as well as the negative impact it might have on the missionaries from his church: "That their message may be given in peace, we beseech thee, O God, to stabilize the Chinese government. Thou knowest how it is torn with dissension at the present time, and how faction contends against faction to the oppression of the people and the strangling of the nation's life." Like many other Westerners in this era, McKay was not confident that the

24. Herbert Henry Gowen, *An Outline History of China: Part I: From the Earliest Times to the Manchu Conquest, A.D. 1644*, 10. He notes in a footnote on page that "Immediately after the Revolution (1911) Mongolia asserted its independence and elected an ecclesiastical ruler."

25. To better appreciate the longevity of the geographical and cultural concept of the "Chinese Realm," see Scott Pearce, Audrey Spiro, and Patricia Ebrey, *Culture and Power in the Reconstitution of the Chinese Realm, 200–600*.

Chinese people were capable of continued self-rule and national improvement. "Holy Father, may peace and stability be established throughout this Republic, if not by the present government, then through the intervention of the allied powers of the civilized world."

Additionally, both visitors from Utah were appalled and distraught by the poverty and disease that seemed to be all around them in the once mighty Chinese nation. Having left modernized Japan just days earlier, McKay saw the economic disparity between the Japanese and Koreans and then the Chinese as they traveled by train to Peking. He references the impoverished masses in the eighth paragraph: "Heavenly Father, manifest thy tender mercy toward thy suffering children throughout this famine-stricken realm! Stay the progress of pestilence, and may starvation and untimely death stalk no more through the land."

While McKay was clearly devastated over the tremendous temporal challenges the Chinese were then facing, he was also concerned with the nation's spiritual well-being. "Break the bands of superstition, and may the young men and young women come out of the darkness of the Past into the Glorious Light now shining among the children of men," he pleaded with God. McKay anticipated the day when the Chinese would teach their own families and friends the Latter-day Saint message, including performing temple ordinances on behalf of their deceased ancestors who had passed away. After pleading in support of the Chinese people who were then under terrible socioeconomic distress, McKay turns his supplication to the future missionaries that would be called to evangelize the Chinese in the future. In paragraph nine, he prays that those assigned elders and sisters may "have keen insight into the mental and spiritual state of the Chinese mind. Give them special power and ability to approach this people in such a manner as will make the proper appeal to them." McKay further prays that evangelism among the Chinese would "prove joyous, and a rich harvest of honest souls bring that peace to the workers' hearts which surpasseth all understanding."

In paragraphs ten and eleven, McKay focuses his thoughts on the leaders of the church, as well as beloved family and friends back home. Nearing the end of his prayer, McKay implores, "Hear us, O kind and Heavenly Father, we implore thee, and open the door for the preaching of thy Gospel from one end of this realm to the other, and may thy servants who declare this message be especially blest and directed by thee." He then paraphrases the Lord's Prayer: "May thy kingdom come, and thy will be done speedily here on earth among all peoples, kindreds and tongues preparatory to the winding up scenes of these Latter days!" Finally, in the concluding two paragraphs, the apostle closes by praising God the Father and his Son Jesus Christ and saying amen.[26]

As McKay and Cannon returned to their hotel that night, the apostle reflected on the day in his journal. He looked to both the past and the future, writing, "This day is a memorable one in our lives, and we hope it may prove so to the church and do this nation much good."[27] Cannon described McKay's apostolic dedicatory ordinance as "an act destined to affect the lives of four hundred and fifty millions of people now living, as well as of millions and perhaps billions yet unborn." Yet he rightly acknowledged that "the vast majority of those affected may die in ignorance of the event."[28] McKay likewise appreciated the magnitude of what they had done in the heart of China. The following week, in a letter to his friend John Watson from Ogden, Utah, McKay described what transpired in Peking's Central Park: "This official act unlocked the door for the entrance of the authorized servants of the Lord into this land at such time in the future as the presiding Authorities feel impressed to call them. It was a most solemn and memorable occasion, one never to be forgotten by the two humble missionaries participating therein."[29]

Sightseeing in and Observations of China

Having reached Peking on schedule and dedicated China as intended, Elders David O. McKay and Hugh J. Cannon slowed down their itinerary and spent the next week sightseeing. They spent the first half of the week in the Chinese capital. Like other Western tourists, they explored the area around the Forbidden City, a palatial complex of sacred buildings that served as the seat of the Qing and Ming dynasties.[30] Though McKay was unimpressed by "the old, dilapidated temples" in China, especially compared to the sights in Japan, he "felt repaid doubly by the Temple of Heaven," which was finished in AD 1420. But he couldn't help noticing a disconnect between the beauty of the Forbidden City and the shortcomings he perceived in modern China: "When one

26. Cannon, Diary, February 23, 1921.

27. McKay, Diary, January 9, 1921.

28. Cannon, "The Land of China Dedicated," 115–16.

29. David O. McKay to John Watson, January 16, 1921, David O. McKay Scrapbook #126, Marriott Special Collections.

30. See Geremie Barmé, *The Forbidden City*.

David O. McKay climbing steps at the Temple of Heaven, January 1921. Church History Library, The Church of Jesus Christ of Latter-day Saints.

contemplates what the magnificence of this mighty empire must have been centuries and centuries ago, as evidenced by the mute monuments on every hand, and then sees what it is today, one can only exclaim, 'How have the mighty fallen.'"[31]

On Tuesday, McKay and Cannon spent the morning on a three-hour train ride from Peking to Ching-lung-chiao to experience the Great Wall of China, the famed structure dating back to the third century BC. "It is a common Japanese saying that 'Until you have seen Nikko, never say splendid!' We are convinced that until you have climbed up the Chinese wall and followed it up and down one of the mountainsides, you will never know the meaning of *stupendous*!" the apostle exclaimed, finally praising the Chinese above the Japanese. "How the huge stones composing the double walls were placed so evenly and permanently, over mountain peaks, across hollows and chasms, and stretching in a circuitous manner over mountain range after mountain range for 2,500 miles is truly a world wonder!"[32] The next day they toured the Winter Palace back in Peking. Located northwest of the Forbidden City, the Winter Palace was once a winter's retreat for various Chinese emperors. The landscape was immaculately groomed, replete with lakes, bridges, pagodas, towers, and

31. McKay, Diary, January 10, 1921.
32. McKay, Diary, January 11, 1921.

Hugh J. Cannon on the Great Wall of China, Ching-lung-Chiao, China, January 11, 1921. Courtesy Church History Library, The Church of Jesus Christ of Latter-day Saints.

flowers.[33] "I think in point of landscape beauty, attractive approach, and natural and artificial excellency in art, it ranks first, although in architectural beauty and symmetry it comes second to the Temple of Heaven," McKay reported.[34]

On Wednesday, the two Latter-day Saint men departed Peking for the last time, heading south toward Shanghai, which bordered the East China Sea. As they traveled to Tientsin and toward the Yangtze River, McKay continued to be disturbed by the ever-present, famine-induced devastation he saw. "Poor old China! She is most certainly in a senile condition," he wrote.[35] Recognizing the tragic circumstances facing the nation, he nevertheless found himself annoyed by the beggars at the railroad station at Pukou, a port near Nanjing. "Bro. Cannon and I, having only a satchel each, answered them all with 'Bu-Tao,' and avoided a great deal of unpleasantness. The trouble is that when you pay them, they stand and beg for more, saying, 'Not enough, not enough,' and this, too, after you have given them twice the usual tip!" McKay complained.[36] Their train continued eastward on to Shanghai, where they arrived late that evening eager to sleep. But they once again found that the Chinese did not meet their expectations. They had telegraphed the Palace Hotel ahead of time to secure rooms, but once they arrived there via the unconventional method of *jinrikisha*, there was no room available there nor anywhere else in town. "Finally," the clerk "put up two beds in the drawing room for ladies, so at midnight we stretched our somewhat tired muscles," the apostle grumbled.[37]

During their final weekend in China, McKay and Cannon explored Shanghai, which McKay noted was "a modern city—a city in which 'Occident meets and mingles with the Orient.'"[38] The following Sunday morning, McKay and Cannon boarded the steamer *Tenyo Maru,* bound for Yokohama. With Korea and China behind them, the two men discussed what they had just experienced while in mainland Asia, where they had traveled nearly 2,500 miles by land and water. McKay outlined in his

33. Maggie Keswick and Alison Hardie, *The Chinese Garden: History, Art, and Architecture*, 71.

34. McKay, Diary, January 12, 1921.

35. McKay, Diary, January 13, 1921.

36. McKay, Diary, January 14, 1921.

37. McKay, Diary, January 14, 1921.

38. McKay, Diary, January 15, 1921.

Postcard of the *Tenyo Maru* on which David O. McKay and Hugh J. Cannon sailed from Shanghai, China, back to Yokohama, Japan, January 1921. Church History Library, The Church of Jesus Christ of Latter-day Saints.

diary seven of their major observations from their recent travels among the Chinese.

McKay and Cannon's first four reflections were more critical of China and the Chinese. First, "China is a disintegrating nation." McKay explained, "Faded is the glory of her past, impotent, the power of her once-mighty government! The art and splendor of her picturesque temples, like the old Wall, are permitted to go to decay; so is the manhood and womanhood of the nation." The duo believed that China required a modern-day Confucius, Kublai Khan, or Theodore Roosevelt to lead the rising Chinese generation.

Next, "China is a mercenary nation." The apostle lamented the "mercenary spirit" that seemed to permeate the Chinese mindset: "Everybody's sole aim, seemingly, is to get money; and the system of 'squeezing' operating from the central government to the provinces, and then from the Mandarins down through the various castes and classes, until the poor, wretched producer who cannot squeeze is crushed hopelessly and sometimes lifelessly to the ground." McKay insisted that the Chinese needed to embrace the virtues of national "loyalty and unity" to rescue their long-standing civilization.

Third, "China is a land of beggars and parasites!" Although McKay and Cannon had great compassion for those they believed to be the truly poor Chinese citizens suffering through famine, they still had no sympathy or pity for those they considered opportunistic panhandlers. "Beggars here are organized, with a King of Beggars at their head. Individuals even resort to self-mutilation in order to prey more successfully on the sympathies of the public. How indifferent and careless and impotent that government which permits such human parasites to ply their trade on every street and near every public place," McKay complained in his diary about the career mendicants.

Fourth, "China appears to be made up of not a religious but a superstitious people." McKay viewed the Chinese religious syncretism of Taoism, Confucianism, and Buddhism as a "so-called religion" inferior to Christianity, especially the restored gospel of Jesus Christ. But the apostle was confident that their blended belief systems "will not be an insurmountable obstacle in their way of accepting the Gospel, once their superstition regarding evil spirits can be overcome."[39]

McKay's final three observations were more positive and hopeful regarding China and the Chinese. To begin with, "the Chinese are a polite, courteous people." Reflecting on his recent travels in both Japan and China, the apostle complimented the Chinese: "This admirable trait is almost as evident among the better classes as it is among the Japanese. Nice distinctions and considerations in deportment that show a sense of true refinement."

Next, McKay expressed the widespread American sentiment that China could not rise up on its own power: "The Chinese nation needs the friendship and protection of the United States." Like other Westerners, the apostle believed that only Euro-American military powers had the capacity to uplift the nations of East Asia. "I hope Old Glory may ever be seen waving in the breeze at every principal port and in all the principal cities of the Celestial Empire, now the struggling young Republic, of China."

Finally, McKay offered his assessment of contemporary missionary opportunities for the church in China, as that had been one of the two purposes the First Presidency had given for his tour of the country. His conclusion: "The Chinese people cannot be successfully Christianized by the usual missionary propaganda."[40] Something would need to change

39. McKay, Diary, January 16, 1921.
40. McKay, Diary, January 16, 1921.

David O. McKay and Hugh J. Cannon with American Latter-day Saint missionaries and Japanese church members, Japan, January 1921. Courtesy Church History Library, The Church of Jesus Christ of Latter-day Saints.

in the church's proselyting approach if they hoped to make a difference among the Chinese.

The two Latter-day Saint representatives, together with their fellow passengers, steamed away from Shanghai on the Huangpu River, a tributary of the Yangtze River. They reached the East China Sea and came into the Japanese archipelago, where they would spend their final seventeen days in East Asia on a concluding tour of the Japan Mission. Their steamer arrived in the Nagasaki harbor after a "pleasant voyage" of about six hundred miles.[41] Back in Japan they were again impressed by what they encountered, especially the Japanese citizens. "Certain it is that thirty days in Japan and China have completely changed my views hitherto entertained of the Orient and Oriental people," McKay exclaimed.[42] Amid their responsibilities of making recommendations for improving the island's missionary labors, navigating a change in mission leadership, and attending meetings, McKay took time to note some additional observations from his inaugural foray into transpacific Asia.

On January 26, McKay and Cannon again boarded the steamship *Tenyo Maru*, this time bound for the Hawaiian Islands, where they arrived on February 4. McKay and Cannon spoke at well-attended conferences across the islands, visited church-owned plantations and schools,

41. McKay, Diary, January 17, 1921.
42. McKay, Diary, January 24, 1921.

and immersed themselves in the local culture. Their tour of Hawaii was especially moving for Cannon, whose father, George Q. Cannon, was one of first Latter-day Saint missionaries called to serve in the islands seven decades earlier. McKay noted the multicultural composition of the local church membership, enjoyed luaus prepared by local Latter-day Saints, offered guidance to young missionaries, and marveled at the variety of geographic landforms, including volcanoes, coral reefs, and waterfalls.

Finally, on February 23, McKay and Cannon boarded a steamer in Honolulu Harbor, bound for San Francisco, California.[43] That evening, their first onboard the *Maui*, Cannon noted, "Tonight, we are sitting together and alone in our stateroom." After months of travel in foreign lands, they took a moment to catch their breath and reflect on the experiences on their world tour thus far. It was that evening that Cannon drew upon his earlier notes to draft what would become the official text of McKay's dedicatory prayer over the Chinese realm more than six weeks earlier.[44]

Return to Utah and Reaction to News of the Dedicatory Prayer

The *Maui* and its two Latter-day Saint passengers arrived in the San Francisco harbor on March 1, 1921. Elders David O. McKay and Hugh J. Cannon anticipated stopping over for only two days before departing on another steamer for French Polynesia. But because of problems with their passports, President Heber J. Grant invited them to return home to Utah for two weeks while their travel papers were put in order. This allowed them to be temporarily reunited with their families and loved ones and to attend the funeral for Anthon H. Lund, a member of the First Presidency and the Church Historian, on March 6, held in the Salt Lake Tabernacle.[45] The two travelers remained in Utah for a little over three weeks until their departure on March 26 for San Francisco, when they resumed their around-the-world tour.[46]

Latter-day Saints in Utah were anxious to learn more about McKay and Cannon's experiences abroad, especially the recent dedication of the Chinese realm. Given that only one other Asian nation—Japan—had been dedicated by an apostle up to this point, it is not surprising that McKay's

43. McKay, Diary, February 23, 1921.

44. Cannon, Diary, February 23, 1921.

45. Frank W. Otterstrom, "Report of Funeral Services for President Anthon H. Lund," *Deseret News*, March 12, 1921.

46. Cannon, Diary, March 26, 1921.

special prayer created a stir among church members in America. During their unanticipated sojourn in Utah, McKay shared his feelings about the prospects for evangelism among the Chinese. One observer reported a speech he gave at the Weber Normal College in Ogden, informing readers, "The ground for a new mission in China has been dedicated and the mission will be built in the near future, according to Apostle McKay. The feasibility of using Chinese missionaries from Hawaii for that field has been considered favorably by the church authorities."[47] Apparently, McKay had shared such hopes with the First Presidency and Quorum of the Twelve Apostles; however, no action to open a Chinese Mission would be taken at this time.

While stopping over in Salt Lake City, Cannon shared his account of McKay's dedicatory prayer and experience in Peking with the editors of the various church organizations' periodicals, and his narrative was published in the *Improvement Era* (Young Men's Mutual Improvement Association), *Juvenile Instructor* (adult Sunday School), *Young Woman's Journal* (Young Ladies' Mutual Improvement Association), and the *Relief Society Magazine* (adult women's organization).[48] The Latter-day Saints were anxious to learn more about their activities in China, as evidenced by the publication of Cannon's account in all of the church's major magazines.

Of all these auxiliary organizations, the female Relief Society gave McKay's dedication of the Chinese realm the most attention. "The opening of the Chinese mission is of peculiar significance to the Latter-day Saints, and especially to the women of the Relief Society, because the women of China have long needed the enlightening influences of the gospel to correct the stultifying condition which always obtains when a people live without the light of pure revelation," the editors of the *Relief Society Magazine* began their lead article of the April 1921 issue. After

---

47. "Missionaries Describe Travels: Observations Made in Far East by Officials of Mormon Church," *Salt Lake Telegram*, March 7, 1921. See also McKay's comments to the students at the Weber Normal College in Ogden, Utah, in "Students Hear David O. McKay: Ogden Church Educator Returns from Visit Before Resuming World Tour," *Ogden Standard-Examiner*, March 11, 1921.

48. See Appendix D, herein, for the complete text of his syndicated letter. Hugh J. Cannon, "The Chinese Realm Dedicated for the Preaching of the Gospel: The Act Accomplished by Elder David O. McKay, in the Authority of the Holy Apostleship," reprinted as Cannon, "The Land of China Dedicated"; Hugh J. Cannon, "China Dedicated for Preaching of the Gospel"; and "Opening of the Chinese Realm for the Preaching of the Gospel," *Relief Society Magazine*.

referencing a contemporary historian's supposition on the origin of the Chinese race from the days of biblical Noah, they then discussed the Chinese and their Asian neighbors, the Japanese.[49] The Relief Society authors published a two-part article on the history of the church in these two East Asian lands, highlighting the long-standing Japanese Mission and the anticipated Chinese Mission, including "the dedication services performed by Elder David O. McKay and his companion, Elder Hugh J. Cannon, on their recent trip around the world."[50] The editors then included Cannon's own account of the experience, as he did his best to convey to church members in Utah the historical significance of McKay's nation dedicatory ordinance: "Notwithstanding her present pitiably inane condition, we have met some admirable Chinese people, and cherish the sincere hope that at no very distant day the light of the gospel may penetrate the present overwhelming darkness."[51] Cannon's hopes for China mirrored those of the editors of the magazine.

By the time the *Relief Society Magazine* published their feature articles on China and Japan, McKay and Cannon had already left Utah to resume their world tour. Yet the reports of their work in China would continue to reverberate among the Saints. At the conclusion of the article about China, the sisters had positioned the dedication of China in a millenarian framework, as an event that moved the world closer to the Second Coming of Jesus Christ: "Latter-day Saints realize that there are but few nations left, now that China has opened her doors, in which the gospel must be preached, before the end shall come; perhaps only Russia, Egypt, and the Congo regions of dark Africa. How glorious are the prospects for the Latter-day Saint who lives his religion and observes the signs of the times."[52] Despite the hope among these magazine editors and the Latter-day Saints in general, however, McKay had only "unlocked the door" to the Chinese realm. The First Presidency determined to not open evangelism to China at this time.

---

49. "Opening of the Chinese Realm for the Preaching of the Gospel," 191.
50. "Opening of the Chinese Realm for the Preaching of the Gospel," 194.
51. "Opening of the Chinese Realm for the Preaching of the Gospel," 196–98.
52. "Opening of the Chinese Realm for the Preaching of the Gospel," 196–98.

CHAPTER SIX

Echoes of David O. McKay's Dedicatory Prayer

Elders David O. McKay and Hugh J. Cannon's time in China may have ended, but they still had many miles to go in their tour of the greater Pacific Rim and beyond. Their stopover in northern California and Utah was bittersweet; the unanticipated blessing of seeing loved ones for a few weeks alleviated their homesickness, yet both knew more than eight months would pass before they would reunite again with their families. After returning to San Francisco in late March 1921, they resumed their journey to the South Pacific—a region with a rich heritage for The Church of Jesus Christ of Latter-day Saints.

Proselytizing efforts in Tahiti began in the mid-nineteenth century when Addison Pratt and his two companions arrived on Tubuai on May 4, 1844, three years before the Latter-day Saint pioneers arrived in Utah. Thousands of natives soon joined the church in French Polynesia. In 1853, a new local government expelled the Latter-day Saint missionaries, and the local church fell into disarray. Missionaries returned four decades later, in 1892, and resumed their proselyting efforts. In the summer of 1915, the secretary of the Tahitian Mission reported that they had baptized their first Chinese immigrant.[1] Thus, the church was well established in French Polynesia by the time McKay and Cannon arrived in the capital city of Papeete on April 9, 1921, ready for their tour of the Tahitian Mission. Their stay was brief; they spent only three days traveling through the islands of Tahiti and Rarotonga before heading onward to New Zealand. However, the archipelago had a profound impact on McKay, who observed firsthand the challenges of missionary work, the costliness of transportation, and the severity of the weather.

McKay and Cannon's steamship plied into the port at Wellington, New Zealand, before dawn on April 21. They spent just over a week on the North Island, visiting missionaries, local members of European descent (known as "Pakeha"), and native Māori Latter-day Saints. By the time of McKay's visit, Māori converts and their descendants composed the majority of Latter-day Saints in New Zealand. Their traditions enamored McKay—most notably the Hui Tau, an annual, multiday conference that

1. Feng Xi, "A History of Mormon-Chinese Relations: 1849–1993," 51.

included dances, feasts, and community discussions on topics ranging from church administration to local needs and ecclesiastical unit organization. On many occasions, McKay was "hongied" by Māori members—given an intimate nose-to-nose greeting. He bid farewell to the New Zealand Saints on April 30 and departed for the next leg of his journey.

McKay and Cannon arrived in Samoa on May 10 and spent time on all three principal islands—Savai'i, Upolu, and Tutuila. During their visit, they toured plantations, humble meetinghouses, and two of the church's schools in Mapusaga and Sauniatu. McKay and Cannon were repeatedly feted as honored guests by local tribal chiefs at cultural celebrations, concerts, and dances; they received ornate handmade gifts and were well fed by local members. For McKay and Cannon, leaving such company was never an easy task, and in one instance, bidding farewell to a village of Latter-day Saint islanders resulted in a historic occasion. As he left Sauniatu, McKay felt impressed to turn back to a group of church members and give them his apostolic blessing, a special prayer given by priesthood authority. In memory of this act, the local saints erected a concrete obelisk. For decades, May 31 was thereafter referred to and celebrated as McKay Day.

It was also here in Samoa that McKay and Cannon encountered a faithful Latter-day Saint Chinese immigrant family, which caused McKay to reflect deeply on the fact that there were possibilities for evangelism among the Chinese people throughout the larger Pacific region, beyond the Chinese realm. About a decade before the apostle and his companion toured the Samoan Mission, a number of Chinese immigrants began joining the church there. In the winter of 1910, Robert M. Forrest, secretary of the Samoan Mission, reported that there were several Chinese and Chinese-Samoan people in the mission who loyally paid tithing, understood Latter-day Saint doctrines, and "are indeed a great help to us in our work."[2]

On June 4, 1921, McKay and Cannon were invited to dine at the home of church member Ah Ching and his wife. Also present was their son Arthur and his wife, Telese. They were among Polynesia's Chinese converts to the church. "All the Elders were invited, and we had a most enjoyable feast and afternoon entertainment, not the least interesting of which was old Bro. Ah Ching's narration of his early experiences in Samoa," the apostle noted in his diary. According to McKay's account of the convert's story, Ah Ching left Pu Chow, Fukien Province, China, in his teens as a crewman on a sailing vessel in the South Pacific. After a decade at sea,

2. Robert M. Forrest, "Chinese as Latter-day Saints," *Deseret Evening News*, March 26, 1910.

Mission President John Q. Adams, David O. McKay, and Hugh J. Cannon dressed in traditional Samoan attire, Samoa, May 1921. Courtesy Church History Library, The Church of Jesus Christ of Latter-day Saints.

saving his money all the while, he ended up in Apia, Samoa. After a close business associate took advantage of him, robbing him of every penny, he began selling wares in the street and eventually established himself as a prosperous merchant and owner of multiple shops. Eventually, he married the daughter of a local chieftain, giving him the title of chief through lineage. It is clear from McKay's praiseworthy tone that he was inspired by the story and admired Ah Ching's thrift, honesty, and wisdom. The apostle would later write an article about the family for the church's periodical the *Improvement Era*, which was published while he was still abroad.[3] He would also tell the First Presidency about his memorable experience with this Chinese family in Samoa.

After touring the Samoan Mission, McKay and Cannon briefly separated. While Cannon sailed to New Zealand to secure their future travel itinerary and steamship tickets, McKay headed to neighboring Tonga alone. Before he could set foot in the Tongan Mission, however, the apostle and his fellow steamship passengers were forced to endure two weeks of quarantine on the remote five-acre islet of Makahaa, near Nuku'alofa. They did so at the behest of the local Tongan government, who feared an outbreak of measles brought by outsiders. McKay's long, hot days were enlivened by exploring the coral beds, reading Shakespeare, and holding religious services. When the mandatory confinement ended, McKay visited the islands of Tongatapu, Vava'u, and Ha'apai to inspect church plantations, schools, and the mission home. He spoke at several spiritual meetings with the missionaries and Saints. These interisland voyages were often conducted on subpar boats, led by less-than-sober captains, in perilous weather. At the end of his tour in Tonga, McKay boarded a steamer for New Zealand via Samoa and Fiji.

McKay's return to New Zealand was punctuated by several reunions, one with his travel companion Cannon, and others with members and missionaries he had met on his earlier visit. Upon arrival, McKay deliberated over the possibility of securing a boat for the mission. McKay and Cannon then visited Māori villages, the Māori Agricultural College at Korongata, and member congregations in cities like Dannevirke, Auckland, and Wellington. The apostle enjoyed the rugged scenery as he toured the North Island. Impressed by certain church leaders and their families, the Māori people and their culture, and the enterprising missionaries he encountered on this leg of his journey, McKay noted several

3. David O. McKay, "Ah Ching," 992–97. See Appendix E, herein.

ongoing challenges facing the Māori Agricultural College and made recommendations in his diary about the school's fate. The two visitors remained in New Zealand from July 18 to August 2. From Auckland, the pair set sail aboard the SS *Ulimaroa* for Australia.

The Australian Mission marked the last official visit of McKay and Cannon's ecclesiastical tour of the Pacific Basin. Before their three-month journey home via South Asia, the Middle East, and Europe, the two men spent nearly a month gauging the state of church affairs in Oceania. At the outset of their Australian tour, McKay and Cannon took a rare break from their arduous meeting schedule to make a foray to the Blue Mountains, visiting the Jenolan Caves and Mount Victoria. The apostle was struck by the distinct variety of terrains, plants, and animals. In the following weeks, they spoke at meetings across Tasmania, Sydney, Melbourne, Adelaide, and Brisbane. McKay recognized the difficulties faced by Latter-day Saint missionaries in Australia—prejudice, religious apathy, and English conservatism. On September 6, 1921, McKay and Cannon said goodbye to Australian Mission president Don C. Ruston, to several of his missionaries, and to local church members gathered at the Brisbane harbor.

During the ten months since they had embarked on their tour of the Pacific, McKay and Cannon had visited the Japanese Mission, the Hawaiian Mission, the Tahitian Mission, the New Zealand Mission (twice), the Samoan Mission, the Tongan Mission, and the Australian Mission—thereby fulfilling their primary Pacific Isles assignment from the First Presidency. "This practically completes our mission, and now, I'm ready for home," McKay wrote in his diary that night.[4] Cannon likewise considered their official obligation over. "This is the last organized mission that we are called to visit. Of course, we are expected to visit the Saints in India and if possible those in Armenia, but in neither place have we an organized Mission," he journaled that same evening. "In looking back over the work we have accomplished, I feel that the money has been well spent, and that it has been a real blessing to the work to have one of the Twelve visit among them and encourage and strengthen them."[5]

McKay and Cannon boarded the *Marella*, a steamer from the Australian Philp Burns-Philp shipping line, bound for South Asia and the Middle East. After passing through Singapore, Malaysia, Burma (Myanmar), and India, the two men then boarded another steamer, which ferried them across the Arabian Sea and through the Gulf of Aden into the

4. David O. McKay, Diary, September 6, 1921, Marriott Special Collections.
5. Hugh J. Cannon, Journal, September 6, 1921, Church History Library.

Hugh J. Cannon and David O. McKay on camelback in front of the Sphinx, Cairo, Egypt, October 26, 1921. Courtesy Church History Library, The Church of Jesus Christ of Latter-day Saints.

Red Sea. After traveling up the Suez Canal, they reached Port Said, on the Mediterranean Sea, in late October 1921.

While in the Near East, they visited the antiquities of Egypt, including the spectacular pyramids and monumental sphinx on the outskirts of Cairo. McKay was eager to tour Palestine and the lands of the Bible, given his own church calling as an apostle. McKay later related his experience to the First Presidency, saying, "Our visit to Jerusalem and the Holy Land was an appreciated privilege and an excellent educative experience. I had heard a number of tourists express disappointment over their tour of this most memorable land, but I experienced no such feeling." He continued, "The site of the Holy City on the four picturesque and frequently mentioned mounts and its relative position to other Biblical places have been so clearly impressed upon my mind that this geographical significance alone is quite sufficient reward for the journey."[6] The two men also traveled to Aleppo and Aintab, where they ministered to the Armenian Latter-day Saints suffering in the aftermath of World War I.

Home for Christmas and a Report to the First Presidency

After a year abroad, the weary Elders David O. McKay and Hugh J. Cannon finally made their way by ship and train to Europe, where they spent time in the Swiss-German, Belgium-Netherlands, and British missions. They boarded the *Cedric* on December 10 and steamed away from the European coast, bound for the docks of Manhattan. Before leaving, however, McKay sent President Heber J. Grant a cablegram from Liverpool, letting church leaders and their families know that they would be home for Christmas. Their steamer reached the New York harbor nine days later, and there they sent a telegram to the First Presidency updating them on their westward progress.[7] "The brethren had been stirred by the sight of colorful Japan, of the mammoth Chinese wall, of historic pyramids, the chaste Taj Mahal," Cannon described. "But surpassing all else is the thrill which comes to an American when, after a long absence, he sees the inspiring Statue of Liberty at the entrance to New York harbor, and behind this his own native land."[8] Eager to make it home for the winter holidays, McKay and Cannon embarked on a train for Salt Lake City, where they arrived on December 23. McKay finally reached his home in Huntsville, Utah, on Christmas Eve. Their world tour had lasted a year and twenty days.

Christmas 1921 fell on a Sunday, and McKay delivered a sermon in the Ogden Tabernacle, his first public remarks since returning from his world tour.[9] Two Sundays later, McKay spoke in the Salt Lake Tabernacle on Temple Square about his experiences abroad as the First Presidency's global ambassador.[10] McKay and Cannon were asked to lecture many more times in the ensuing months—Latter-day Saints were eager to learn more about their fellow church members scattered across the Pacific and

---

6. David O. McKay, "Summary and Report: Tour of Inspection of Missions and Schools," Church History Library.

7. "Mormon Travelers Reach New York," *Salt Lake Telegram*, December 21, 1921.

8. Quoted in Hugh J. Cannon, *To the Peripheries of Mormondom: The Apostolic Around-the-World Journey of David O. McKay, 1920–1921*, 153.

9. "Apostle M'Kay Tells of Trip," *Salt Lake Telegram*, December 26, 1921.

10. "M'Kay Talks at S. L. Tabernacle," *Ogden Standard-Examiner*, January 9, 1922.

other foreign missionary fields, including evangelism prospects in East Asia.

The First Presidency was likewise anxious to learn from McKay's lengthy world tour, and they asked for a formal synopsis. In his type-written report to church leaders, the apostle attempted to summarize and analyze more than a year's worth of experiences. Among other important moments, he highlighted his meaningful time in the Chinese capital city. "In the heart of old historic Peking, acting upon the suggestion of the President of the Church, and under the inspiration of the Lord, as one of the Council of the Twelve, I offered the dedicatory prayer setting apart the Chinese realm for the preaching of the Gospel," McKay described to the First Presidency. "Subsequently, in our visits to the missions, we have met Chinese converts, actively engaged in this great Latter-day work." He continued by describing the immigrant Chinese, including Ah Ching and his family, they encountered during their travels (see Appendix E):

> Their faith in the Gospel seems to be unquestioned, and their zeal most commendable. Without exception, they hold not only the confidence but esteem of their presiding officers. They are industrious, intelligent, prosperous, and willing to sacrifice time and means for the advancement of the Truth.

After spending time with these East Asian converts, McKay shared with his fellow apostles in Utah that he believed that God appeared to be working in the Chinese realm and among the overseas Chinese living beyond East Asia. Beginning in the mid-nineteenth century, for example, a number of Chinese immigrants joined the church in the Hawaiian Islands, some of whom he had met there.[11] In his report, McKay also pointed to the Chinese family he had met in Samoa in June 1921 as a sign of evangelism prospects among the overseas Chinese. "I mention this," he said, "because it would seem that the Lord has already opened the way for the taking of the initial steps toward the preaching of the Gospel to the millions in that land who have never heard the message of salvation."[12]

McKay appreciated the significance of his world tour, including the ecclesiastical, historical, and cultural insights he had personally gained while abroad. Going forward, he felt that such journeys should be a regular occurrence. "Brethren, I desire to suggest that these missions be permitted to

---

11. See Russell T. Clement and Sheng-Luen Tsai, "East Wind to Hawai'i: Contributions and History of Chinese and Japanese Mormons in Hawaii," 89–106; and R. Lanier Britsch, *Moramona: The Mormons in Hawaii*, 168–69.

12. McKay, "Summary and Report," 292–[300].

go at longest no more than two years without another visit from a member or members of the General Authorities of the Church," he recommended to the First Presidency in his formal report, emphasizing the need for apostles to fulfill their local and global responsibilities. "I plead that more frequent visits be given to these missions, that the Presidents thereof may be benefitted and strengthened by personal contact with members of the General Authorities. The good thus to be accomplished cannot be overestimated." McKay expressed gratitude for his tour, which he called "one of the greatest privileges and blessings of my life."[13] It was an experience that would shape his apostolic ministry and presidential years.

When McKay and Cannon returned to Utah that winter, both men were subsumed into their former lives. McKay returned to his apostolic duties and assignments as church commissioner of education, while Cannon resumed his responsibilities as president of the Liberty Stake. At the next general conference, in April 1922, McKay reflected on his experiences abroad, including his apostolic dedicatory prayer for the Chinese people. "I want to testify to you that God was with us when we stood beneath that tree in old China and turned the key for the preaching of the gospel in the Chinese realm," the apostle witnessed to the Latter-day Saint audience gathered in the Salt Lake Tabernacle. "My words may not convince you of the fact, but no disputant can convince us that our souls were not filled to overflowing with the Spirit of God on that occasion."[14] In subsequent decades, McKay labored to help fulfill his own divine petition as he oversaw the spread of the church's message and programs throughout East Asia in his role as a member of the Quorum of the Twelve Apostles, then as a counselor in the First Presidency, and finally as president of the church.

Echoes of McKay's Peking Dedicatory Prayer

In the century since Elder David O. McKay formally blessed China for the church in 1921, several of his fellow Latter-day Saint apostles have echoed his prayer language as they dedicated lands and temples within the Chinese realm. While serving as a second counselor in the First Presidency, McKay helped organize missionary work among the Chinese in Hong Kong, for example. He called Hilton A. Robertson, who had presided over the early Japan Mission in Tokyo (1923–24) and the Japanese Mission in Honolulu (1937–40), as the inaugural president of the newly created

13. McKay, "Summary and Report," 292–[300].
14. David O. McKay, *Conference Report* (1922), 65.

Chinese Mission, with Henry Aki, a Chinese-American church member living in Hawaii, as his counselor in the new mission presidency. McKay and his fellow First Presidency members then assigned Matthew Cowley of the Quorum of the Twelve Apostles to travel to China to rededicate the land for the preaching of the gospel.[15] These three church leaders and their wives sailed from Tokyo to Manila and then to Hong Kong, which was then still a British colony and dependent territory. Fortunately for historians, Cowley's wife, Elva, wrote a first person account of the trip. "We were now looking forward to going to China, where Matthew would dedicate that land for missionary work. We were all looking forward to that event," she recalled in her autobiography.[16]

Cowley's apostolic blessing would ultimately be given in Hong Kong, not mainland China. "At last [on July 10, 1949], we sailed into the Hong Kong harbor," Elva narrated their travels. "Hong Kong is built on a peak. It made a beautiful picture, with its apartment house lights encircling the hills and glistening in the night." The following day they went sightseeing and searching for a potential dedication site: "We went on the cable car up on the [Victoria] peak to decide where Matthew would dedicate the land. He was giving it a lot of thought. He needed a little time to decide." But her apostle-husband continued to be unsettled. "Matthew decided he wanted to dedicate China proper," Elva Cowley wrote, "so he got airplane tickets for Canton [Guangzhou], one of the oldest and largest seaport towns. We flew over and saw how they build their houses in clusters and went out of their little communities to farm." Once in Canton, a port city to the northwest of Hong Kong, they took a bus tour and surveyed the surrounding area for a suitable dedication location. Elva recounted that during dinner that evening, "Matthew said to us, 'Well, we have traveled a lot of miles today, I don't know about you folks, but I haven't seen a hallowed spot to dedicate the land.' We all agreed. He said, 'We will go back to Hong Kong, and tomorrow morning, we will go up on the peak and open up China for missionary work.'"[17] They all flew back to Hong Kong that evening.

On July 14, 1949, the three Latter-day Saint couples once again rode the cable car up to the top of Victoria Peak. "We got off and walked for a little distance and came to a huge boulder and indentation in the path," Elva wrote. "Matthew stopped and said, 'This is the place we will

---

15. R. Lanier Britsch, *From the East: The History of the Latter-day Saints in Asia, 1851–1996*, 231–33.

16. Elva T. Cowley, "My Life, A Love Story," 293, Perry Special Collections.

17. Cowley, 295–97.

have our meeting.' We could see the beautiful harbor, the peninsula and China proper in the distance. It was a beautiful, sunshiny day." There Elder Cowley offered an apostolic prayer of rededication. "Then Matthew dedicated the land. When he finished, there was dead silence. The Holy Spirit enfolded all of us and the land," his wife described. "The silence was broken when Hilton Robertson took his pocket knife out of his pocket, went over to the huge boulder and wrote on it, July 14, 1949. That was the day that would never be forgotten."[18] In the years following this prayer, Latter-day Saints in Hong Kong would visit this spot and run their fingers over the still visible etchings in the stone face in commemoration.

Months later, during the faith's October general conference, the Cowleys described that memorable moment on Victoria Peak:

> There we officially opened the mission by a brief service, each of us praying in turn. I will never forget the prayer of Brother Henry Aki, who, as he stood there, facing his homeland, with its four hundred and sixty-five million inhabitants, poured out his soul to God that he might be the means of bringing salvation to his kindred people. . . . In our prayers we included by reference the dedicatory prayer offered by President McKay in 1921, I think it was, when he asked God to open up the way for the gospel to be brought to that great nation. We will need missionaries for China—those who are willing to serve among a people who have not yet received the light and knowledge of the gospel.[19]

The Chinese Mission operated out of Hong Kong from 1949 until 1953. Two years after its closure, church president McKay assigned Joseph Fielding Smith, then president of the Quorum of the Twelve Apostles, to travel to East Asia and tour the church's missions and dedicate additional lands for the preaching of the gospel. Smith first toured the church units in Japan and then continued to South Korea, which he dedicated for evangelism on August 2, 1955. While in East Asia, he also divided the sprawling Far East Mission into the Northern Far East Mission (encompassing Japan, South Korea, and Okinawa) and the Southern Far East Mission (comprising the nations of Guam, Hong Kong, the Philippines, Taiwan, and the unevangelized lands of South and Southeast Asia). On August 14, Smith dedicated the island of Okinawa, a former prefecture of Japan, which was then being occupied by the United States following World War II. On August 21 he dedicated the Philippines for preaching, and on

18. Cowley, 298.

19. Matthew Cowley, "The Language of Sincerity," 715. See also, Henry Aki, *Conference Report* (October 1951), 46–47.

August 25, Guam. Smith, however, was unable to make it to Taiwan that summer for an anticipated apostolic dedication.[20]

Four years later, McKay assigned Elder Mark E. Peterson to survey church progress in Taiwan on behalf of the First Presidency. While in Taipei, Peterson met with mission leaders and church members on Chung Shan North Road, immediately south of the landmark Grand Hotel, and there dedicated the island of Formosa on June 1, 1959.[21] He prayed,

> Father, Thou knowest that work has been carried on in the Far East now for many years. Thou dost remember that Thy great prophet [McKay] who is President of the Church passed through the Far East many years ago, and dedicated here these lands for the preaching of the gospel. We remember the journeys made by President McKay and President Cannon in those days. . . . We are grateful for them and we are grateful for the general dedication of the Far East for the preaching of the everlasting gospel.

Peterson also acknowledged the recent apostolic dedications by Joseph Fielding Smith in North and Southeast Asia but noted that Taiwan was still undedicated:

> It was not his privilege to dedicate this island or rededicate it, so it is for this reason that we have assembled here today, and we acknowledge the general dedication of the entire area by President McKay. Therefore we realize that we are offering a prayer of rededication and particularly to dedicate this particular island unto Thee.[22]

By the end of the 1950s, nearly all of the lands of East Asia and some neighboring islands had been dedicated or rededicated by an apostle for missionary work, including Japan (1901), Hong Kong (1949), South Korea (1955), the Philippines (1955), Guam (1955), Okinawa (1955), and Taiwan (1959).

During the final years of his presidential ministry, one of McKay's priorities was the translation of the Book of Mormon into Chinese and other East Asian languages. Although the original Japanese translation was published in 1909, he presided over its retranslation and republication in 1957. McKay was delighted when on January 16, 1966, Elder Gordon B. Hinckley presented him the Latter-day Saint scripture in Chinese, the language of seven hundred million people at the time. He was thrilled to

---

20. Britsch, *From the East*, 98–100, 176–78.
21. Britsch, *From the East*, 255–56.
22. As quoted by Reid L. Nielson in Grant H. Heaton and Luana C. Heaton, *A Documentary History of the Chinese Mission*, 658–59.

David O. McKay served as the ninth president of The Church of Jesus Christ of Latter-day Saints from 1951 until 1970. Courtesy Church History Library, The Church of Jesus Christ of Latter-day Saints.

read Hinckley's inscription that referred to his 1921 dedicatory prayer and ended thus: "The Book of Mormon is now available in the language which is the mother tongue of more people than any other on earth. May it go forth among them as a witness of the Son of God, the Savior of the World." McKay recorded in his diary: "With great emotion I gratefully received this inscribed copy, and commented upon the publication of the Chinese Book of Mormon, saying: 'This is a great event in the history of the Chinese people. This brings back many fond and delightful memories, and especially of a warm and most delightful day in the early morning 45 years ago when I went with Brother Hugh J. Cannon into the Cypress Grove [in Peking]. We were all alone as we offered the prayer, dedicating China for the reception of the Gospel.'" The church president was also pleased to learn from Hinckley that the Korean edition would soon be published, making the Book of Mormon available in the three major East Asian languages.[23]

President McKay passed away in 1970, but his hopes of evangelizing the Chinese people did not die with him. Several of his younger fellow

23. McKay, Diary, January 19, 1966. The Korean translation of the Book of Mormon was published in 1967.

apostles continued to seek for missionary openings for China, especially Elders Spencer W. Kimball and Gordon B. Hinckley. Kimball, who had been called to the Quorum of the Twelve Apostles in 1943 when McKay was a counselor in the First Presidency, appears to have begun thinking about the Chinese realm in 1945, when he had a puzzling dream in which he found himself traveling to China. Kimball recorded in his journal, "After I had awakened I seemed to continue to be obsessed with the idea that I might be sent to China for missionary service." According to the biography written by his son and grandson, the young apostle "mulled it over for another hour in bed, wondering if it were prophetic, then finally got up and dressed, still unsure."[24] Despite Kimball's uncertainty regarding the dream's divine origin, one thing was clear: the Chinese people were on the new apostle's mind.

After becoming the church's president in December 1973, Kimball consistently shared his vision of global evangelism with his fellow church leaders. According to his biographers, Kimball believed that the church could strategize its growth by establishing strongholds in places such as Japan, Korea, and the Philippines. Once the Latter-day Saint presence was strong enough, these nations could provide their own missionaries instead of relying on representatives from North America. Eventually, missionaries from the United States and these other countries would have the numbers to bring their message to nations that were as yet closed to proselytizing, including China, India, and Russia.[25] Kimball shared this message repeatedly in succeeding years.

For instance, at a seminar for senior church leaders in April 1974, Kimball offered an address, entitled "When the World Will Be Converted," on the faith's global efforts. He hoped that Japan, Taiwan, and Hong Kong could produce enough missionaries to staff their own lands and provide a surplus of elders and sisters to preach in China, Mongolia, Vietnam, and Cambodia.[26] Four years later, in June 1978, Kimball revoked a long-standing church policy that prohibited people of African ancestry from receiving the faith's priesthood or entering its temples. This policy change had significant implications for evangelizing in the nations of Africa, and

---

24. Edward L. Kimball and Andrew E. Kimball, *Spencer W. Kimball: Twelfth President of The Church of Jesus Christ of Latter-day Saints*, 229.

25. Kimball and Kimball, 405–7.

26. Spencer W. Kimball, "When the World Will Be Converted," *Ensign*, October 1974, 12.

Kimball also kept reminding the Saints that China remained high on his list of evangelistic priorities.

Spencer W. Kimball served as the twelfth president of The Church of Jesus Christ of Latter-day Saints from 1973 until 1985. Courtesy Church History Library, The Church of Jesus Christ of Latter-day Saints.

At a seminar in September 1978, he pointed out that China was undergoing "major changes" and that the church needed to be ready to welcome any missionary opportunities that might become available on the mainland.[27] And the following spring, the church president invited Latter-day Saints to pray for global peace, especially for China, "that we might make entry with our missionaries." Kimball further reminded his audience of the dedication of the Chinese realm by David O. McKay and Hugh J. Cannon, nearly six decades earlier: "They walked through shrines, pagodas, and temples fast falling into decay. Finally they came to a grove of cypress trees. A reverential feeling came and a presence seemed to be upon them. They were sure that unseen holy beings were directing their footsteps. There at Peking, in the heart of the most populous nation in the world, undisturbed by the multitudes, they offered the dedicatory prayer."[28] He continued to keep China and McKay's earlier dedicatory prayer alive in the memory of Latter-day Saints.

Diplomatic relations between the United States and China had stabilized in January 1979, prompting officials from church-owned Brigham Young University to send its renowned performance group Young Ambassadors on a tour through China that summer.[29] They were accompanied to Beijing (formerly Peking) by a member of the Quorum of the Twelve Apostles, James E. Faust, who had an additional assignment from

27. Spencer W. Kimball, "'The Uttermost Parts of the Earth,'" *Ensign*, July 1979, 7.

28. Marvin K. Gardner, "President Kimball Shares Missionary Vision with Leaders," *Ensign*, May 1979, 105–6. See also Dell Van Orden, "'Door to China May Be Opening,'" *Church News*, April 7, 1979.

29. See John Hilton III and Brady Liu, "'This Is Very Historic': The Young Ambassadors 1979 Tour of China," 134–64.

Gordon B. Hinckley served as the fifteenth president of The Church of Jesus Christ of Latter-day Saints from 1995 until 2008. Courtesy Church History Library, The Church of Jesus Christ of Latter-day Saints.

the First Presidency to offer a prayer of rededication.[30] In his prayer, given in Beijing's Forbidden City on July 4, 1979, Faust recognized and ratified McKay's 1921 prayer text as a fellow apostle.[31]

Moreover, McKay's 1921 dedicatory prayer has been invoked and quoted from as church leaders have built and dedicated temples within the Chinese realm. Not content to merely pray for missionary opportunities among the Chinese, Kimball announced plans to construct the Taipei Taiwan Temple in the April 1982 general conference.[32] It was the church's third temple built in Asia—and the first temple built in what McKay had called the Chinese realm. Gordon B. Hinckley, then one of Kimball's counselors in the First Presidency, dedicated the structure for church members in November 1984. In this prayer, Hinckley quoted extensively from McKay's 1921 dedicatory prayer and expressed gratitude for his fellow apostle's earlier invocation.[33] This would set a precedent and pattern for subsequent temple dedicatory prayers in East Asia.

A decade following the announcement of the Taipei Taiwan Temple, Hinckley shared in the church's October 1992 general conference "that property has been designated for the construction of a new temple in Hong

---

30. Dallin H. Oaks, "Getting to Know China," 97. See also James P. Bell, *In the Strength of the Lord: The Life and Teachings of James E. Faust*, 154–55.

31. Carol Clark Ottesen, "Waking the Sleeping Giant: A History of the China Teachers Program, Brigham Young University David M. Kennedy Center for International Studies," 16.

32. Spencer W. Kimball, "Remember the Mission of the Church," *Ensign*, May 1982, 4.

33. "'Glorious Light Now Shining,'" *Church News*, November 25, 1984. See also "First Temple in Chinese Realm," *Church News*, November 25, 1984.

The Taipei Taiwan Temple was dedicated by Gordon B. Hinckley on November 17–18, 1984. Courtesy Church History Library, The Church of Jesus Christ of Latter-day Saints.

The Hong Kong China Temple was dedicated by Gordon B. Hinckley on May 26–27, 1996. Courtesy Church History Library, The Church of Jesus Christ of Latter-day Saints.

Kong to serve the needs of our people in that great area of Asia."[34] The Hong Kong Temple, today known as the Hong Kong China Temple, would become the first temple built in China and the second temple in mainland Asia, after the Seoul Korea Temple in 1985. About sixteen months later, McKay's dedicatory prayer was again mentioned during the Hong Kong China Temple's groundbreaking ceremony. Elder John K. Carmack of the Seventy shared his opinion with the assembled Latter-day Saints that three milestone events had culminated in a temple being made available to worthy Hong Kongers: McKay's dedicatory prayer in 1921, Elder Matthew Cowley's apostolic prayer in 1949, and this temple groundbreaking in 1994. "Thus, China has been dedicated, and that dedication was reinforced by solemn prayers at the [Victoria] Peak. When the complete gospel plan is on the earth and among a people, a temple is at the center of it," concluded Carmack. "This, then, is the third great historic event for China and Asia—the breaking of ground for the Hong Kong Temple."[35]

By May 1996, construction of the Hong Kong Temple was complete, and the structure was ready for its apostolic dedication. President Hinckley traveled to Asia for the dedicatory prayer and held a meeting for the missionaries serving in Hong Kong. "The creation of this temple represents one of the great dreams of my life, at least for the last thirty-five years of my life. I first came here thirty-six years ago. Hong Kong was a different place then from what it is now," the prophet began. "I never could have dreamed, back in those early days when the work was just struggling along here, that the time would come when we would have Latter-day Saints gathered together in such numbers as we have seen." He then recounted the experience of McKay in 1921 when "he and his companion found a quiet place in the Forbidden City of Beijing. I have been there, and I think we have found the area where he offered the dedicatory prayer. He pleaded with the Lord to touch the great Chinese realm by the power of His Holy Spirit."[36] The next day, Hinckley dedicated the Hong Kong Temple.[37] The

34. Gordon B. Hinckley, "The Sustaining of Church Officers," *Ensign*, November 1992, 21.

35. "Ground is Broken for Hong Kong Temple to Serve 18,400 Members in Mission, Four Stakes," *Church News*, February 5, 1994.

36. Gordon B. Hinckley, *Discourses of President Gordon B. Hinckley, Volume 1: 1995–1999*, 327.

37. Gordon B. Hinckley, "Hong Kong Temple: 'May Thy Watch Care Be Over It,'" *Church News*, June 1, 1996. See also "President Hinckley Visits Asian Saints, Dedicates Hong Kong Temple," *Ensign*, August 1996, 74–77.

following year, in July 1997, the United Kingdom handed back Hong Kong, their former colonial outpost, to the People's Republic of China, after 156 years of British governance.

The Contemporary Church in the Chinese Realm

Since Brigham Young assigned the first group of elders to evangelize in Hong Kong in August 1852, missionary-minded Latter-day Saints have observed China with great interest. In March 1991, Elder Dallin H. Oaks of the Quorum of the Twelve Apostles gave a speech at Brigham Young University titled "Getting to Know China," in which he discussed the past, present, and future of the church in the Chinese realm. "The Chinese who are members of our Church make up such a tiny fraction of the total population of the People's Republic of China that we could not really say that we have fulfilled our scriptural duty to teach that nation. This is especially clear when we do not have any missionaries in the People's Republic of China," the apostle began. "It is currently against the law to send foreign missionaries to China or to proselyte in that country. And because our Church observes the laws of each nation, we have no plans to send missionaries or to engage in proselyting activities in that great land."[38] Oaks then shared many of the positive contacts and exchanges that the church, including the Brigham Young University community, had enjoyed with Chinese officials and citizens over the past several decades. Moreover, he observed that the Chinese realm had changed since Elder David O. McKay's prayer in Peking in 1921.[39]

Over the past century, a growing number of Chinese have joined the church, especially those who live in places where evangelism is allowed, outside of mainland China. By the centennial of McKay's 1921 dedicatory prayer, the church had more than 61,000 members in Taiwan, more than 25,000 members in Hong Kong, and more than 1,000 members in Macau. Greater Asia had over a million church members, many of whom are overseas Chinese Latter-day Saints.[40] There were also dozens of Chinese-language church units (both Mandarin and Cantonese) meeting beyond East Asia in the United States, including congregations in the states of California, Florida, Maryland, Massachusetts, New York, Texas, Utah,

38. Oaks, "Getting to Know China," 93.
39. Oaks, "Getting to Know China," 97.
40. See Church Newsroom, "Facts and Statistics: Asia."

Virginia, and Washington, and in other countries, including Australia, Canada, Malaysia, New Zealand, Singapore, and the United Kingdom.

Furthermore, Mandarin Chinese is officially used by Latter-day Saint missionaries in more than forty missions, and Cantonese is spoken by elders and sisters in about a half dozen additional missions today. The church's four books of scriptures—the Bible, Book of Mormon, Doctrine and Covenants, and Pearl of Great Price—have been translated into Chinese, along with its official magazine and basic curriculum. Nevertheless, Chinese remains a very minor language used by the global church membership when compared to English, Spanish, and Portuguese, which combined accounts for about 90 percent of the languages spoken by Latter-day Saints worldwide.[41]

In April 2020, church president Russell M. Nelson made history when he announced that a temple was planned for construction in Shanghai, China. "For more than two decades, temple-worthy members in the People's Republic of China have attended the Hong Kong China Temple," he explained to astonished church members during general conference. "But in July 2019, that temple was closed for long-planned and much-needed renovation. In Shanghai, a modest multipurpose meeting place will provide a way for Chinese members to continue to participate in ordinances of the temple—in the People's Republic of China—for them and their ancestors." The prophet clarified that church operations and gathering protocols would remain unaffected in mainland China: "Expatriate and Chinese congregations will continue to meet separately. The Church's legal status there remains *unchanged.* In an initial phase of facility use, entry will be by appointment only. The house of the Lord in Shanghai will *not* be a destination place for tourists from other countries."[42] The planned construction of a Latter-day Saint temple in mainland China for Chinese nationals—even with its unprecedented constraints—was something unimaginable in previous decades.

According to independent Latter-day Saint demographer Matt Martinich, the church's announced Shanghai temple "was a major surprise given that the Church operates under significant legal restrictions in the PRC [People's Republic of China], and there [remain] no stakes in the PRC at present." After reiterating Nelson's rationale to construct a temple in mainland China, Martinich points out that the church now

41. Larry Richman, "Church Membership and Languages Worldwide."

42. Russell M. Nelson, "Go Forward in Faith," *Ensign*, May 2020, 115; emphasis in original.

has membership in most major Chinese cities, most of whom are likely citizens of the PRC.[43] In 2021, Nelson also announced plans for a temple in Kaohsiung, Taiwan.[44] When these two Chinese temples are dedicated, it is likely that McKay's 1921 dedicatory prayer over the Chinese realm will continue to play an important rhetorical role in the story of Latter-day Saints in East Asia.

---

43. "Eight New Temples Announced—Analysis," Growth of The Church of Jesus Christ of Latter-day Saints (blog), April 5, 2020.

44. Russell M. Nelson, "Make Time for the Lord," *Liahona*, November 2021, 121.

APPENDIX A

Hosea Stout, Report on China Mission in the Salt Lake Tabernacle, December 1853

Hosea Stout, Report, December 25, 1853, Papers of George D. Watt, Church History Library. Transcribed from Pitman shorthand by LaJean Purcell Carruth and verified by Silvia Ghosh.

All punctuation and capitalization have been added for readability. Words enclosed in [ ] are editorial additions for readability. Words enclosed in [?] indicate a transcription that is somewhat uncertain. Two or more words enclosed in [?] indicate different possible readings of the shorthand.

Tabernacle Sunday 25th 1853.

Hosea Stout, late from China, where he had been on a mission.

I have been called upon to address the congregation for few moments this morning. I can truly say that I am very much rejoiced to be in your midst once more. I never knew what it was to be separated from the Saints since I first became acquainted with them until I went on mission to China. During our absence I felt as though I was away from home; how to express my feelings on returning again I hardly know how to begin.

I suppose that you would all be anxious to hear something about what we done, and perhaps something about what we did not do. [It is a] very short story to tell what we done: the fact is, we did not do anything worth naming. We went there and back and had no difficulty in finding the way. We had a long trip, and it was a singular country, and [the] people [were] something naturally different from anything I had ever been acquainted with; [a] person [has] got to go there and see things before they can know anything about it. I will give you a faint sketch, I will do my best. There is one thing here I have had to console myself with: that is, we had exceeding great faith when we went. I never undertook a thing that I had more faith in than that mission; it was over me. That we did. It would have been a lonesome business if we had not had exceeding great faith.

We were blessed in everything we undertook in going and coming. When we got to California, there was 38 of us together going to different parts of the world. We went to San Francisco. We found a small branch of church there and one across the bay, and brethren came forward to fit out the different missions. We were not put to the trouble in calling on them for assistance, [or?] the fact few of the missionaries expected any, but thought they would have to gather means to fit themselves out, but the brethren came forward and fitted us out. John M. Horner took the lead and Brother [Quartus] Sparks. He came forward like a man, and said he realized [the] importance of [our] mission, that the elders should [not] be detained to work to fit out [themselves], and it was necessary [that] brethren come forward and advance the means. He also said if brethren did not follow along to do [that], he would do it himself, he was able to take all the doing and fit out the mission which he would do before they should be detained. I can say I was much [disappointed] in feelings I found among the brethren there. Brother John M. Horner came over to meet with us. He stated he [had] made arrangements in San Jose for the brethren to fit out the mission, [to hand] all they felt like subscribing for it over to him, and he would pay over the balance. When it was counted up it almost scared me: [it] made up [an] amount of nearly 7000 [dollars]. Brethren, many call themselves Mormons, but few brethren there. Horner came forward like Sparks and said he would fit out the entire missions than the rest. He give drafts on the [illegible] and raised the money, [made our own?] his portion he put in; over 2900 dollars came out of Brother Horner. I do not know exactly how much Brother Sparks paid. But it was a pretty large sum. We met our own friend Thomas S. Williams there and he paid over 500 dollars; that was also a voluntary contribution, for no one asked him for it, but he considered it a privilege to do [it].

The missionaries accordingly took their departure [on] the first [available] vessels. The China Mission did not start until the 8th of March; that was first vessel we had the opportunity to sail on. (Those other missions you know as much about as I do; all I have learned about them was through the *Deseret News*.) We left on 8 of March and [were] 49 days going out; [we] had [an] agreeable journey. When we got to Hong Kong, we found things naturally different from what we expected. We found that board was $40 month in any respectable society; if we [would] go below that, we had to go into the lowest depths of corruption and degradation that I believe exists on [the] face of [the] earth. I never saw the like. [There are] only two classes of inhabitants there, that is, those that consider themselves [the] greatest men in [the] world and those that are the lowest creatures I believe are on the face of the earth.

We looked around to see what chance there was for preaching the gospel, and we found it [a] pretty difficult show. People all received us very friendlily, [they were] kind and courteous to us, but they all bore testimony that hospitality was unknown among them. They said we would be kindly treated as long as [we had] money to pay, [but] that after that no one [would] have further business with us. [They said] that was the fashion of country, and we found it to be the fact. We looked around and finally took a room. In getting a room, we found a friend gave us [the] use of [a] room for nothing. We set up housekeeping on our own cook.

After that we commenced making arrangements for preaching the gospel. We found that it was impossible to get a house to preach in. There was a difficulty in getting a chapel or any place kept by any religious denominations, and those who were the most friendly to us informed us [it would] be impossible to get a congregation into a house any way. An English man told me he did not think there was a preacher on [the] face of earth [who could] get the inhabitants of Hong Kong but natural power of stories. We advertised and went to preaching on [the] parade ground close to the barracks where the English [military] has a garrison. [At the] first appointment there was a good turnout in that place; the most of them was soldiers. They paid good attention and heard all we had to say. We advertised again and again and preached until our congregations dwindled down until not a single soul [was] attending us. We would advertise still and go and sit on [a] big rock until sun down; we gave [out our message] that way. We learned the people had heard as much of our [religious] principles as they wished to know, their curiosity was satisfied, and that was all they wanted to know. We then commenced going around from house to house and preaching to individuals [and] we followed that up until we could no longer get [into] a house. When we quit, we did not know one individual [in] any place we could talk [with] upon the principles of the gospel. All this time they were extremely courteous and cavalier, rather too much so to suit me, and they all wished us success. They all told me that they were glad we came, and they hoped we would have good success; they really [did] believe if we could convert the China nation to Mormonism, [they] felt [it would] better the condition of [the] nation much, and they said they believe it be a better religion for them than the other [Christian] sects of day.

Their testimony was not favorable in relation to [Protestant] missionaries. They say they are a corrupt people; they only mean to live an indolent, corrupt, life. This is the testimony of all the people in Hong Kong; I had no reason to dispute it. The Catholic missionaries do the best they can to bring people to their faith and they have [the] best credit. As to the Chinese being converted to Christianity, I saw no one that ever believed that the Chinaman ever had been converted; they say it is a thing they never saw. The missionaries themselves do not believe they can bring any [Chinese] over to the faith, and what they expect to do there is more than I can tell. They never gave me any reasons or told me what they do expect to bring to pass. But they are living there and have a handsome salary, enough to support them in indolence and luxury, and that is all they care for.

The Chinese themselves are [a] singular people in their attributes, manners, and customs, and all their associations and habits of life differ from anything I have ever been acquainted with. They very strictly adhere to their manners and customs. I suppose they dress as they did thousands years ago. They never vary from ancient customs in their dress and mechanical [point?], they are most tenacious of their customs as any people I ever did see. They consider all foreigners [a] degraded, barbarous race, and totally beneath their notice. They are celestial beings, they say their forefathers came down from [the] sun, [the] celestial planet and they settled in China, and they are their descendants. The outside barbarians, as they term them, say their forefathers was made in the adobe yard. They consider themselves naturally superior than people that descended from such low parentage. They are very tenacious about letting foreigners come amongst them.

They are the most thievish people I ever saw. [They] take everything a man has when he is watching. They take a man's watch handkerchief every day course. They will cheat the worst Yankee that ever went out to trade, and he cannot help himself. I never did trade with them, but I got shaved, and I knew it. One little boy actually put some bogus money upon me one day. I did not notice until I wanted to pass it. He cheated me out of ¾ cent; pretty good [pace/race?] for [a] Chinaman. The servants cheat you in market; [they] take a little slice of meat, tea, [or] wood, and you have to buy all of what you use and [they] cheat you out of that. Your money is discounted 10 percent to begin [or again?] a man counts all lost. He only gets about one half of his money, when he counts up all the shaves he goes through. They say when a merchant buys goods and sells it, he makes percents, and when they buy provisions, anything to write, they make a percent too. This is a knock down argument, and they cannot help themselves. If they go to market themselves, they will ask foreigners about a third more, and they are all agreed in this thing. If you go and ask price of article, [they will] tell you how much it was and tell the coolie to buy it, and he will get it for one third less, [right] before my face. As to the character of [the] Chinese, they are a very industrious people; they work hard, but they are slow. They are very ingenious but not enterprising. If they can get 16 cents per day for hardest work [they are] perfectly satisfied and feel they are doing well and will board themselves into the bargain.

There is a rebellion going on there that keeps the country in [a] considerable state of excitement. The foreign parties are all times on the lookout and expecting that peradventure they will have to go to Hong Kong for safety; several ships [are] kept on hand for that purpose. I have no doubt but what the rebellion will succeed. I have no doubt but what the Tartar dynasty will be overthrown, and the ancient laws and customs of China will be established, if foreign powers do not interfere. The rebel chief does well while [the] emperor does not try to defend himself. The rebel chief says he is commanded by the God of heaven to set matters right, to expel the Tartars and restore the ancient customs. When he gets the revelations to conquer provinces, and he always acts according to the creed and talks in name of [the] God of heaven, it works very well, and he has kept his word so far and I believe will. What [the] effect will be after he does succeed, I cannot tell. They are not a warlike people; they sometimes have battles [where] there are thousands of people on each side, [but] not more than 10 killed. The leaders, when the battle commences, flee, and the commanders either kill themselves or the emperor kills him for losing the battle. They are perfectly contented to be tyrannized over and be bound down; it is the spirit of the nation and always has been. They know but little about the world. For instance, when the rebel chief took the province of [Nanking?], and the city fell into his hands, he turned towards the interior. [The] province of China was joining [Nanking?], and the reason he did not go to conquer [was] that he did not know there was such a province there. He knew nothing about the country any further than beyond as he discovered it in traveling over it.

We found that it was totally impractical for us to go from one part [of China] to another. It would cost us as much to go to Shanghai as it was to go to [San] Francisco, $100; for less than that I could [pay to] get to California. When we found we had no means to go upon and have to go from one part another to get a [company?], we concluded [that] we would come back to California and then report ourselves to president [Brigham Young] again and see what further orders [we received] when we got there. It was concluded for me to come home and make reports, but Brother [James] Lewis and [Chapman] Duncan stayed there. They concluded what ever an [establishment?], they would go at it until [we] got further orders. I went to San Bernardino and there remained two months. In that time Lewis came down and found me there and came home with me. He is now in [Parowan]; Duncan is in [San] Francisco.

That is about the sum and substance of [our] mission [to China]. By what means the Lord will introduce the gospel to that nation is more than I know. It is on that account [that] I came home, that I might find out. I believe the gospel will be established among them and many of them [will] embrace it. If [they] do embrace it and ever realize the blessings of gospel, they will be useful people: they will be contented with their lot, whatever they are set to do they will do, and be contented about it. There is no disposition to run about and wander. But there is more degradation and misery there [than] I ever conceived of. I have often heard the Saints grumble about our times poor, and [how they are] oppressed in Zion. A great many [Saints] go to California because of it. I can say I never saw people suffering until I [went?] to China, never saw people tyrannized over until I went there. Those brethren [that have] gone to California [be]cause of oppression ought to go further [to China] to see it. I have seen the policemen whip the poor on their bare backs. I have seen hundreds sitting on [illegible] because nothing to do. Policemen would go to work and whip as many of them he could get at, and they do not consider themselves abused because [they have] always been used to be[ing] cuffed and kicked about. The streets and sidewalks [are] full of Chinamen out of employ[ment], seeking for something to do to get victuals. I have seen them on my door[step], and when I come out, they bow half across the street. They expected to be kicked because he was in my door. It is common for gentlemen to [get] kicked. When the sidewalk gets blocked, up they jump out of the way for fear of being abused. They bow down to the most servile oppression in the world. They have been raised to it; they know nothing about anything else.

When I saw all these things and came to reflect back at the blessings now in Utah, I was more astonished than ever [at] those [who] rise up and going away [to California] and report evil about the inhabitants of Utah and talk about oppression. I know really that [all?] set to grumbling at the richest blessings of heaven. Before they get through, those that go to California, they will wish they were back [in Utah] again. I saw hundreds of brethren in California that went off boasting [of the] great things they were going [to] accomplish when got there, one in particular, [and said that from] this time henceforth [they were] going be free, independent men, and they would show the world and [the] church [that] they were men of calculation. They have calculated themselves out of everything they possessed on earth. I have seen men there [that] do not know where [to get] the next meal of victuals. I heard them say if [they] ever get back to Utah, [it will] take more [than] hard times and oppression to get them away, and I know it. I make mention of this so that you may think of it. All those [who] want to go there, [who] believe it is good plan for them to go and try it awhile and when they come back, they will be better satisfied, I hope.

I have never seen any suffering [from] poverty in Utah. I have seen thousands of men in [San] Francisco laying on the sidewalk sick, and men running over them, and no one think enough of them to take them to hospital, and I have been told [it is] common to find them dead on the streets, for in a city where more money [is] in circulation than in [the] world, if a man is out of money there he is out of luck. I met several brethren that left Coal Creek [Iron County, Utah] in consequence of extreme rigor of martial law. We told them they had 90 miles to pass without [illegible] and water, [and warned them to] be careful and earnest. They were believing [aye?] and said they could go out [of Utah] and were glad [they] got out of oppression, etc., [illegible] like Carthage was to Nauvoo. All our old mobocratic friends in [the] east mixing up; they are all going fine now, [but] after [a] while it will gather and burst, and I pity those brethren that may be found in their midst when it takes place. Elements gathering in lower California [will] make many Saints suffer; [they are] bound to do it. In upper California I saw but little prejudice against the Mormons; many good women, gentlemen. Sam Brannon is there; he is known as [an] apostate Mormon that has been cut off [from] the church for rascality. He is very wealthy and is elected into the [California] senate and is considered honorable, although they say he is great rascal. Brother [John] Horner [is] considered one of [the] best men in California, and he is considered a good Mormon in full fellowship, and they say he is a good man. But religion is a matter they do not trouble themselves about. Well, brethren, that is about all I have to say to you. I say may the Lord bless you all. Amen.

APPENDIX B

Alma O. Taylor, "Report of Our Visit to China," 1910

Alma O. Taylor, "Report of Our Visit to China," [1910], Church History Library.

His original typewritten report totals thirty-two double-spaced pages. This reproduction retains original spelling and punctuation. Taylor's handwritten edits appear within slashes (//), while editorial additions, including Chinese place names that have changed since 1910, appear within brackets ([]). I have included Taylor's introduction and four of his eight sections, which are most relevant to prospective evangelizing. The sections not included below are "Races and Political Conditions," "Military Condition," and "Educational Condition." For an annotated version, see Reid L. Neilson, "Alma O. Taylor's 1910 Fact Finding Mission to China," 176–203.

Report of Our Visit to China

Written by Alma O. Taylor

. . . On the morning of January 26th [1910] we crossed the Yalu River [Yalujiang] on ice sleds and arrived at Antung [Dandong] in Manchuria. At Antung we took the train for Mukden [Shenyang]. Although the distance is only 191 miles, owing to the poor condition of this light-railroad, which was hurriedly built by the Japanese during their war with the Russians, it took two days to reach Mukden, one night being spent at the half-way station, Tsaohokon. Mukden is the chief city of Manchuria and the sacred city of the present Imperial Family of China. It has an interesting history connected with the Manchus, and here we find some of the tombs of the Imperial Ancestors.

After an interesting three days visit at Mukden we boarded the train going south. At night we reached Shanhaikwan [Shanhaiguan]. The next morning we visited that wonderful monument to the genius and endurance of the Chinese—the great wall of China—which terminates at this place.

Proceeding by the early forenoon train, we reached Tientsin [Tianjin] that afternoon. Tientsin is the outlet to Peking [Beijing], holding the same relation to it that Osaka does to Kyoto or Yokohama to Tokyo. It is interesting because of the massacre of whites enacted here in 1870 and because of the part it played in the Boxer War—the battle of Tientsin deciding the fate of the foreigners in Peking.

After two days we proceeded to Peking, the capital of China and the most interesting and most cosmopolitan city in the Empire. We spent four full days here in busy inquiry and educational sight seeing.

From Peking to Hankow [Hankou/Wuhan] is a ride by rail of 750 miles, and there is nothing on the way that the ordinary tourist cares or ventures to see. For these there is only one through train a week. All the other trains are locals and by these it takes three days to reach Hankow, two stops at night in Chinese inns being necessary. The chance to stop in a Chinese inn and get in closer touch with their food and life tempted us, so we left Peking on the slow schedule.

Paotingfu [Baoching] is the capital of Chihli Province and the scene of a bloody massacre of Christians during the Boxer War. This was made the first stop and we had half a day to visit the resident foreigners and see the city. We boarded and lodged in a Chinese inn. The next day we got as far as Changtefu and had another experience in Chinese life. It was the night before Chinese New Year and the noisy celebration, together with uncomfortable slab-beds, made sleep difficult. After another day in a train as dusty as a desert stage, we reached Chumatien and spent New Year's night in a Chinese inn where a Western idea or two had been poorly applied. The next day we reached Hankow.

From a point about 30 miles the other side of Mukden to Hankow our journey was mostly through extensive plains seldom broken by mountains or hills. At this time of the year (last of January and first of February) scarcely a green leaf or blade of grass is seen. The broad fields are dry and dusty. The cold winds that blow almost every day pick up the dust and carry it over the open country with such fury that the atmosphere is colored and the houses and trains are constantly coated with dust both inside and out.

Across the river from Hankow is the city of ~~Uri~~/Wu/chang [Wuhan], the educational center of middle China. ~~Uri~~/Wu/chang, Hankow and Hangyang [Hanyang] three cities all in one group, form the great metropolis of central China. We had a profitable three days' sojourn here. Leaving the dusty, uncomfortable trains of North China, we took steamer down the great Yangtse [Yangtze] river for Nanking [Nanjing].

Nanking was the capital of China during the Ming dynasty, and it was the scene of the bloodiest tragedy of the Taiping Rebellion, which rebellion, it is said, resulted in the death of 100,000,000 of China's inhabitants.

A day and a half were spent investigating conditions at Nanking, then we proceeded by rail to Suchow [Suzhou], called by some, the Venice of China. The visit here was limited to sight-seeing. The next day we took the train to Shanghai. This ended our railroad experiences in China. From Chinkiang to Suchow the railroad runs parallel with the grand canal, another of the great engineering feats of the Chinese.

A wait for the proper southbound coast steamer made it necessary to spend eight days in Shanghai. Shanghai is a great commercial city populated by men of all nations and creeds, whose principal aim in life seems to be money-making. Here also a mixture of Western and Eastern life can be seen to good advantage; the foreign city standing alongside the native gives a good chance to draw comparisons. While the Westerner is showing the Chinese a good example in material affairs, his influence morally is absolutely degrading.

Leaving Shanghai we proceeded down the coast to the city called Foochow [Fuzhou], on the Min River. At last we have found a spot in China w[h]ere the scenery looks fresh and beautiful! Our disgust with the poverty of scenic landscape in north and central China is partially forgotten when we behold the magnificence of the scenery from the mouth of the Min up to the city of Foochow. Unfortunately we had to leave Foochow early the following morning.

The next stop was at Amoy [Xiamen], situated in a beautiful harbor. The native city is the filthiest and foulest in China so far as our experience permits us to judge. In this harbor a part of the American Atlantic Fleet was royally entertained by the Chinese in 1908.

Our steamer called next at Swatow [Shantou], where we had a few hours' stay and then proceeded to Hongkong [Hong Kong]. Hongkong has a delightful situation and its life and activities are much like those of Shanghai.

We went up the river to Canton [Guangzhou], the city of the greatest population in China. There are more people in Canton to the square rod than in any other spot on the globe. Most of the Chinese in America emigrated from the country surrounding Canton. After two days of study, inquiry and sight-seeing we went back to Hongkong, allowing one day to prepare for the start home. Our steamer sailed from Hongkong Saturday, March 12th, at noon. The next Tuesday we had seven hours at Shanghai, where we said farewell to China.

China is commonly spoken of as North China and South China, the Yangtse River being the dividing line. Our sojourn in the north lasted seventeen days, and we were seventeen days in the south, while fifteen days were spent in cities on the banks of or near the Yangtse, for, when we reached this river at Hankow, we were about 600 miles inland from the Pacific. The entire journey in North China of 1463 miles was made by rail—railroads owned by the Chinese, but still directed more or less by foreigners. The rest of our journey in China, with the exception of the distance from Nanking to Shanghai, 193 miles, was made by steamer, and from Shanghai to Canton was limited to the coast. In all, our travels by land and water in and about China, including the return from Hongkong to Shanghai, covered a distance of about 4,385 miles. . . .

Social Conditions.

The home is the foundation of Chinese society. The family interests are greater than the interests of the individual. Individual liberty is, to a degree, curtailed because of the supremacy of the family.

While traveling in China we have heard considerable of the Chinese lack of real love in the family circle. Much has been said and written about family quarrels and sorrows. But, after all, in a land where so much stress is laid upon filial piety and ancestor worship and the perpetuation of the family lines, there must be a strong loving bond somewhere. After living in Japan and studying the Japanese for over eight years, we feel safe in judging that in China also the surface appearances are poor indications of the inner life. We are therefore inclined to accept the view of the minority which is best stated in the words of Dr. McGowan:

> "There is no doubt that husband and wife in the great majority of homes in China are bound to each other by genuine, undoubted love. At first sight this seems difficult to be believed. Not only do the young people never catch sight of one another until the moment that they stand side by side as man and wife in the husband's home, but it is an undoubted fact that the great mass of the women of this land are very deficient in personal charm. Fortunately, good looks are not the things that cause love to grow in a man's or woman's heart. As time goes by, other forces come into play that make the plain face shine with a beauty of its own; and soon the hearts are knit together as though Cupid himself had twined the golden chain that bound them in a common love. . . .
>
> "That there are unhappy homes in China, where husbands and wives dispute and quarrel with each other I do not doubt. The same is the case in countries where men and women fall in love and willingly marry each other. . . .

> ["]As far as a long experience would enable me to judge, I verily believe that the majority of homes in this country are reasonably happy ones, and the wives hold a position not of sufference but of love."

'Tis true that marriages are performed in what, to a Westerner, may seem an arbitrary, mechanical, loveless way, but the Oriental is used to Oriental customs, and a person cannot safely theorize on Chinese love-knots while holding up the Western custom as a standard.

We discovered, however, some decidedly barbaric practices in connection with the family life of China, which moral principles all over the world condemn: such as /the/ killing of infants, especially girl babies, or casting them away, or selling them as slaves. That this has been an all too general custom in the past and is an all too common sin at present every speaker and writer admits. But justice demands that the world be informed that this sin has greatly decreased of late years and hope is bright that it will, ere long, cease entirely. Poverty, the honor that comes to the parents with the birth of a male child, and the disgrace and humiliation which custom and perverted Confucianism frequently attaches to the birth of a female child are the chief reasons assigned for this crime.

The use above of the word "slaves" may imply that slavery exists in China, in fact some men so view it, but from our readings and observations, we would be more inclined to refer to it as a severe apprenticeship, because whips and lashes and bloodhounds are not in evidence, and freedom and independence are not impossible if worked for. Still it is not uncommon for this apprenticeship to continue from father to son, making the system appear like an inherited bondage.

One would expect to find in a country like China a pronounced class distinction, but we were agreeably surprised to find that the high and low mingle together with less restraint than Oriental society in most places demands. As already noted in the remarks on education, according to the old system, every man, except the sons of those engaged in degraded business, could aspire to and, by their own diligence and genius, reach the highest honors this side [of] the Imperial throne. Wealth and poverty makes less distinction between men than learning and ignorance do. It remains to be seen whether or not the program for a new China will result in more or less caste in her society.

Ideas of propriety in the intercourse between men and women in China are different from the Western ideas. The women are separated from the men in most public places. The churches in North China are provided with curtains that hang through the centre of the assembly rooms and the men are seated on one side and the women on the other, preventing even a view of each other. In all churches where the curtains are not used, the sexes are assigned different parts of the room, a mixture of sexes in the same tier being carefully avoided, let alone a mixture on the same bench. The inns where we stopped, the public places where we visited (aside from the shrines), the stores where we made purchases; all these are manned, giving everything an indelicate, inartistic, rough, masculine appearance and air. The women in the house also have no special part to play in the entertainment of a male guest. This condition makes it impracticable and dangerous, therefore quite impossible, for a male missionary to do work among the women; and they, being generally too illiterate, he cannot reach them with the written word. The female missionary is therefore a necessary adjunct to missionary work in China.

There is a class of females, known as singing girls, who dance and play and sing before male audiences in certain public and private entertainments. These girls are common attendants upon real swell restaurants, tea houses, etc., but their profession is decidedly shady.

The theatre is the chief source of amusement in China, and all performances, whether good or bad, elevating or demoralizing, are well patronized by both men and women. The actors are all men; women being prohibited from going on the stage.

Private gatherings are no doubt common among the wealthier people, but we have had only the faintest hints as to their nature, except that feasting at the other fellow's expense is the Chinaman's delight.

Although we have not recognized it by sight, polygamy is a common institution in China. The importance of the family, the necessity of continuing the family line and keeping up the worship at the ancestral tombs and tablets according to Confucian principles, are cited as the basic reason for polygamy: Since the beginning of the practice, however, the reasons have been found to justify individual cases and now concubinage has also become common as an appendage to a perversion of polygamy.

The terrible graft that is carried on in official circles, because every official is so badly paid and squeezed by his superiors that he in turn has to squeeze and steal right and left in order to live and maintain the standard of his position, has had a demoralizing effect upon aristocratic society. And the commoners have found in this an excuse and precedent for similar immoral, high-handed schemes in their part of society. Thus there are evidences that one rank of society is suspicious of the other and a mutual suspicion and jealousy exists alarmingly among individuals. The President of the largest Christian University in China said that the students' distrust in the government and official promises was so great that free education in government schools was no attraction to the young men of the nation, who are too fearful of what the results might be to themselves. This common suspicion is one of the important sociological problems of the Celestial Empire.

Moral State.

The statements we have heard about the Chinaman's morality are many and often quite contradictory. Foreigners of long residence in North China unhesitatingly applaud the personal purity of the people and declare their condition to be equally as clean if not cleaner, than conditions found in Europe or America. The story in South China, told by men of equally long experience is that the Chinese are terrifically loose in their morals, and the seclusion of women (it is not so marked in the south as in the north) so much applauded, is not the white flower of virtue that it is often said to be. One veteran, living in central China, recited what he called actual discoveries of immorality which, if true, certainly rank well with the startling revelations of sexual rottenness in the Occident. Doctors in middle and south China claim that syphilis and kindred diseases are unusually common but are not of the most virulent type.

One fact, which, we judge, would have a bearing on this question is that marriage, being considered of utmost importance, is urged upon everyone. Bachelors and old maids are the scapegoats of society. The result is that the Chinese marry young, the girls' years are especially tender. This custom, to our minds, reduces the temptations of young manhood and young womanhood, and surely prevents much impurity which would otherwise exist.

The Chinese are known all over the world as men of their word. Honesty in business—commercial integrity, have made them almost a proverb in the mouths of Westerners. To know the basis of this reputation has been one of the objects of our search and study in China. After all, we conclude, from the evidence to hand, that honesty with the Chinese is not a moral asset to his character—it is not a matter of conscience with him; it is only a policy which he has recognized to be essential in obtaining the most coveted thing in the world—money. The Chinese keenly recognizes that in order to get the foreigner's money he must first get his confidence. And the policy that gets and holds a merchant's confidence, is honesty in business deals. Now the basis of a man's honesty and reliability in business is not a question about which the Western merchant cares much, therefore they have praised the Chinese so loudly that people take it for granted that honesty is a characteristic virtue of the Chinese. But it is not.

The Chinaman is a born gambler. He would rather play games of chance than eat, and he likes a feast very much. It was no uncommon thing for us to see little boys and girls not yet big enough to go to school playing juvenile games of chance in the streets, preparatory, it seemed, to following in the footsteps of their sires. Their intense passion to play for luck is illustrated by one writer who says it is not uncommon for the people of a certain district who have received a tax notice, say, for $17.00, to sink the $17.00 in a game of chance in the hope of getting $20.00, but only come out with $14.00 rather than go directly to the collector and pay the $17.00. Gambling is no doubt one of the curses of China.

Another curse is opium smoking. It has been prohibited by law, but a majority of the officials are said to be secretly continuing the practice, while hundreds of thousands of the common people are slaves to the habit—a habit which, it is claimed does more harm to the nation than floods, pestilences and famines combined.

We have been deeply interested in learning of the Chinese sincerity of heart and purpose when he enters the Christian church. Missionaries, questioned on this point, have naturally spoken in defense of their convert's sincerity, but there has been an occasional shy acknowledgment of exceptions to the rule. The history of a Baptist missionary's (not Dr. McGowan) experiences in China during 50 years, which has been read with keen interest, records happenings which clearly prove that the Chinese have weaknesses in common with their neighbors, and there is more or less ulterior motive in the sympathetic attitude of many towards religion. This is not limited to the professing Christians—it is seen in the professing Buddhists and others. In justice to the Chinese Christians, their heroic stand at the time of the Boxer War should not be forgotten. A Bible was placed at their feet and they were commanded to trample upon it and renounce Christianity. Not complying, they were threatened with death. It is said that practically every soul thus tested chose death. We are told by missionaries generally that apostasy is uncommon, but lukewarmness and inactivity in Christian duties is one of the worries of the work.

Religious Condition.

The Chinese being such faithful students of the classics, we were not surprised to hear of their high esteem for Confucius and Mencius. Ancestor worship, so common in every part of the Empire, and in every grade of society is the chief product of Confucianism. It, in fact, is the soul of religion in China, if indeed China has any distinct religion, and around this worship of the dead have gathered Buddhistic and Taoistic rites and ceremonies embracing varied conceptions of strange gods and spirits both good and bad, beautiful and ugly, gentle and ferocious.

Confucianism should exist as an independent code of ethics. It cannot logically or consistently admit Buddhism or Taoism, for the very nature of these systems is antagonistic to Confucius' doctrines. But the remarkable ability of the Chinese to mix oil with water, as it were, has mixed the metaphysics of Buddhism, the superstitions of Taoism and the ethics of Confucianism into one incongruous, but, to the Chinese mind, quite harmonious mass. Thus in some rites of worship the people may be strictly Buddhists, while in others, Taoists, and still again in others Confucianists. Dr. Arthur H. Smith states his observations of this condition as follows:

> . . . Any Chinese who wants the services of a Buddhist priest, and who can afford to pay for them, will hire the priest, and thus be 'a Buddhist.' If he wants a Taoist priest, he will in like manner call him, and this makes him 'a Taoist'. It is of no consequence to the Chinese which of the two he employs, and he will not improbably call them both at once, and thus be at once [']a Buddhist" and 'a Taoist'. Thus the same individual is at once a Confucianist, a Buddhist, and a Taoist, and with no sense of incongruity. Buddhism swallowed Taoism, Taoism swallowed Confucianism, but at last the latter swallowed both Buddhism and Taoism together, and thus 'the three religions are one!'"

Our own observations lead to the belief that the Chinese are polytheists. They seem to have a god for every occasion. It seems also that pantheism is a characteristic of their faith, for objects in nature, if not nature itself, are deified and worshipped. It may be, however, indeed our observations suggest, that idolatrous polytheism and idolatrous pantheism are more eagerly followed by the ignorant classes than by the scholars, for the latter have their brains well soaked in the teachings found in the classics. Some understand the Confucian classics to deny the existence of God, hence say that atheism is common among the scholars of China.

However it all may be, what our own eyes have seen, our noses smelled, and our ears heard, while visiting Buddhist, Taoist and Confucian shrines in China, all goes to prove that the religions of China are, in practice, unclean, without order, superstitious, immoral, idolatrous, retrogressive and unenlightening. No matter how beautifully their theology may be recorded, Confucius, Mencius, Guatama and Laotse are not honored by the worship done in their names.

It is said that the Chinese have never been anti-Christian, that is, hostile to Christianity itself. It is the foreigner and the foreign influence that accompanies Christianity into China that the Chinese have opposed and do still oppose. Still it does not seem to us reasonable that Christianity, as such, should not be more or less resisted. It is no doubt true that the common people, unacquainted with the classics are not anti-Christian, but the scholars, from the very nature of their textbooks must recognize Christianity as antagonistic to their beloved sage's analects. In a book entitled "China's Only Hope," written by Chang Chih-Tug, one of China's greatest Vice-roys, and approved by Imperial edict, the idea of Christianity for the West and Confucianism for China is plainly set forth. The following paragraphs are significant:

> "We would here state that there are now three things necessary to be done in order to save China from revolution. The first is to maintain the reigning Dynasty; the second is to conserve the Holy Religion; and the third is to protect the Chinese Race. These are inseparably connected; in fact they together constitute one; for in order to protect the Chinese Race we must first conserve the Religion, and if the Religion is to be conserved we are bound to maintain the Dynasty.
>
> "Our Holy Religion has flourished in China several thousand years without change. The early Emperors and Kings embellished our tenets by their noble examples and bequeathed to us the rich legacy which we now possess. The sovereigns were the teachers. The Han, the T'ang and all the Chinese Dynasties to the Ming (embracing a period of 1800 years) honored and revered the religion of Confucius. Religion is the government, and the Emperors of our Dynasty honor Confucianism with a still greater reverence[.] . . . For government and religion are inseparably linked together and constitute the warp of the past and present, the woof of intercommunication between China and the West.
>
> "The foundations of our State are deep and durable. Protected by Heaven, the superstructure will certainly stand secure! But supposing this absurd gossip about the partition of China by Europeans were true and the country were cut up, be it ever so exalted and excellent, would foreigners respect the Holy Doctrine of Confucius? Far from it. The Classics of the Four Philosophers would be thrown out as refuse, and the Confucian cap and gown would never more cherish the hope of an official career. Our clever

> scholars would figure as clergymen, compressors, and clerks, whilst the common people would be required to pay a poll-tax and be used as soldiers, artisans, underlings, and servants. That is what would happen. And the more menial our people became, the more stupid they would be; until being both menial and stupid, they would become reduced to wretched poverty and at last perish miserably. Our Holy Religion would meet the same fate that Brahmanism in India did. Its adherents would be found skulking away, or crouching among the cavernous hills, but clinging fast the while to some tattered remnants of the truth!
>
> "Buddhism and Taoism are decaying, and cannot long exist, whilst the Western religion is flourishing and making progress every day. Buddhism is on its last legs, and Taoism is discouraged, because its devils have become irresponsive and inefficacious. If there be a renaissance of Confucianism, China will be brought to order and Buddhism and Taoism will receive secure protection from the Sect of the Learned.
>
> "The old and new must both be taught; by the old is meant the Four Books, the Five Classics, history, government, and geography of China; by the new, Western government, science, and history. Both are imperative, but we repeat that the old is to form the basis and the new is for practical purposes.
>
> "Chinese learning is moral. Western learning is practical. Chinese learning concerns itself with moral conduct. Western learning, with the affairs of the world. What matters it, then, whether Western learning is mentioned in the Classics or not, if it teaches nothing repugnant, or antagonistic, to the genius of our books? If the Chinese heart throbs in unison with the heart of the sages, expressing the truth in irreprovable conduct, in filial piety, brotherly love, honestly, integrity, virtue; if government is loyalty and protection, then let government make use of foreign machinery and the railway from morning to night and nothing untoward will befall the disciples of Confucius."

There is one point that should not be overlooked in discussing the religious conditions in China; that is, the passionate love of the Chinaman for money. We are told that a Chinese will almost forsake his ancestors, if such an act will bring him a bag of money, and he can be persuaded that the spirits will not destroy him for his unfiliality. Therefore, one of the fears, in South China especially, is that if the Chinese are convinced of the absurdities of their superstitions and ancestor worship, that they will put the dollar in place of Confucius' tablet and Buddha's idol and prostrate themselves before the altar of filthy lucre.

In regard to Christian missionary work in China, we have heard much, seen a little and read considerable. Certainly the pathway has been rough and is dotted with the grave mounds of thousands of martyrs. The way is still hard.

Catholic Missions have been operating in China since the Ming Dynasty (1368–1628). They have a large following. There are historical facts that show that in the past they have wielded great influence—great enough to attract Imperial attention and call forth the government's praise or restrictions as the case might be. Catholic cathedrals, orphanages, and schools represent an immense outlay which one priest said was nearly all subscribed by Christians in Europe.

The oldest Protestant Mission was started in 1807. There are now representatives of 91 different sects or societies in the Protestant wing of missionary work. Protestant stations having resident foreign missionaries are established in over 600 cities and towns throughout the empire. In nearly every instance schools are run in connection with the evangelizing work. Hospitals are established to show the practical benevolence of the doctrine and to act as a bait for the "heathen". Many churches with native pastors are said to be entirely self-supporting. The table of statistics submitted at a Protestant Conference, January 1st, 1907, while incomplete, may serve to give an idea in figures of Protestant strength:

Foreign Missionaries	3,719
Native Helpers	9,998
Stations	706
Sub or out Stations	3,794
Communicants	154,142
Schools	2,394
Students in attendance	52,965
Hospitals and Dispensaries	366

Since the Boxer War the work in North China is reported to have grown more rapidly than ever before. Some think the stand of the native Christians who chose death rather than deny the faith, made a great impression on the non-Christians, stirring them up to an investigation of Christianity. Others think that the liberty with which the missionaries have been able to pursue their work since the war is naturally bearing its fruit. The war didn't affect the people of South China much. There missionary work seems to be going on at the same old pace. One thing in the South which makes progress slow is the commercial spirit of the people. They are more worldly, material and mercenary than the people of the North. Yet, in Fukien Province perhaps the greatest response to the Christian call has been observed. The people of this province are nearly all men of the soil, with little ability for or tendency towards commercialism.

The following two or three fragmentary ideas are submitted by way of conclusion on religious conditions:

Dr. C. D. Tenney at present Chinese Secretary of the U. S. Legation at Peking, an ex-missionary who has perhaps been broadened in his views by experience and study in the East, declared that Christianity unrelieved of its dogmatism and unrationalized would never be generally accepted by the Chinese.

Rev. Timothy Richard, a man of decided views, after a long experience in China, is very optimistic in his estimate of the influence of the principles of Christianity is having on the trend of Chinese thought and life, but he doesn't boast much over the condition of the concrete Church in China.

It seems that the upper class and officials have hardly been touched by Christianity. Some lament this condition, while a number of prominent church men say it is a blessing, because the so-called gentry are generally so corrupt and unreliable that their sympathy would do Christianity more harm than good.

Miscellaneous.

The Chinaman has been born and raised in such an unsanitary, foul-smelling, filthy and badly aired houses and cities, that we wonder if he would thrive outside of an atmosphere filled with the germs of plague and disease. It is useless to attempt a description of the terribly dirt-infected cities and houses of China. One can only marvel that pestilence does not annihilate more millions than it does. It was seldom, in fact only once, did we find the foreigner living right in among the Chinese. They have had to get up on some hill, out of the cities, or on a different island, or somewhere where they could find room to breathe and space to walk without inviting contagion. Sure it is that if cleanliness is next to godliness, that the Chinese are not even within telegraphing distance of it. But in personal appearance the Chinese men, and especially the women, are neat and clean. It is a miracle how they can come out of so much surrounding filth with so few soiled spots.

We are told everywhere that there exists a strong anti-foreign feeling. But, by sore experience and loss of money, influence and territory, the officials have learned that murdering the foreigner is no way of getting rid of him, hence their hate for the foreigner has not asserted itself so freely since the great lesson of 1900. The common people, however, are easily excited and when once a riot arises it requires a quick and powerful official to protect life and property. The Chinese are more or less converted to the need of civilization educationally, politically, and materially, but they don't want any more of the foreigner than they can possibly avoid. In a few instances, such as in the railroads, customs service, and army, they have had to use foreigners, but we are told that the present tendency is to discharge and get rid of the foreign employees and advisers. Of course, if China were as able to get along without outside teachers and leaders as Japan is, then the dismissal of foreigners would be a good thing. The future will prove China's wisdom or folly in her present tendency.

To sum up the condition: China is in an uncertain, transitional state. The probability of revolution is not past. The program for the establishment of a constitution and parliament is drawn up. Will the constitution grant religious liberty, and the laws and officials protect every man in his worship? Or will it make a state religion of Confucianism and put a ban on all others? The Chinese are extremely self-proud and their national conceit, at such a critical period, is a huge stumbling block to their progress. China's friends are earnestly and prayerfully awaiting the time when she will be united within, friendly to other nations and peoples, truly appreciative of and consistently working for modern education and a healthful, sanitary life.

It appeals to us that the Latter-day Saints will not be neglecting their duty to the world nor allowing any golden opportunity to slip by if they postpone the opening of a mission in China until the present chaotic, transitory state changes sufficiently to assure the world that China really intends and wants to give her foreign friends protection and a fair chance.

APPENDIX C

David O. McKay, Dedicatory Prayer on the Chinese Realm, January 9, 1921

Hugh J. Cannon, Diary, February 23, 1921, Church History Library. Paragraph numbering added for ease of reference.

[¶1] Our Heavenly Father: In deep humility and gratitude, we thy servants approach thee in prayer and supplication on this most solemn and momentous occasion. We pray thee to draw near unto us, to grant us the peace asked for in the opening prayer by Brother Cannon; and to let the channel of communication between thee and us be open, that thy Word may be spoken, and thy Will be done. We pray for forgiveness of any folly, weakness or lightmindedness that it may not stand between us and the rich outpouring of thy Holy Spirit. Holy Father, grant us thy peace and they inspiration, and may we not be disturbed during this solemn service.

[¶2] For thy kind protection and watchful care over us in our travels by land and by sea, we render our sincere gratitude. We are grateful, too, for the fellowship and brotherly love we have one for the other, that our hearts beat as one, and that we stand before thee this holy Sabbath day with clean hands, pure hearts, and with our minds free from all worldly cares.

[¶3] Though keenly aware of the great responsibility this special mission entails, yet we are thankful that thou hast called us to perform it. Heavenly Father, make us equal, we beseech thee, to every duty and task. As we visit thy Missions in the various parts of the world, give us keen insight into the conditions and needs of each, and bestow upon us in rich abundance the gift of discernment.

[¶4] With grateful hearts, we acknowledge thy guiding influence in our travels to this great land of China, and particularly to this quiet, and secluded spot in the heart of this ancient and crowded city. We pray that the petition setting this spot apart as a place of prayer and dedication may be granted by thee and that it may be held sacred in thy sight.

[¶5] Holy Father, we rejoice in the knowledge of the Truth, and in the restoration of the Gospel of the Redeemer. We praise thy name for having revealed thyself and thine Only Begotten Son to thy servant, Joseph the Prophet, and that through thy revelations the Church, in its purity and perfection, was established in these last days, for the happiness and eternal salvation of the human family. We thank thee for the Priesthood, which gives men authority to officiate in thy holy name.

[¶6] In this land there are millions who know not thee nor thy work, who are bound by the fetters of superstition and false doctrine, and who have never been given the opportunity even of hearing the true message of their Redeemer. Countless millions have died in ignorance of thy plan of life and salvation. We feel deeply impressed with the realization that the time has come when the Light of the Glorious Gospel should begin to shine through the dense darkness that has enshrouded this nation for ages.

[¶7] To this end, therefore, by the authority of the Holy Apostleship, I dedicate and consecrate and set apart the Chinese Realm for the preaching of the Gospel of Jesus Christ as restored in this dispensation through the Prophet Joseph Smith. By this act, shall the key be turned that unlocks the door through which thy chosen servant shall enter with Glad Tidings of Great Joy to this benighted and senile nation. That their message may be given in peace, we beseech thee, O God, to stabilize the Chinese government. Though knowest how it is torn with dissension at the present time, and how faction contends against faction to the oppression of the people and the strangling of the nation's life. Holy Father, may peace and stability be established throughout this Republic, if not by the present government, then through the intervention of the allied powers of the civilized world.

[¶8] Heavenly Father, manifest thy tender mercy toward thy suffering children throughout this famine-stricken realm! Stay the progress of pestilence, and may starvation and untimely death stalk no more through the land. Break the bands of superstition, and may the young men and young women come out of the darkness of the Past into the Glorious Light now shining among the children of men. Grant, our Father, that these young men and young women may, through upright, virtuous lives, and prayerful study, be prepared and inclined to declare this message of salvation in their own tongue to their fellowmen. May their hearts, and the hearts of this people, be turned to their fathers that they may accept the opportunity offered them to bring salvation to the millions who have gone before.

[¶9] May the Elders and Sisters whom thou shalt call to this land as missionaries have keen insight into the mental and spiritual state of the Chinese mind. Give them special power and ability to approach this people in such a manner as will make the proper appeal to them. We beseech thee, O God, to reveal to thy servants the best methods to adopt and the best plans to follow in establishing thy work among this ancient, tradition-steeped people. May the work prove joyous, and a rich harvest of honest souls bring that peace to the workers' hearts which surpasseth all understanding.

[¶10] Remember thy servants, whom thou hast chosen to preside in thy Church. We uphold and sustain before thee, President Heber J. Grant, who stands at the head at this time, and his counselors, President Anthon H. Lund and President Charles W. Penrose. Bless them, we pray thee, with every needful blessing, and keep them one in all things pertaining to thy work. Likewise bless the Council of Twelve. May they continue to be one with the First Presidency. Remember the Presiding Patriarch, the First Council of Seventy, the Presiding Bishopric, and all who preside in Stakes, Wards, Quorums, organizations, Temples, Church Schools, and Missions. May the spirit of purity, peace, and energy characterize all thy organizations.

[¶11] Heavenly Father, be kind to our Loved Ones from whom we are now separated. Let thy Holy Spirit abide in our homes, that sickness, disease and death may not enter therein.

[¶12] Hear us, O kind and Heavenly Father, we implore thee, and open the door for the preaching of thy Gospel from one end of this realm to the other, and may thy servants who declare this message be especially blest and directed by thee. May thy kingdom come, and they will be done speedily here on earth among all peoples, kindreds and tongues preparatory to the winding up scenes of these Latter days!

[¶13] And while we behold thy guiding hand through it all, we shall ascribe unto thee the praise, the glory and the honor, through Jesus Christ our Lord and Redeemer, Amen.

APPENDIX D

Hugh J. Cannon, "The Chinese Realm Dedicated for the Preaching of the Gospel," 1921

Hugh J. Cannon, "The Chinese Realm Dedicated for the Preaching of the Gospel: The Act Accomplished by Elder David O. McKay, in the Authority of the Holy Apostleship," Improvement Era *24, no. 5 (March 1921): 443–46. Reprinted as Hugh J. Cannon, "The Land of China Dedicated,"* Juvenile Instructor *56, no. 3 (March 1921): 115–17; Hugh J. Cannon, "China Dedicated for Preaching of the Gospel,"* Young Woman's Journal *32, no. 4 (April 1921): 221–24; and "Opening of the Chinese Realm for the Preaching of the Gospel,"* Relief Society Magazine *8, no. 4 (April 1921): 194–96.*

Elder David O. McKay, of the Council of the Twelve, and the writer, arrived in Peking, the chief city of China, Saturday evening, January 8, 1921. The horde of ragged and revolting mendicants, grimy porters and insistent jinrikisha men, who fought noisily for possession of us, as we emerged from the station, was not such as to inspire a feeling of affectionate brotherhood. However, we had gone to Peking to do the Lord's will, as nearly as we could ascertain what it was. His inspiration rested upon his servant in charge, and Elder McKay decided that the land should be dedicated and set apart for the preaching of the gospel of the Master.

It seemed most desirable that this should be done on the following day, as that was the only Sabbath we should be in Peking. But where, in the midst of that clamor and confusion, could a suitable spot be found? The city lies on a level, barren plain. There are no forests, and, as far as we knew, no groves nor even clumps of trees. We were wholly unfamiliar with the city and had met no one who could enlighten us. If we went outside the surrounding walls, there was reason to believe no secluded spot could be found nor the ever-present crowd of supplicants avoided.

January 9 dawned clear and cold. With no definite goal in mind, we left the hotel and walked through the legation quarter, under the shadow of dear Old Glory, out into what is known as "The Forbidden City," past the crumbling temples reared to an "Unknown God." Directed, as we believe, by a Higher Power, we came to a grove of cypress trees, partially surrounded by a moat, and walked to its extreme northwest corner, then retraced our steps until reaching a tree with divided trunk which had attracted our attention when we first saw it.

"This is the spot," said Elder McKay.

A reposeful peace hovered over the place which seemed already hallowed; one felt that it was almost a profanation to tread thereon with covered head and feet.

Two men were in sight, but they seemed oblivious to our presence, and they soon left the grove. There, in the heart of a city with a million inhabitants, we were entirely alone, except for the presence of a divinely sweet and comforting Spirit.

An act destined to affect the lives of four hundred and fifty millions of people now living, as well as of millions and perhaps billions yet unborn, calls forth feelings of profound solemnity, and that, too, despite the fact that the vast majority of those affected may die in ignorance of the event.

After a prayer had been offered and the spot dedicated as a place of supplication and for the fulfilment of the object of our visit, Elder David O. McKay, in the authority of the Holy Apostleship, dedicated and set apart the Chinese Realm for the preaching of the gospel of the Lord Jesus Christ, whenever the Church authorities shall deem it advisable to send out missionaries for that purpose. Never was the power of his calling more apparent in his utterances. He blessed the land and its benighted people, and supplicated the Almighty to acknowledge this blessing. He prayed that famine and pestilence might be stayed, that the government might become stable, either through its own initiative, or by the intervention of other powers, and that superstition and error, which for ages have enveloped the people, might be discarded, and Truth take their place. He supplicated the Lord to send to this land broad-minded and intelligent men and women, that upon them might rest the spirit of discernment and the power to comprehend the Chinese nature, so that in the souls of this people an appreciation of the glorious gospel might be awakened.

It was such a prayer and blessing as must be recognized in heaven, and though the effects may not be suddenly apparent, they will be none the less real.

And never, perhaps, has there been a land more greatly in need of heavenly aid. One cannot help but feel that if it were not for the watchful and unselfish attitude of the United States, China's national rights would very quickly be invaded. With the largest population of any country in the world, she is wholly impotent, and in addition to her own helplessness, a curse seems to overshadow her. Millions of her people are starving. It is estimated by the committee in charge of the relief work that five dollars will save a life, but the five dollars must come from abroad.

And yet, if this nation would observe one of the simplest of the Lord's commandments, that of the monthly fast, and give the meals thus saved to those in need, the famine problem would be solved. This would furnish two meals daily to each of the fifteen million sufferers.

The cypress tree is a symbol of sorrow and sadness in China, and this cypress grove seemed a peculiarly fitting place in which to invoke the blessing of heaven upon this oppressed and sorrowing people. The accompanying picture shows the tree, and Brother McKay, where the dedicatory prayer was offered.

At Shan-Hai-Quan, the point at which that wonder of wonders, the great Chinese wall, meets the sea, and on the frontier of the famine district, we took a picture which we are presenting herewith. Though the morning was bitterly cold, we judged it to be zero weather, some of these people were nearly naked. The shreds of patches which only partially covered their emaciated and shivering bodies might well feel complimented at being called rags.

One contemplates China's past accomplishments with a feeling akin to awe. We respect old age, and especially so when, with antiquity, we see achievement; and it is well to remember that this land had a highly developed civilization nearly twenty-five centuries before the Christian era.

Notwithstanding her present pitiably inane condition, we have met some admirable Chinese people, and cherish the sincere hope that at no very distant day the light of the gospel may penetrate to present overwhelming darkness. Though the abject misery we beheld appealed to our tenderest sympathies, gold and silver we could not give, but the door was unlocked for them through which they may enter into eternal life.

APPENDIX E

David O. McKay, "Ah Ching," 1921

David O. McKay, "Ah Ching," Improvement Era *24, no. 11 (September 1921): 992–97.*

"For great and low there's but one test,
'Tis that each one shall do his best.
Who works with all the strength he can
Shall never die in debt to man."

Confucius once said, "All my knowledge is strung on one thread;" and on that "one connecting thread," we learn from his disciple, Tsang Tsu, were hung the principles, Self control and Charity to one's neighbor. These are certainly two fundamental elements in character building, without which no man can justly claim true nobility.

I thought I saw the fruits of these two principles exemplified in the life of Ah Ching as I listened to him one day, when he and his wife, his son Arthur and Telese (Mrs. Arthur Ah Ching), acted as host and hostesses to a number of missionaries. That Saturday afternoon and evening, June 4, are numbered among the most pleasant of the many delightful days and nights spent in "dear old" Samoa. Every hour seemed rich in fruition of profitable intercourse and valued friendships, or inspirational experiences, not the least interesting of which was Ah Ching's narration of his early life in these islands. I wish my pen could reproduce his accent, and his nervous, animated facial expression as he spoke, in his "pidg'n" English mixed with Samoan words, of the trials and reverses and service of those struggling years. But that were wishing the impossible: so I must be content to write in that old prosaic style which, I fear is "dry, stale and unprofitable."

Ah Ching is small of stature, about five feet, five, I should say, and rather lightly built at that. His muscular movement like his thoughts, indicate a highly nervous temperament. I fancy his temper in his early youth was of the gunpowder type; when touched off, it would go with a flash; and, yet, today, I believe he can endure imposition and ignominy if necessary, as patiently as any of his brethren.

If you were to meet him on the street, or could see him move unobtrusively into a rear or side seat of church, you would think him, if you gave him even a passing thought, one of the most humble of Chinamen—I'm not sure that your opinion would change, either, if you chanced to see him in his modest three-roomed house in the rear of his little store in Apia; and yet, if you were to offer him a cashier's check of $50,000 for his property interests, he would undoubtedly smile at you, shake his head, and turn to his busy, unassuming life with a view of adding a few more pounds sterling to his comfortable fortune.

This prosperous little business man "no can lead," he "no can lite;" but he can "speakee China, and speakee Samoa." He keeps no books, and has never kept an account in his business transactions; but he has never purchased an article in his life without paying spot cash for it. He has never "owed a man a penny." He quickly remarked, "If any man no payee me, please himself, me no care."

Now, undoubtedly, in this old work-a-day, business world, which, in many of its aspects seems a long way from that anticipated time when every man will esteem his neighbor as himself, and there shall be no rogues to defraud and to steal, an X-ray examination into Ah Ching's business might reveal the fact that not a few men have "pleased themselves" not to "payee" all they owe him. At any rate there was one who deliberately planned to defraud him, and whose dastardly treachery was the means of testing Ah Ching in life's crucible. Had his character not possessed more pure gold than dross, he would perhaps even now be deprived of life, or be still wearing the stripes of a condemned felon.

Ah Ching was a young man in his teens when he left Pu Chow, Fukin province, China, and enlisted as one of the crew of a small vessel sailing for the South Seas. True to his thrifty nature, acquired by heredity, and necessity, he saved nearly every penny of his fair wage. Thus after ten years constant service with the ship's company, he had accumulated a thousand pounds sterling or more. A business friend whom he had met during his not infrequent visits to Apia, induced him to invest his hard earned savings in a hotel and store, he to furnish the money, his friend to furnish the brains and business acumen required, and the two to divide the profits upon a proportionate basis acceptable to both. Ah Ching invested his money, only to discover in a year or two that he had been robbed of every penny of his hard-earned savings. In certain transfers of the property, it seems his friend had appropriated everything to himself. Trusting Ah Ching, couldn't "leadee," couldn't "litee," so he became an unsuspecting victim to the treachery of one to whom he had entrusted practically his life; for "you take one's life, when you take away the means whereby one lives," and up to that time Ah Ching had had but one object and that was to make money; though he had always made it honestly.

When he realized that he had been robbed of all the savings of his young life, when he sensed the villainy of the dishonest scoundrel whom he had called friend, all the fire in his Chinese nature flashed forth and showed him but one more thing for which to live, and that one thing, revenge. He truly wished that his enemy "had forty thousand lives—one was too poor, too weak, to satisfy his revenge."

"He cheatee me all my money: I killee him;" he hissed in his rage, "I sharpee a knife like a lacee," he narrated, indicating the length of the knife by touching with his right hand the elbow of his left arm, which he stretched full length. His knife sharpened, he cried in his agonized rage:

"Me killee him!"

"Something inside-e me say, 'No killee him;' I stop; and it say again 'no killee him.'"

"Then I know God, he helpee me, so I no killee him. I cly, that is all—just cly." (Cry.)

Who can deny that God did "helpee" him in this great crisis of his life? Whether that help sprang from an unsullied conscience, or gave strength in a moment of weakness to a will that once more assumed the mastery of a passion, or whether his spirit responded to the promptings of the Infinite—the fact remains that his frenzy was overpowered, his spirit subdued and he just "clied."

"Yes, thou art ever present, Power Supreme;
Not circumscribed by time, nor fix'd to space,
Confined to altars, nor to temples bound,
In wealth, in want, in freedom, or in chains,
In dungeons or on thrones the faithful find thee."

Unfortunately, too, many fail to heed the gentle "something inside", and follow the lead of blinded passion whether mental or physical—to their inevitable end, unhappiness and unescaped misery.

It was not an easy matter for Ah Ching to cry "down" to his injured and revengeful spirit; but once he became victor, he felt, though he did not then know, that,

"Vengeance is mine, saith the Lord and I will repay."

It was a real joy to all who heard him relate his experience to see his face light up as he said:

"Me gladee from that day to this."

Truly, the fruits of that spirit are love, joy and peace.

"Well, how did the man prosper with his stolen money, Brother Ah Ching?" I asked.

"That house he burnee down," he answered, "man in the stleet—all bowed down—nobody likee him—die poor." This intimation that God had avenged his enemy, recalled the lines:

"I know that each sinful action, as sure as the sun brings shade,
Is somewhere, sometime punished ahead of him, though the hour be long delayed."

With prospects of success ahead of him, Ah Ching had married a Chieftain's daughter. Now they were homeless and penniless, except for the money earned day by day at odd jobs. To add to his difficulty, he had voluntarily proffered support to two of his fellow countrymen, one of whom was sickly and unable to supply the least of his necessities. I do not now recall if I learned at all, what claim the other man had.

"Were they your relatives?" I inquired, knowing the strong ties of family relationship in the Chinese mind.

"No," was his reply, "no lelation—just Chunamen, that's all—needee help, and I give him—I findee wolk sometimee; my woman she takee in washing. Sometimee me have no lice for all (rice), but me givee Chinamen lice alle samee."

Sharing his last kernel of rice with a fellowman in need, and that, too, without any recompense or desire for reward—is not that true service? No doubt the gratitude whispered by the sick and dying man fully repaid Ah Ching for his years of gratuitous food and shelter; but there will be further recompense when one who takes note of all such kindnesses will some day say,

"These deeds shall thy memorial be—
Fear not thou didst them unto me."

It is no wonder that the sound of the gospel struck a responsive chord in this humble man's heart. Conscientiousness, self-mastery, service among its principal themes.

His church record like his life is marked not in words but in deeds. You may know his annual income by his tithes and offerings which are freely and thankfully given as expressions of his gratitude for the manifest goodness of God to him.

His rise from poverty to opulence began about the time that he joined the Church, the turning point being marked in his mind as undoubtedly it was in reality, by a singular dream that came to him.

"I dleamed one night," he narrated, "that the Lord, he say to me, 'Plenty money in the stleet, why you no pick him up?' Next morning I get up, lookee the stleet—no money. I could see no money in the stleet. Then I thought; I sellee things in the stleet, and makee money."

With the little savings he and his wife had horded, he purchased by paying cash in full, One case of salmon, one sack of sugar, one gross of matches, 5 plugs of Samoan tobacco, one hundred pounds of Samoan Kava, and 900 pounds of flour. When this was sold he purchased more. Thus began his little business, which today includes three separate stores, and a bakery, all free from encumbrances, and carrying on a thriving trade.

His faithful wife, who shared his struggles in poverty, lived to share only a part of his prosperity. A year or so after her death he married her sister, who evidently is an excellent help-meet and companion to him and in whom we thought we could detect the same admirable qualities of womanhood as those elements of manhood which have contributed to the commendable life of her husband. Through her lineage he now holds the title of chief among her people.

Of his sons and daughters, we learned but little. His son Arthur, who is now a partner in the business, was educated in China where his father supported him seven years. He and his wife Telese are also members of the Church, and seem to hold the confidence and esteem of the mission authorities and elders who know him. They are certainly as bounteous in their desires to please and to serve others as their father Ah Ching; for after eighteen or more feasted that afternoon with all the delicacies Samoa produces, all the Sauniatu band boys, were feted to their appetites' content.

As we sat in his flower-bedecked home in Tulaele, with evidences of thrift and opulence on every hand, as we thought of the number of men and women whom it is in his power now to bless; as we heard him express his gratitude for what the gospel has brought him and for what it means to him, there passed quickly in my mind, in striking contrast to this scene of success and sweet contentment, a picture of a possible felon's cell with all its associated misery and ignominy.

Conscientiousness, service, thrift, honesty, and obedience to other principles of the gospel, have given Ah Ching this comfort; and self mastery in a moment when he stood blindly at the parting of life's ways, kept him from the felon's cell.

With the results of his industry around him, and the fruit of the Spirit in his soul, it was indeed gratifying to hear him acknowledge God's guidance and inspiration in this simple sentence:

"Me knowee God, he helpee me."

Suva, Fiji

APPENDIX F

Chronology of The Church of Jesus Christ of Latter-day Saints in East Asia, 1852–2025

East Asia encompasses China, Hong Kong, Japan, Macau, Mongolia, North Korea, South Korea, and Taiwan. The major events featured in the chronology below are adapted from R. Lanier Britsch, *From the East: The History of the Latter-day Saints in Asia, 1851–1996*; Reid L. Neilson, *Early Mormon Missionary Activities in Japan, 1901–1924*; Po Nien Chou and Petra Chou, *Voice of the Saints in Mongolia*; Po Nien Chou and Petra Chou, *Voice of the Saints in Taiwan: A History of the Latter-day Saints in Taiwan*; and "Global Histories," The Church of Jesus Christ of Latter-day Saints.

Year	Milestone Church Events in East Asia
1852	August 28. President Brigham Young announces assignment of several missionaries to China at a special missionary conference held in Salt Lake City, Utah.
1853	April 28. Hosea Stout, James Lewis, and Chapman Duncan arrive in Hong Kong as missionaries but are unsuccessful and return home after a few weeks.
1854	First overseas Chinese are baptized church members in Hilo, Hawaii.
1901	February 14. First Presidency announces opening of the Japan Mission with Elder Heber J. Grant as its first president.
1901	August 12. The first group of Latter-day Saint missionaries arrives in Yokohama, Japan.
1901	September 1. Grant dedicates Japan for the preaching of the gospel in Yokohama.
1902	March 8. Hajime Nakazawa becomes the first convert to the church in Japan.
1907	April 7. Church membership endorses Relief Society resolution to send twenty tons of flour to famine-stricken China.
1909	October 6. The first copies of the Book of Mormon in Japanese are printed and bound in Tokyo.
1910	January–March. Missionaries Alma O. Taylor and Frederick A. Caine tour Korea and China for the First Presidency to see what evangelism opportunities might exist for the church.
1917	May 30. The first Relief Society in Japan is organized in Tokyo.

1921	January 9. Elder David O. McKay of the Quorum of the Twelve Apostles dedicates the "Chinese Realm" for the preaching of the gospel in Peking (Beijing).
1924	June 9. Due to rising tension between the United States and Japan, Heber J. Grant, president of the church, discontinues the Japanese Mission in Tokyo.
1927	September 20. Kim Chai Han is baptized abroad in Hawaii, becoming the first known Korean to be baptized.
1934	July–December. Takeo Fujiwara, who was set apart earlier that year as "presiding elder and special missionary" to Japan, organizes branches in Tokyo, Osaka, Kofu, and Sapporo.
1937–45	The Japanese Mission oversees the affairs of the church in Japan from its headquarters in Honolulu, Hawaii.
1947	October 22. Edward L. Clissold is called to reopen the Japanese Mission.
1949	July 10. A Chinese Mission is established with Hilton A. Robertson as president in Kowloon, Hong Kong.
1949	July 14. Elder Matthew Cowley of the Quorum of the Twelve Apostles rededicates Hong Kong for the preaching of the gospel.
1949	July 17. While visiting Japan, Cowley prophesies that the church will build many buildings, including temples, in Japan.
1950	February 25. Missionaries H. Grant Heaton and William Pa'alani arrive in Hong Kong.
1950–53	During the Korean War, additional groups of Latter-day Saints serving in the United States military worship and share the gospel in South Korea and North Korea.
1951–53	Chinese Mission headquarters in Hong Kong is moved to Hawaii and then to San Francisco, where work is conducted among the Chinese-American population.
1955	August. Elder Joseph Fielding Smith divides the Far East Mission into the Northern Far East Mission (encompassing Japan, South Korea, and Okinawa) and the Southern Far East Mission (comprising Guam, Hong Kong, the Philippines, and Taiwan).
1955	August 2. Smith dedicates South Korea for the preaching of the gospel. He also creates the country's first district, which includes Korean-speaking branches in Seoul and Busan.
1955	August 14. Smith dedicates Okinawa for the preaching of the gospel.

1955	The Doctrine and Covenants and the Pearl of Great Price are published in Japanese in Tokyo for the first time.
1955	August. H. Grant Heaton and Luana Carter Heaton are called to preside over the newly organized Southern Far East Mission in Hong Kong, serving Hong Kong, Taiwan, India, the Philippines, Macau, Singapore, and Guam.
1956	June 3. The first four missionaries to Taiwan, Duane W. Degn, Keith A. Madsen, Weldon J. Kitchen, and Melvin C. Fish, arrive in Taipei after nine months of studying Mandarin Chinese in Hong Kong.
1956	September 26. The first literature printed in Chinese, a tract containing the Joseph Smith story from the Pearl of Great Price, is received by missionaries in Taipei, Taiwan.
1956	A Chinese hymnal is compiled and 500 copies are printed in Taipei, Taiwan.
1957	April 11. With the help of district president Kim Ho Jik, the church secures legal recognition from the government of the Republic of Korea in Seoul.
1959	March–June. Missionaries and local members work together to build a small meetinghouse at Tiu Keng Leng, Hong Kong, the first church-built meetinghouse in Asia since the 1850s.
1959	June 1. Elder Mark E. Peterson of the Quorum of the Twelve Apostles dedicates Taiwan for the preaching of the gospel.
1962	March–August. The church's registration as an ecclesiastical body in Taiwan is approved, followed by registration as a corporation (a requirement in order to buy land) in August 1962.
1962	July. The Korean Mission is organized in South Korea.
1962	A translation of 3 Nephi from the Book of Mormon is published in Korean. A complete Korean translation of the Book of Mormon is published in 1967 in South Korea.
1963	The first Latter-day Saint hymnbook in Korean is published in South Korea.
1964	April 26. The Tokyo North Branch meetinghouse is dedicated, the first Latter-day Saint meetinghouse constructed in Asia.
1964	July 2. Missionaries from the Hong Kong Mission begin work in Macau.
1964	August. Steven Lau is the first person in Macau to be baptized, and missionaries begin holding regular church meetings.

1965	July. Japanese church members make the first of many temple excursions to the Laie Hawaii Temple to participate in temple ordinances.
1965	December. The Book of Mormon is printed in Chinese in Hong Kong.
1966	September 10. The Seoul East Chapel, the first church-built meetinghouse in South Korea, is dedicated.
1966	October 16. The first church-owned meetinghouse in Taiwan is dedicated in Taipei.
1970	March 15. The first stake of the church in Asia, the Tokyo Stake in Japan, is organized with Kenji Tanaka as president.
1973	March 8. The Seoul Korea Stake, the first stake in mainland Asia, is organized, with Rhee Ho Nam as president.
1974	The Doctrine and Covenants is published in Chinese by both the Hong Kong and Taiwan mission offices.
1975	August 9. Spencer W. Kimball, president of the church, announces that a temple will be built in Tokyo, Japan.
1976	April. The Pearl of Great Price is published in Chinese in Hong Kong and Taiwan.
1976	April 22. The Taipei Taiwan Stake is created with Chang I-ch'ing serving as first stake president.
1976	April 25. The Hong Kong Stake is created with Poon Shiu-Tat as president.
1977	January 1. The Macau Branch is organized.
1980	October 27–29. Kimball dedicates the Tokyo Japan Temple, the first temple in Asia.
1984	November 17–18. The Taipei Taiwan Temple is dedicated by President Gordon B. Hinckley of the First Presidency.
1985	December 14–15. The Seoul Korea Temple is dedicated by Hinckley.
1992	September 17. The first missionary couple, Kenneth H. and Donna Beesley, arrive in Ulaanbaatar, Mongolia.
1993	February 6. Purevsuren Lamjav and Bat-Ulzii Tsendkhuu are the first converts baptized in Mongolia.
1993	April 15. Elder Neal A. Maxwell of the Quorum of the Twelve Apostles dedicates Mongolia for the preaching of the gospel.
1995	July 1. The first mission in Mongolia is established with Richard E. Cook as the first president of the Mongolia Ulaanbaatar Mission, accompanied by his wife, Mary N. Cook.

1996	May 26. The Hong Kong Temple is dedicated by Hinckley, now the church president.
2000	June 11. The Fukuoka Japan Temple is dedicated by Hinckley.
2001	October. The translation of the Mongolian Book of Mormon is completed.
2001	The Book of Mormon is published in simplified Chinese characters.
2005	New Korean translations of the Book of Mormon, Doctrine and Covenants, and Pearl of Great Price are released in Seoul, South Korea.
2007	December 16. The new Mongolian triple combination (the Book of Mormon, Doctrine and Covenants, and Pearl of Great Price) is distributed throughout the Mongolia Ulaanbaatar Mission.
2007–08	A revised translation of the Book of Mormon, Doctrine and Covenants, and Pearl of Great Price is published in traditional and simplified Chinese characters in Hong Kong.
2009	June 7. President Donald H. Hallstrom of the presidency of the Seventy organizes the Ulaanbaatar Mongolia West Stake with Odgerel Ochirjav as the first stake president in Mongolia.
2015	May 17. The Macau China District is formed, with Hong Wai Tak as president.
2016	August 21. President Russell M. Nelson of the Quorum of the Twelve Apostles dedicates the Sapporo Japan Temple.
2019	April 7. Nelson, now the church president, announces future construction of the Okinawa Japan Temple.
2020	April 5. Nelson announces future construction of the Shanghai People's Republic of China Temple.
2021	October 3. Nelson announces future construction of the Kaohsiung Taiwan Temple.
2022	October 2. Nelson announces future construction of the Busan Korea Temple.
2023	October 1. Nelson announces future construction of the Osaka Japan Temple.
2023	October 1. Nelson announces future construction of the Ulaanbaatar Mongolia Temple.
2023	November 12. Elder Gary E. Stevenson of the Quorum of the Twelve Apostles dedicates the Okinawa Japan Temple.

Bibliography

Abbreviations

Church History Library, The Church of Jesus Christ of Latter-day Saints, Salt Lake City, Utah (hereafter cited as Church History Library).

Family History Library, The Church of Jesus Christ of Latter-day Saints, Salt Lake City, Utah (hereafter cited as Family History Library).

L. Tom Perry Special Collections, Harold B. Lee Library, Brigham Young University, Provo, Utah (hereafter cited as Perry Special Collections).

Special Collections, J. Willard Marriott Library, University of Utah, Salt Lake City, Utah (hereafter cited as Marriott Special Collections).

Archival Sources

Bullock, Thomas. Minutes (LaJean Carruth shorthand version). Historian's Office General Church Minutes. Church History Library.

Cannon, Abraham H. Journal. Perry Special Collections.

Cannon, George Q. Journal. Church History Library.

Cannon, Hugh J. "Around-the-World Travels of David O. McKay and Hugh J. Cannon." Church History Library.

———. Diary. Church History Library.

———. Papers. Church History Library.

Cannon, Sylvester Q. Diary. Church History Library.

Clawson, Rudger. Diary. Church History Library.

Cowley, Elva T. "My Life, a Love Story." Autobiography. Matthew Cowley Collection. Perry Special Collections.

Duncan, Chapman. Biography. Perry Special Collections.

Grant, Heber J. Journal. Church History Library.

Japan Mission Letterpress Copybooks. Church History Library.

Jarvis, G. Stanford. "The Far East: Footprints and Fulfillments." Unpublished manuscript in author's possession.

Journal History of The Church of Jesus Christ of Latter-day Saints. Church History Library.

Lund, Anthon H. Diary. Church History Library.

Lunt, Henry. "Life of Henry Lunt and Family, Together with a Portion of His Journal." Typescript, Special Collections, Southern Utah State University.

McKay, David O. Diary. Marriott Special Collections.

———. Scrapbooks. Church History Library.

———. "Summary and Report: Tour of Inspection of Missions and Schools." In David O. McKay scrapbooks, 1928–1970, MS 4640, box 127, pp. 292–[300]. Church History Library.

Ottesen, Carol Clark. "Waking the Sleeping Giant: A History of the China Teachers Program, Brigham Young University David M. Kennedy Center for International Studies." Unpublished manuscript, n.d.

Taylor, Alma O. Journals and Papers. Perry Special Collections.

———. "Report of Our Visit to China." Church History Library.

Thatcher, Moses. Journal. Perry Special Collections.

Woodruff, Wilford. Journal. Church History Library.

Young, Brigham. Office Files. Church History Library.

Newspapers and Newsletters

Conference Reports. Salt Lake City, Utah.

Contributor. Salt Lake City, Utah.

Deseret Evening News. Salt Lake City, Utah.

Desert News. Salt Lake City, Utah.

Deseret Weekly News. Salt Lake City, Utah.

Elder's Journal. Atlanta, Georgia. and Chattanooga, Tennessee.

Ensign. Salt Lake City, Utah.

Evening and Morning Star. Kirtland, Ohio.

Improvement Era. Salt Lake City, Utah.

Journal of Discourses. Liverpool, England.

Juvenile Instructor. Salt Lake City, Utah.

Latter-day Saints' Millennial Star. Liverpool, England.

Messenger and Advocate. Kirtland, Ohio.

Millennial Star. Manchester, England.

New Era. Salt Lake City, Utah.

Ogden Standard. Ogden, Utah.

Ogden Standard-Examiner. Ogden, Utah.

Relief Society Magazine. Salt Lake City, Utah.

Salt Lake Telegram. Salt Lake City, Utah.

Salt Lake Tribune. Salt Lake City, Utah.

Times and Seasons. Nauvoo, Illinois.

Websites and Internet Databases

"China: Two apostles visit, assured that religious freedom exists and people are free to worship as they choose." *Church News*. January 28, 1989. https://www.thechurchnews.com/1989/1/28/23263292/china-two-apostles-visit-assured-that-religious-freedom-exists-and-people-are-free-to-worship-as-the/.

Church History Department. Church History Biographical Database. https://history.churchofjesuschrist.org/chd/landing.

Church History Topics. "Dedication of the Holy Land." The Church of Jesus Christ of Latter-day Saints. https://churchofjesuschrist.org/study/history/topics/dedication-of-the-holy-land.

———. "Temple Dedications and Dedicatory Prayers." The Church of Jesus Christ of Latter-day Saints. www.churchofjesuschrist.org/study/history/topics/temple-dedications-and-dedicatory-prayers.

Church Newsroom. "Facts and Statistics: Asia." The Church of Jesus Christ of Latter-day Saints. https://newsroom.churchofjesuschrist.org/facts-and-statistics.

———. "New Church Website Will Help Chinese Nationals, Church Leaders Around the World." The Church of Jesus Christ of Latter-day Saints. March 15, 2013. https://newsroom.churchofjesuschrist.org/article/china-website-mormons.

———. "Style Guide—The Name of the Church." The Church of Jesus Christ of Latter-day Saints. https://newsroom.churchofjesuschrist.org/style-guide.

"The Church of Jesus Christ of Latter-day Saints in China." The Church of Jesus Christ of Latter-day Saints. https://www.churchofjesuschrist.org/China.

"Eight New Temples Announced—Analysis." Growth of The Church of Jesus Christ of Latter-day Saints (blog). April 5, 2020. https://ldschurchgrowth.blogspot.com/2020/04/eight-new-temples-announced-analysis.html.

Family History Department. FamilySearch. https://familysearch.org.

"Global Histories." The Church of Jesus Christ of Latter-day Saints. https://www.churchofjesuschrist.org/study/history/global-histories.

The Joseph Smith Papers. https://www.josephsmithpapers.org/.

Richman, Larry. "Church Membership and Languages Worldwide." LDS 365. January 14, 2022. https://lds365.com/2022/01/14/church-membership-and-languages-worldwide/.

"Statistics: Temple Dimensions." Temples of The Church of Jesus Christ of Latter-day Saints. https://churchofjesuschristtemples.org/statistics/dimensions/.

"Temples." The Church of Jesus Christ of Latter-day Saints. https://www.churchofjesuschrist.org/temples.

Periodicals

Aki, Henry. Address. *One Hundred Twenty-Second Semi-annual Conference of The Church of Jesus Christ of Latter-day Saints* (The Church of Jesus Christ of Latter-day Saints, 1951): 46–47.

"American and Japanese Flags." *Deseret Evening News* (June 19, 1901).

"Apostle M'Kay Tells of Trip." *Salt Lake Telegram* (December 26, 1921).

"Are They of Israel?" *Millennial Star* 49, no. 3 (January 17, 1887): 33–36.

"Are They of Israel?" *Millennial Star* 58, no. 31 (August 2, 1906): 479–80.

Ballard, Melvin J. "Dedicating the Lands of South America to the Preaching of the Gospel." *Improvement Era* 29, no. 6 (April 1926): 575–77.

Cannon, Abraham H. "A Future Mission Field." *Contributor* 16, no. 12 (October 1895): 764–65.

Cannon, George Q. "Editorial Thoughts." *Juvenile Instructor* 7, no. 4 (February 17, 1872): 28.

———. Address. *Seventy-First Semi-annual Conference of The Church of Jesus Christ of Latter-day Saints* (The Church of Jesus Christ of Latter-day Saints, 1900): 63–64, 66–68.

Cannon, Hugh J. "The Chinese Realm Dedicated for the Preaching of the Gospel: The Act Accomplished by Elder David O. McKay, in the Authority of the Holy Apostleship." *Improvement Era* 24, no. 5 (March 1921): 443–46.

———. "China Dedicated for Preaching of the Gospel." *Young Woman's Journal* 32, no. 4 (April 1921): 221–24.

———. "The Land of China Dedicated." *Juvenile Instructor* 56, no. 3 (March 1921): 115–17.

"Church Sends Flour to China." *Deseret Evening News* (April 8, 1907).

Cowley, Matthew. Address. *One Hundred Twentieth Semi-annual Conference of The Church of Jesus Christ of Latter-day Saints* (The Church of Jesus Christ of Latter-day Saints, 1949): 45–46.

———. "The Language of Sincerity." *Improvement Era* 52, no. 11 (November 1949): 715.

Cowley, Matthias F. Address. *Seventy-First Annual Conference of The Church of Jesus Christ of Latter-day Saints* (The Church of Jesus Christ of Latter-day Saints, 1901): 16.

———. Address. *Seventy-Second Semi-annual Conference of The Church of Jesus Christ of Latter-day Saints* (The Church of Jesus Christ of Latter-day Saints, 1901): 18.

"Elder Spencer W. Kimball Dedicates Land of Central America as a Mission." *Church News* (December 13, 1952): 5–6, 13.

Eyre, Aubrey. "President Nelson's 36 Years of Influencing World Leaders and Sharing the Gospel throughout the Globe." *Church News* (September 11, 2019).

"A Farewell Reception." *Improvement Era* 4 (August 1901): 796.

"First Temple in Chinese Realm." *Church News* (November 25, 1984): 3, 14.

Gardner, Marvin K. "President Kimball Shares Missionary Vision with Leaders." *Ensign* (May 1979): 105–6.

"General Conference of the Relief Society." *Woman's Exponent* 35, no. 9 (May 1907): 70–71.

"'Glorious light now shining.'" *Church News* (November 25, 1984): 4.

"The Gospel in the United States, &c." *Millennial Star* 15, no. 14 (April 2, 1853): 216–17.

"Ground is Broken for Hong Kong Temple to serve 18,400 members in mission, four stakes." *Church News* (February 5, 1994).

Hartley, William G. "Adventures of a Young British Seaman, 1852–1862." *New Era* 10 (March 1980): 38–47.

Hinckley, Gordon B. "Hong Kong Temple: 'May Thy Watch Care Be Over It.'" *Church News* (June 1, 1996): 4.

———. "The Sustaining of Church Officers." *Ensign* (November 1992): 21.

"The Japanese Mission Benefit." *Deseret Evening News*, May 30, 1901.

Kimball, Spencer W. "Remember the Mission of the Church." *Ensign* (May 1982): 4.

———. "'The Uttermost Parts of the Earth.'" *Ensign* (July 1979): 7.

———. "When the World Will Be Converted." *Ensign* (October 1974): 12.

Lee, Harold B. "Report on the Orient." *Improvement Era* 57, no. 12 (December 1954): 926–30.

"Letter from Apostle Grant." *Millennial Star* 63, no. 40 (October 3, 1901): 654.

McKay, David O. "Ah Ching." *Improvement Era* 24, no. 11 (September 1921): 992–97.

———. Address. *Ninety-Second Annual Conference of The Church of Jesus Christ of Latter-day Saints* (The Church of Jesus Christ of Latter-day Saints, 1922): 65.

"Missionaries Describe Travels: Observations Made in Far East by Officials of Mormon Church." *Salt Lake Telegram* (March 7, 1921).

"M'Kay Talks at S. L. Tabernacle." *Ogden Standard-Examiner* (January 9, 1922).

Mostert, Mary, and Gerry Avant. "Prayers of Dedication Offered on 4 Nations in Central, Southern Africa." *Church News* (September 26, 1992).

"Mormon Travelers Reach New York." *Salt Lake Telegram* (December 21, 1921).

Nelson, Russell M. "Go Forward in Faith." *Ensign* (May 2020): 115.

———. "Let God Prevail." *Ensign* (November 2020): 92–95.

———. "Make Time for the Lord." *Liahona* (November 2021): 120–21.

"Opening of the Chinese Realm for the Preaching of the Gospel." *Relief Society Magazine* 8, no. 4 (April 1921): 194–96.

"Opening of a Mission in Japan." *Deseret Evening News* (April 6, 1901).

Orden, Dell Van. "Door to China May Be Opening." *Church News* (April 7, 1979): 3, 9.

Otterstrom, Frank W. "Report of Funeral Services for President Anthon H. Lund." *Deseret News* (March 12, 1921).

Perkins, Anthony D. "Go Forth in Faith." *Ensign* (April 2015): 16–20.

"Plan Visit to Island Missions." *Deseret News* (October 23, 1920).

Pratt, Parley P., and Franklin D. Richards. "An Epistle of the Twelve to President Orson Pratt, and the Church of Jesus Christ of Latter-day Saints in the British Isles." *Millennial Star* 11, no. 16 (August 15, 1849): 246–47.

"President Hinckley Visits Asian Saints, Dedicates Hong Kong Temple." *Ensign* (August 1996): 74–77.

Roberts, Brigham H. Address. *Seventy-Seventh Annual Conference of The Church of Jesus Christ of Latter-day Saints* (The Church of Jesus Christ of Latter-day Saints, 1907): 59.

Smith, Joseph F. "The Last Days of President Snow." *Juvenile Instructor* 36 (November 15, 1901): 689–90.

Smoot, Reed. Address. *Seventy-First Annual Conference of The Church of Jesus*

Christ of Latter-day Saints (The Church of Jesus Christ of Latter-day Saints, 1901): 6.

"Students Hear David O. McKay: Ogden Church Educator Returns from Visit Before Resuming World Tour." *Ogden Standard-Examiner* (March 11, 1921).

"Two Church Workers Will Tour Missions of Pacific Islands." *Deseret News* (October 15, 1920).

Vidi. "A Progressive People." *Juvenile Instructor* 28 (October 1, 1893): 595–97.

Wells, Emmeline B. "Earthquake and Fire." *Woman's Exponent* 34, no. 10 (May 1906): 68.

Young, Seymour B. Address. *Seventy-Second Semi-annual Conference of The Church of Jesus Christ of Latter-day Saints* (The Church of Jesus Christ of Latter-day Saints, 1901): 40.

Books, Chapters, and Articles

Alexander, Thomas G. *Mormonism in Transition: A History of the Latter-day Saints, 1890–1930.* University of Illinois Press, 1986.

Allen, James B., Ronald K. Esplin, and David J. Whittaker. *Men with a Mission: The Quorum of the Twelve Apostles in the British Isles, 1837–1841.* Deseret Book, 1992.

Allen, James B., and Glen M. Leonard. *The Story of the Latter-day Saints.* Deseret Book, 1976.

Allen, James B., Ronald W. Walker, and David J. Whittaker. *Studies in Mormon History, 1830–1997: An Indexed Bibliography.* University of Illinois Press, 2000.

Arkush, R. David, and Leo O. Lee, eds. and trans. *Land Without Ghosts: Chinese Impressions of America From the Mid-Nineteenth Century to the Present.* University of California Press, 1989.

Arrington, Leonard J. *Great Basin Kingdom: An Economic History of the Latter-day Saints, 1830–1900.* 1958. University of Utah Press and Tanner Trust Fund, 1993.

———. *The Price of Prejudice: The Japanese-American Relocation Center in Utah during World War II.* The Faculty Organization, Utah State University, 1962.

———. "Utah's Ambiguous Reception: The Relocated Japanese Americans." In *Japanese Americans: From Relocation to Redress*, edited by Roger Daniels, Sandra C. Taylor, and Harry H. L. Kitano. University of Utah Press, 1986, 92–97.

Bagley, Will, ed. *"Cities of the Wicked": Alexander Badlam Reports on Mormon Prospects in California and China in the 1850s.* Arthur H. Clark Company, 1999.

Barmé, Geremie. *The Forbidden City.* Harvard University Press, 2008.

Bays, Daniel H. *A New History of Christianity in China.* Wiley-Blackwell, 2012.

Beecher, Maureen Ursenbach, and Paul Thomas Smith. "Snow, Lorenzo."

In *Encyclopedia of Mormonism*, edited by Daniel H. Ludlow. 4 vols. Macmillan, 1992.

Bell, Catherine. *Ritual Theory, Ritual Practice*. Oxford University Press, 1992.

Bell, James P. *In the Strength of the Lord: The Life and Teachings of James E. Faust*. Deseret Book, 1999.

Belnap, Daniel L. "Latter-day Saints and the Perception of Ritual." In *By Our Rites of Worship: Latter-day Saint Views on Ritual in Scripture, History, and Practice*, edited by Daniel L. Belnap. BYU Religious Studies Center, 2013.

Bredon, Juliet. *Peking: A Historical and Intimate Description of its Chief Places of Interest*. Kelly and Walsh, 1922.

Britsch, R. Lanier. "Church Beginnings in China." *BYU Studies* 10, no. 2 (Winter 1970): 161–72.

———. "The East India Mission of 1851–56: Crossing the Boundaries of Culture, Religion, and Law." *Journal of Mormon History* 27 (Fall 2001): 150–76.

———. *From the East: The History of the Latter-day Saints in Asia, 1851–1996*. Deseret Book, 1998.

——— *Moramona: The Mormons in Hawaii*. Institute for Polynesian Studies, 1989.

———. *Nothing More Heroic: The Compelling Story of the First Latter-day Saint Missionaries in India*. Deseret Book, 1999.

———. *Unto the Islands of the Sea: A History of the Latter-day Saints in the Pacific*. Deseret Book, 1986.

Brown, Samuel. "A Sacred Code: Mormon Temple Dedication Prayers, 1836–2000." *Journal of Mormon History* 32, no. 2 (Summer 2006): 173–96.

Butler, Wendy. "Eyes Only for the Orient: Early Twentieth-Century Mormon Neglect of Salt Lake City Japanese." Paper presented at "A Centennial Celebration: The History of The Church of Jesus Christ of Latter-day Saints in Japan 1901–2001." Brigham Young University, Provo, Utah, October 2001.

———. "The Iwakura Mission and its Stay in Salt Lake City." *Utah Historical Quarterly* 66 (Winter 1998): 26–47.

———. "Strategies, Conditions, and Meaning of Early Japanese Labor in Salt Lake City, Utah, 1890–1920." Master's thesis, Brigham Young University, 2002.

Callister, Tad. "Dedications." In *Encyclopedia of Mormonism*, edited by Daniel H. Ludlow. 4 vols. Macmillan, 1992.

Cannon, Donald Q. "Joseph Smith in Salem (D&C 111)." In *Studies in Scripture, Vol. 1: The Doctrine and Covenants*, edited by Kent P. Jackson and Robert L. Millet. Deseret Book, 1989.

Cannon, Hugh J. *To the Peripheries of Mormondom: The Apostolic Around-the-World Journey of David O. McKay, 1920–1921*, edited by Reid L. Neilson. University of Utah Press, 2011.

Carter, Kate B., comp. *Our Pioneer Heritage*. 20 vols. Daughters of Utah Pioneers, 1958–77.

Chang Chih-Tung, *China's Only Hope*, trans. Samuel I. Woodbridge. F. H. Revell, 1900.

Chester, S. H. *Lights and Shadows of Mission Work in the Far East: Being the Record of Observations Made during a Visit to the Southern Presbyterian Missions in Japan, China, and Korea in the Year 1897.* Presbyterian Committee of Publication, 1899.

Chinn, Thomas W., ed., *History of the Chinese in California: A Syllabus.* Chinese Historical Society, 1969.

Choi, Dong Sull. "A History of the Church of Jesus Christ of Latter-day Saints in Korea, 1950–1985." PhD dissertation, Brigham Young University, 1990.

Chou, Po Nien, and Benjamin K. Tsai. *Montgomery Chinese Branch: Voice of the Chinese Saints in Washington DC, 1992–2022.* Po Nien (Felipe) Chou and Benjamin K. Tsai in cooperation with the Montgomery Chinese Branch, [2022].

Chou, Po Nien, and Petra Chou. *Voice of the Saints in Taiwan: A History of the Latter-day Saints in Taiwan.* BYU Religious Studies Center, 2017.

Clement, Russell T., and Sheng-Luen Tsai. "'East Wind to Hawaii: Contributions and History of Chinese and Japanese Mormons in Hawaii." In *Voyages of Faith: Explorations in Mormon Pacific History,* edited by Grant Underwood. Brigham Young University Press, 2000.

Clement, Russell T. *Mormons in the Pacific: A Bibliography.* Institute for Polynesian Studies, 1981.

Condie, Spencer J. *Russell M. Nelson: Father, Surgeon, Apostle.* Deseret Book, 2003.

Conkling, J. Christopher. "Members without a Church: Japanese Mormons in Japan from 1924 to 1948." *BYU Studies* 15 (Winter 1975): 191–214.

Conley, Don C. "The Pioneer Chinese of Utah." Master's thesis, Brigham Young University, 1976.

Crawley, Peter. *Descriptive Bibliography of the Mormon Church, Volume Two.* Religious Studies Center, 2005.

Cutler, Charleen, ed. *The Life of William Willes: From His Own Personal Journals and Writings.* Family Footprints, 2000.

Daniels, Roger. *Asian America: Chinese and Japanese in the United States Since 1850.* University of Washington Press, 1988.

Daynes, Kathryn M. *More Wives Than One: Transformation of the Mormon Marriage System, 1840–1910.* University of Illinois Press, 2008.

Deseret Morning News 2004 Church Almanac. Deseret News, 2003.

Deseret News 2013 Church Almanac. Deseret Book, 2012.

Dew, Sheri. *Insights from a Prophet's Life: Russell M. Nelson.* Deseret Book, 2019.

Douglas, Norman. "The Sons of Lehi and the Seed of Cain: Racial Myths in Mormon Scripture and their Relevance to the Pacific Islands." *The Journal of Religious History* 8 (June 1974): 90–104.

———. "'Unto the Islands of the Sea': The Erratic Beginnings of Mormon Missions in Polynesia, 1844–1900." In *Vision and Reality in Pacific Religion,* edited by Phyllis Herda, Michael Reilly, and David Hilliard. Macmillan Brown Centre for Pacific Studies, University of Canterbury, 2005.

Drummond, Richard H. *A History of Christianity in Japan*. William B. Eerdmans, 1971.

Eidelberg, Joseph. *The Biblical Hebrew Origin of the Japanese People*. Gefen Publishing House, 2005.

Embry, Jessie L. "Relief Society Grain Storage Program, 1876–1940." Master's thesis, Brigham Young University, 1974.

Fairbank, John K. ed. *The Missionary Enterprise in China and America*. Harvard University Press, 1974.

Faulconer, James E. "The Mormon Temple and Mormon Ritual." In *The Oxford Handbook of Mormonism*, edited by Terryl L. Givens and Philip L. Barlow. Oxford University Press, 2015.

Fields, Larry. "The Eurocentric Worldview: Misunderstanding East Asia." *Asian Studies: Journal of Critical Perspectives on Asia* 19 (April–December 1981): 37–55.

Finamore, Daniel. "Displaying the Sea and Defining America: Early Exhibitions at the Salem East India Marine Society." *Journal for Maritime Research* 4, no. 1 (May 2002): 40–51.

Garr, Arnold K., Donald Q. Cannon, and Richard O. Cowan, eds. *Encyclopedia of Latter-day Saint History*. Deseret Book, 2000.

Gaskill, Alonzo L. *Sacred Symbols: Finding Meaning in Rites, Rituals, and Ordinances*. Bonneville Books, 2011.

Gibson, Arrell Morgan. *Yankees in Paradise: The Pacific Basin Frontier*. University of New Mexico Press, 1993.

Godfrey, Donald G., and Rebecca S. Martineau-McCarty, eds. *An Uncommon Common Pioneer: The Journals of James Henry Martineau, 1828–1918*. Religious Studies Center, 2008.

Goodwin, K. Shane. "The History of the Name of the Savior's Church: A Collaborative and Revelatory Process." *BYU Studies Quarterly* 58, no. 3 (2019): 5–41.

Gordon, Sarah Barringer. *The Mormon Question: Polygamy and Constitutional Conflict in Nineteenth-Century America*. The University of North Carolina Press, 2002.

Gowen, Herbert Henry. *An Outline History of China: Part I: From the Earliest Times to the Manchu Conquest, A.D. 1644*. Sherman, French and Company, 1913.

Grow, Matthew J. "A Providential Means of Agitating Mormonism: Parley P. Pratt and the San Francisco Press in the 1850s." *Journal of Mormon Studies* 29 (Fall 2003): 158–85.

Gunson, Neil. *Messengers of Grace: Evangelical Missionaries in the South Seas, 1797–1860*. Oxford University Press, 1978.

Halverson, Jared M. "Global Gatherings: Temple Dedications and the Spread of Sacred Space." Paper presented at the LDS Church History Symposium on the Worldwide Church. Brigham Young University, Provo, Utah, March 2014.

Hardy, Arthur Sherburne. *Life and Letters of Joseph Hardy Neesima*. Houghton, Mifflin and Company, 1891.

Haycock, D. Arthur. "Temples: LDS Temple Dedications." In E*ncyclopedia of Mormonism*, edited by Daniel H. Ludlow. 4 vols. Macmillan, 1992.

Hayford, Charles W. "Chinese and American Characteristics: Arthur H. Smith and His China Book." In *Christianity in China: Early Protestant Missionary Writings*, edited by Suzanne Wilson Barnett and John King Fairbanks. Harvard University Press, 1985.

Heaton, Grant H., and Luana C. Heaton, comp. *A Documentary History of the Chinese Mission, 1949–53, Southern Far East Mission, 1955–59*. Privately published, 1999.

Hilton III, John and Brady Liu. "'This Is Very Historic': The Young Ambassadors 1979 Tour of China," *BYU Studies Quarterly* 55, no. 3 (2016): 134–64.

Hinckley, Gordon B. *Discourses of President Gordon B. Hinckley, Volume 1: 1995–1999*. Deseret Book, 2005.

Hing, Bill Ong. *Making and Remaking Asian America Through Immigration Policy, 1850–1990*. Stanford University Press, 1993.

Hutchison, William R. *Errand to the World: American Protestant Thought and Foreign Missions*. University of Chicago Press, 1987.

Hyde, Orson. *A Voice from Jerusalem, or a Sketch of the Travels and Ministry of Orson Hyde, Missionary of The Church of Jesus Christ of Latter-day Saints, to Germany, Constantinople, and Jerusalem*. Parley P. Pratt, Star Office, 1842.

Iglehart, Charles W. *A Century of Protestant Christianity in Japan*. Charles E. Tuttle, 1959.

Inouye, Melissa Wei-Tsing, and Joseph Soderborg. "'We Had A Symbiotic Relationship': The Structure and Texture of Chinese-White Relationships in Depression-Era Utah." *Journal of Mormon History* 50, no. 3 (2024): 73–88.

Irving, Gordon. *Numerical Strength and Geographical Distribution of the LDS Missionary Force, 1830–1974*. Historical Department of The Church of Jesus Christ of Latter-day Saints, 1975.

Iwaasa, David B. "The Mormons and their Japanese Neighbors." *Alberta History* 53 (Winter 2005): 7–22.

Jansen, Marius B. *The Making of Modern Japan*. Belknap Press of Harvard University Press, 2000.

Jensen, Marlin K. "Church History: Past, Present, and Future." *Journal of Mormon History* 34, no. 2 (Spring 2008): 20–42.

Jones, Zachary R. "Conversion amid Conflict: Mormon Proselytizing in Russian Finland, 1861–1914." *Journal of Mormon History* 35, no. 3 (2009): 38–39.

Kang, C. H., and Ethel R. Nelson. *The Discovery of Genesis: How the Truths of Genesis were Found Hidden in the Chinese Language*. Concordia Publishing House, 1979.

Maggie Keswick and Alison Hardie, *The Chinese Garden: History, Art, and Architecture*. Harvard University Press, 2003.

Kimball, Edward L., and Andrew E . Kimball. *Spencer W. Kimball: Twelfth President of The Church of Jesus Christ of Latter-day Saints.* Deseret Book, 1977.

Kume, Kunitake, comp. *The Iwakura Embassy, 1871–1873: A True Account of the Ambassador Extraordinary and Plenipotentiary's Journal of Observation Through the United States of America and Europe*, translated by Martin Collcutt. Princeton University Press, 2002.

Lansing, Michael. "Race, Space, and Chinese Life in Late-Nineteenth-Century Salt Lake City." *Utah Historical Quarterly* 72 (Summer 2004): 219–38.

Latourette, Kenneth Scott. *A History of Christian Missions in China.* Macmillan Company, 1932.

———. *A History of the Expansion of Christianity. Vol. 6: The Great Century: North America and Asia, A.D. 1800–A.D. 1914.* Zondervan Publishing House, 1970.

Lawrence, Bruce B. *New Faiths, Old Fears: Muslims and other Asian Immigrants in American Religious Life.* Columbia University Press, 2002.

Li, Peter S., and Eva Xiaoling Li. "The Chinese Overseas Population." In *Routledge Handbook of the Chinese Diaspora*, edited by Tan Chee-Beng. Routledge, 2013.

Liestman, Daniel. "'To Win Redeemed Souls from Heathen Darkness': Protestant Response to the Chinese of the Pacific Northwest in the Late Nineteenth Century." *Western Historical Quarterly* 24 (May 1993): 179–201.

———. "Utah's Chinatowns: The Development and Decline of Extinct Ethnic Enclaves." In *Chinese on the American Frontier*, edited by Arif Kirlik. Rowman and Littlefield Publishers, 2001.

Lindquist, Jason. "'Unlocking the Door of the Gospel': The Concept of 'Keys' in Mormonism and Early American Culture." In *Archive of Restoration Culture: Summer Fellows' Papers, 1997–1999.* Joseph Fielding Smith Institute for Latter-day Saint History.

Livingston, Craig. "Eyes on 'The Whole European World': Mormon Observers of the 1848 Revolutions." *Journal of Mormon History* 32 (Fall 2005): 78–112.

Ludlow, Victor L. *Principles and Practices of the Restored Gospel.* Deseret Book, 1994.

Lundwall, N. B. *Temples of the Most High.* Deseret Book, 1971.

Luschin, Immo. "Ordinances." In E*ncyclopedia of Mormonism*, edited by Daniel H. Ludlow. 4 vols. Macmillan, 1992.

Lyman, Edward Leo. "From the City of Angeles to the City of Saints: The Struggle to Build a Railroad from Los Angeles to Salt Lake City." *California History* 70 (Spring 1991): 76–93.

Macgowan, John. *Christ or Confucius, Which? or, The Story of the Amoy Mission.* London Missionary Society, 1889.

———. *The Imperial History of China: Being a History of the Empire as Compiled by the Chinese Historians*, 2nd ed. American Presbyterian Mission, 1906.

Maffly-Kipp, Laurie F. "Assembling Bodies and Souls: Missionary Practices on the Pacific Frontier." In *Practicing Protestants: Histories of Christian Life in America, 1630–1965*, edited by Laurie F. Maffly-Kipp, Leigh E. Schmidt, and Mark Valeri. Johns Hopkins University Press, 2006.

———. "Eastward Ho! American Religion from the Perspective of the Pacific Rim." In *Retelling U.S. Religious History*, edited by Thomas A. Tweed. University of California Press, 1997.

———. "Looking West: Mormonism and the Pacific World." *Journal of Mormon History* 26 (Spring 2000): 41–63.

———. *Religion and Society in Frontier California*. Yale University Press, 1994.

Maffly-Kipp, Laurie F., and Reid L. Neilson, eds. *Proclamation to the People: Nineteenth-Century Mormonism and the Pacific Basin Frontier*. University of Utah Press, 2008.

Malone, Michael P. *James J. Hill: Empire Builder of the Northwest.* University of Oklahoma Press, 1996.

Martin, Albro. *James J. Hill and the Opening of the Northwest.* Oxford University Press, 1976.

Matsuda, Matt K. "The Pacific." *The American Historical Review* 111, no. 3 (2006): 758–80.

Mauss, Armand L. *All Abraham's Children: Changing Mormon Conceptions of Race and Lineage.* University of Illinois Press, 2003.

———. "In Search of Ephraim: Traditional Mormon Conceptions of Lineage and Race." *Journal of Mormon History* 25 (Spring 1999): 131–73.

McArthur, Aaron, and Reid L. Neilson, eds. *The Annals of the Southern Mission: A Record of the History of the Settlement of Southern Utah.* Greg Kofford Books, 2018.

McClellan, Robert. *The Heathen Chinee: A Study of American Attitudes Toward China, 1890–1905*. Ohio State University Press, 1971.

McKay, David O. *Ancient Apostles.* Deseret Book, 1964.

McLeod, Nicholas. *Epitome of the Ancient History of Japan.* Rising Sun Office, 1875.

———. *Album and Guide Book of Japan, from Satsuporo [sic] in the North to Kagoshima in the South, with historical and statistical notes.* Compiled by N. McLeod. Seishi Bunsha Co., 1879.

———. *Illustrations to the Epitome of the Ancient History of Japan.* 1878.

———. *Korea and the Ten Lost Tribes of Isreal [sic], with Korean, Japanese and Isrealitish [sic] illustrations.* C. Levy and the Seishi Bunsha Co., 1879.

Mehr, Kahlile B. *Mormon Missionaries Enter Eastern Europe.* Brigham Young University Press, 2002.

Mehr, Kahlile B., Mark L. Grover, Reid L. Neilson, Donald Q. Cannon, and Grant Underwood. "Growth and Internationalization: The LDS Church Since 1945." In *Excavating Mormon Pasts: The New Historiography of the Last Half Century*, edited by Newell G. Bringhurst and Lavina Fielding Anderson. Greg Kofford Books, 2004.

Melville, R. Mark. "The Twenty-Fourth of July: An Overview of Utah's State

Holiday, 1849–2022." *Latter-day Saint Historical Studies* 24, no. 1 (Spring 2023): 69–114.

Millet, Robert L. "Sacramental Living: Reflections on Latter-day Saint Ritual." In *By Our Rites of Worship: Latter-day Saint Views on Ritual in Scripture, History, and Practice*, edited by Daniel L. Belnap. BYU Religious Studies Center, 2013.

Moore, R. Laurence. *Religious Outsiders and the Making of Americans.* Oxford University Press, 1986.

Mowbray, Tate E. *Transpacific Steam: The Story of Steam Navigation from the Pacific Coast of North America to the Far East and the Antipodes, 1867–1941.* Cornwall Books, 1986.

Neill, Stephen. *A History of Christian Missions.* Penguin Books, 1987.

Neilson, Reid L. *Early Mormon Missionary Activities in Japan, 1901–1924.* University of Utah Press, 2010.

———. "'A Fine Intellectual and Spiritual Opportunity': Church Historian Leonard J. Arrington's 1975 Tour of the LDS Church's Asian Area General Conferences." *Journal of Mormon History* 43, no. 2 (Spring 2017): 149–71.

———. "Alma O. Taylor's 1910 Fact Finding Mission to China." *Brigham Young University Studies* 40, no. 1 (2001): 176–203.

———. "Early Mormon Missionary Work in Hong Kong: The Letters of James Lewis to Apostle and Church Historian George A. Smith, 1853–1855." *Mormon Historical Studies* 17, nos. 1 and 2 (Spring and Fall 2016): 1–35.

———. "Elder Alma Owen Taylor: LDS Representative to China, 1910." In *Times of Transition: Proceedings of the 2000 Symposium of The Joseph Fielding Smith Institute for Latter-day Saint History at Brigham Young University*, edited by Thomas G. Alexander. The Joseph Fielding Smith Institute for Latter-day Saint History, 2003.

———. "Foreword." In R. Lanier Britsch, *Moramona: The Mormons in Hawaii*, 2d edition. Jonathan Napela Center for Hawaiian and Pacific Islands Studies, Brigham Young University–Hawaii, 2018.

———. *The Japanese Missionary Journals of Elder Alma O. Taylor, 1901–1910.* Brigham Young University Studies Press and The Joseph Fielding Smith Institute for Latter-day Saint History, 2001.

———. "The Japanese Missionary Journals of Elder Alma O. Taylor, 1901–1910." Master's thesis, Brigham Young University, 2001.

———. "Joseph Smith and Nineteenth-century Mormon Mappings of Asian Religions." In *Joseph Smith: Reappraisals after Two Centuries*, edited by Reid L. Neilson and Terryl L. Givens. Oxford University Press, 2009.

———. "Meetings and Migrations: Nineteenth-century Mormon Encounters with Asians." In *Proclamation to the Pacific: Nineteenth Century Mormonism and the Pacific Basin Frontier*, edited by Laurie F. Maffly-Kipp and Reid L. Neilson. University of Utah Press, 2008.

———. "A Mormon and a Buddhist Debate Plural Marriage: The Letters of Elder Alma O. Taylor and the Reverend Nishijima Kakuryo, 1901." *Brigham Young University Studies Quarterly* 53, no. 2 (2014): 94–120.

———. "Mormonism and the Japanese: A Guide to the Sources." In *Taking the Gospel to the Japanese, 1901–2001*, edited by Reid L. Neilson and Van C. Gessel. Brigham Young University Press, 2006.

———. "Mormonism in the Land of the Morning Calm: A Bibliography of Published Sources on the LDS Church in Korea." *Mormon Historical Studies* 9, no. 2 (Fall 2008): 117–29.

———. "A Priceless Pearl: Alma O. Taylor's Mission to Japan." *Ensign* 32 (June 2002): 56–59.

———. "Strangers in a Strange Land: The Rise and Demise of the Early LDS Japan Mission, 1901–24." PhD dissertation, University of North Carolina at Chapel Hill, 2006.

———, ed. *To the Peripheries of Mormondom: The Apostolic around-the-World Journey of David O. McKay, 1920–1921*. University of Utah Press, 2011.

———. "Traveling and Standing Ministers: The Commandment to Travel (or Not) in the Joseph Smith Era Revelations." *Religious Educator: Perspectives on the Restored Gospel* 17, no. 2 (2016): 15–35.

———. "Turning the Key That Unlocked the Door: Elder David O. McKay's 1921 Apostolic Dedication of the Chinese Realm." *Mormon Historical Studies* 10, no. 2 (Fall 2009): 77–101.

Neilson, Reid L. and Van C. Gessel, eds. *Taking the Gospel to the Japanese, 1901–2001*. Brigham Young University Press, 2006.

Neilson, Reid L. and Scott Marianno, eds. *A Voice in the Wilderness: The 1888–1930 General Conference Sermons of Mormon Historian Andrew Jenson*. Oxford University Press, 2018.

Neilson, Reid L. and R. Mark Melville, eds. *The Saints Abroad: Missionaries Who Answered Brigham Young's 1852 Call to the Nations of the World*. Religious Studies Center, 2019.

Neilson, Reid L., and Riley M. Moffat, eds. *Tales from the World Tour: The 1895–1897 Travel Writings of Mormon Historian Andrew Jenson*. Religious Studies Center, 2012.

Reid L. Neilson and Carson V. Teuscher, eds. *Pacific Apostle: the 1920–21 Diary of David O. McKay in the Latter-day Saint Island Missions*. University of Illinois Press, 2021.

Neilson, Reid L., and Nathan N. Waite, eds. *Settling the Valley, Proclaiming the Gospel: The General Epistles of the Mormon First Presidency*. Oxford University Press, 2017.

Nelson, Terry G. "A History of The Church of Jesus Christ of Latter-day Saints in Japan from 1948 to 1980." Master's thesis, Brigham Young University, 1986.

Newton, Marjorie. *Southern Cross Saints: The Mormons in Australia*. Institute for Polynesian Studies, 1991.

———. *Tiki and Temple: The Mormon Mission to New Zealand, 1854–1958.* Greg Kofford Books, 2012.

Nichols, Murray L. "History of the Japan Mission of The Church of Jesus Christ of Latter-day Saints, 1901–1924." Master's thesis, Brigham Young University, 1957.

Oaks, Dallin H. "Getting to Know China." In *Brigham Young University 1990–91 Devotional and Fireside Speeches.* Brigham Young University Publications, 1991.

Okihiro, Gary Y. *Margins and Mainstreams: Asians in American History and Culture.* University of Washington Press, 1994.

Our Heritage: A Brief History of The Church of Jesus Christ of Latter-day Saints. The Church of Jesus Christ of Latter-day Saints, 1996.

Palmer, A. Delbert and Mark L. Grover. "Hoping to Establish a Presence: Parley P. Pratt's 1851 Mission to Chile." *BYU Studies* 38, no. 4 (1999): 116–19.

Palmer, Spencer J. *The Church Encounters Asia.* Deseret Book, 1970.

———. *The Expanding Church.* Deseret Book, 1978.

Pan, Lynn, ed. *The Encyclopedia of the Chinese Overseas.* Harvard University Press, 1999.

Papanikolas, Helen Z. *The Peoples of Utah.* Utah State Historical Society, 1976.

Pearce, Scott, Audrey Spiro, Patricia Ebrey, eds. *Culture and Power in the Reconstitution of the Chinese Realm, 200–600.* Harvard University Asia Center, 2001.

Perlich, Pamela S. *Utah Minorities: The Story Told by 150 Years of Census Data.* Bureau of Economic and Business Research, David S. Eccles School of Business, University of Utah, 2002.

Plewe, Brandon. "State of the Church in 1852." *Mormon Historical Studies* 16 no. 1 (Spring 2015): 233–43.

Poston Jr., Duley L. and Juyin Helen Wong. "The Chinese Diaspora: The Current Distribution of the Overseas Chinese Population." *Chinese Journal of Sociology* 2, no. 3 (2016): 348–73.

Powell, Allan Kent, ed. *Utah History Encyclopedia.* University of Utah Press, 1994.

Pratt, Parley P. *The Autobiography of Parley Parker Pratt.* Russell Brothers, 1874.

———. *The Essential Parley P. Pratt.* Signature Books, 1990.

Price, Stephen L. *Hosea Stout: Lawman, Legislature, Mormon Defender.* Utah State University Press, 2016.

Proper, David R. "Joseph Smith and Salem." *Essex Institute Historical Collections* 100 (April 1964): 93.

Pyle, Kenneth B. *The Making of Modern Japan.* D. C. Heath and Company, 1996.

Reeve, W. Paul. *Religion of a Different Color: Race and the Mormon Struggle for Whiteness.* Oxford University Press, 2015.

Reilly, Thomas H. *The Taiping Heavenly Kingdom: Rebellion and the Blasphemy of Empire.* University of Washington Press, 2004.

Roberts, B. H. *A Comprehensive History of The Church of Jesus Christ of Latter-day*

Saints, Century One. 6 vols. The Church of Jesus Christ of Latter-day Saints, 1965.

Rogala, Joseph, comp. *A Collector's Guide to Books on Japan in English*. Japan Library, 2001.

Rogers, Brent M., Elizabeth A. Kuehn, Christian K. Heimburger, Max H. Parkin, Alexander L. Baugh, and Steven C. Harper, eds. *Documents, Volume 5: October 1835–January 1838*. Vol. 5 of the Documents series of *The Joseph Smith Papers*, edited by Ronald K. Esplin, Matthew J. Grow, and Matthew C. Godfrey. Church Historian's Press, 2017.

Shaffer, Donald R. "Hiram Clark and the First LDS Hawaiian Mission: A Reappraisal." *Journal of Mormon History* 17 (1991): 94–109.

Shapiro, Sidney, ed. *Jews in Old China: Studies by Chinese Scholars*. Hippocrene Books, 1984.

Shipps, Jan, and John W. Welch, eds. *The Journals of William E. McLellin, 1831–36*. BYU Studies Press and University of Illinois Press, 1994.

Shipps, Jan. *Sojourner in the Promised Land: Forty Years Among the Mormons*. University of Illinois Press, 2000.

Shirts, Morris A. and Kathryn A. Shirts. *A Trial Furnace: Southern Utah's Iron Mission*. Deseret Book, 2020.

Slover II, Robert H. "Resources in the Church Historian's Office Relating to Asia." *BYU Studies* 12 (1971): 107–18.

Smith, Arthur H. *Chinese Characteristics*, rev. and enl. F. H. Revell, 1900.

Smith, Dwight L. "The Engineer and the Canyon." *Utah Historical Quarterly* 28 (July 1960): 263–74.

———. "Robert B. Stanton's Plan for the Far Southwest." *Arizona and the West* 4 (Winter 1962): 369–72.

Smith, Elmer R. "The 'Japanese' in Utah." *Utah Humanities Review* 2 (June 1948): 129–44.

———. "The 'Japanese' in Utah: Part II." *Utah Humanities Review* 2 (July 1948): 208–30.

Smith, Sarah Cox. "Translator or Translated? The Portrayal of The Church of Jesus Christ of Latter-day Saints in Print in Meiji Japan." In *Taking the Gospel to the Japanese, 1901–2001*, edited by Reid L. Neilson and Van C. Gessel. Brigham Young University Press, 2006.

Snodgrass, Judith. *Presenting Japanese Buddhism to the West: Orientalism, Occidentalism, and the Columbian Exposition*. University of North Carolina Press, 2003.

Snow, Lorenzo. *The Italian Mission*. W. Aubrey, 1851.

Spence, Jonathan D. *The Search for Modern China*. 2nd ed. W. W. Norton, 1999.

———. *The Taiping Vision of a Christian China, 1836–1864*. Baylor University Press, 1998.

Staker, Mark L., and Donald L. Enders. "Joseph Smith Sr.'s China Adventure." *Journal of Mormon History* 48, no. 2 (2022): 79–105.

Stapley, Jonathan A. *The Power of Godliness: Mormon Liturgy and Cosmology.* Oxford University Press, 2018.

Stephenson, Barry. *Ritual: A Very Short Introduction.* Oxford University Press, 2015.

Stout, Hosea. *On the Mormon Frontier: The Diary of Hosea Stout.* 2 vols. Edited by Juanita Brooks. University of Utah Press, 1964.

Stout, Wayne. *Hosea Stout: Utah's Pioneer Statesman.* 1953.

Takagi, Shinji. "Mormons in the Press: Reactions to the 1901 Opening of the Japan Mission." *BYU Studies* 40 no. 1 (2001): 141–75.

———. "Tomizo and Tokujiro: The First Japanese Mormons." *BYU Studies* 39, no. 2 (2000): 73–106.

Talbot, Christine. *A Foreign Kingdom: Mormons and Polygamy in American Political Culture, 1852–1890.* University of Illinois Press, 2013.

Taniguchi, Nancy J. "Japanese Immigrants in Utah." In *Utah History Encyclopedia*, edited by Allan Kent Powell. University of Utah Press, 1994.

Taylor, Sandra C. "Leaving the Concentration Camps: Japanese American Resettlement in Utah and the Intermountain West." *Pacific Historical Review* 60 (May 1991): 169–94.

Thomas, Winburn T. *Protestant Beginnings in Japan: The First Three Decades, 1859–1889.* Charles E. Tuttle, 1959.

Thomson, Sandra Caruthers. "Meiji Japan through Missionary Eyes: The American Protestant Experience." *Journal of Religious History* 7 (1973): 248–59.

Toronto, James A., and Richard Neitzel Holzapfel, "The LDS Church in Italy: The 1966 Rededication by Elder Ezra Taft Benson." *BYU Studies Quarterly* 51, no. 3 (2012): 88–90.

Toronto, James A., Eric R Dursteler, and Michael W. Homer. *Mormons in the Piazza: History of the Latter-day Saints in Italy.* Religious Studies Center, Brigham Young University, 2017.

Tsurutani, Hisashi. *American-Bound: The Japanese and the Opening of the American West.* Japan Times, 1989.

Tullis, F. LaMond. *Mormons in Mexico: The Dynamics of Faith and Culture.* Utah State University Press, 1987.

Turley, Richard E., Jr. "Assistant Church Historians and the Publishing of Church History." In *Preserving the History of the Latter-day Saints.*

———. "Collecting, Preserving, and Sharing the Global History of The Church of Jesus Christ of Latter-day Saints." *Journal of Mormon History* 41, no. 1 (January 2015): 125–38.

———. *In the Hands of the Lord: The Life of Dallin H. Oaks.* Deseret Book, 2021,

Tweed, Thomas A. *The American Encounter with Buddhism, 1844–1912: Victorian Culture and the Limits of Dissent.* University of North Carolina Press, 2000.

———. "Introduction." In Hannah Adams, *A Dictionary of all Religions and Religious Denominations.* Scholars Press, 1992.

———, ed. *Retelling U.S. Religious History.* University of California Press, 1997.

Tweed, Thomas A. and Stephen Prothero, eds. *Asian Religions in America: A Documentary History*. Oxford University Press, 1999.

Ulrich, Laurel Thatcher. *A House Full of Females: Plural Marriage and Women's Rights in Early Mormonism, 1835–1870*. Vintage, 2018.

Underwood, Grant. *The Millenarian World of Early Mormonism*. University of Illinois Press, 1993.

———. "Latter-day Saints in the Pacific: A Bibliographic Essay." In *Pioneers in the Pacific: Memory, History, and Cultural Identity among the Latter-day Saints*, edited by Grant Underwood. Religious Studies Center, Brigham Young University, 2005.

van Beek, Walter E. A. "Ritual and the Quest for Meaning." In *By Our Rites of Worship: Latter-day Saint Views on Ritual in Scripture, History, and Practice*, edited by Daniel L. Belnap. BYU Religious Studies Center, 2013.

Van Dyke, Blair G., and LaMar C. Berrett. "In the Footsteps of Orson Hyde: Subsequent Dedications of the Holy Land." *Brigham Young University Studies* 47, no. 1 (2008): 57–93.

Van Sant, John E. *Pacific Pioneers: Japanese Journeys to America and Hawaii, 1850–80*. University of Illinois Press, 2000.

Varg, Paul A. *Missionaries, Chinese, and Diplomats: The American Protestant Missionary Movement in China, 1890–1952*. Princeton University Press, 1958.

Wacker, Grant. "A Plural World: The Protestant Awakening to World Religions." In *Between the Times: The Travail of the Protestant Establishment in America, 1900–1960*, edited by William R. Hutchison. Cambridge University Press, 1989.

Walker, Ronald W. "Strangers in a Strange Land: Heber J. Grant and the Opening of the Japan Mission." In *Taking the Gospel to the Japanese, 1901 to 2001*, edited by Reid L. Neilson and Van C. Gessel. Brigham Young University Press, 2006.

Walz, Eric. "Japanese Immigrants and the Mormons." Paper presented at "A Centennial Celebration: The History of The Church of Jesus Christ of Latter-day Saints in Japan 1901–2001." Brigham Young University, Provo, Utah, October 2001.

Webster, Noah. *American Dictionary of the English Language*. S. Converse, 1828.

Whittaker, David J. "The Bone in the Throat: Orson Pratt and the Public Announcement of Plural Marriage." *Western Historical Quarterly* 18 (July 1987): 293–314.

———. "Brigham Young and the Missionary Enterprise." In *Lion of the Lord: Essays on the Life and Service of Brigham Young*, edited by Susan Easton Black and Larry C. Porter. Deseret Book, 1995.

———. "Mormon Missiology: An Introduction and Guide to the Sources." In *Disciple as Witness: Essays on Latter-day Saint History and Doctrine in Honor of Richard Lloyd Anderson*, edited by Stephen D. Ricks, Donald

W. Parry, and Andrew H. Hedges. Foundation for Ancient Research and Mormon Studies, Brigham Young University, 2000.

———. "Parley P. Pratt and the Pacific Mission: Mormon Publishing in 'That Very Questionable Part of the Civilized World." In *Mormons, Scripture, and the Ancient World: Studies in Honor of John L. Sorenson*, edited by Davis Bitton. Foundation for Ancient Research and Mormon Studies, 1998.

Wilson, Robert A. and Bill Hosokawa. *East to America: A History of the Japanese in the United States*. William Morrow, 1980.

Woo, Wesley Stephen. "Protestant Work among the Chinese in the San Francisco Bay Area, 1850–1920 (California)." PhD dissertation, Graduate Theological Union, 1984.

Xi, Feng. "A History of Mormon-Chinese Relations: 1849–1993." PhD dissertation, Brigham Young University, 1994.

Xi, Lian. *The Conversion of Missionaries: Liberalism in American Protestant Missions in China, 1907–1932*. Pennsylvania State University Press, 1997.

Xu, Shi. "The Images of the Chinese in the Rocky Mountain Region: 1855–1882." PhD dissertation, Brigham Young University, 1996.

Yang, John H., comp. *Asian Americans in Utah: A Living History*. State of Utah Office of Asian Affairs, Asian American Advisory Council, 1999.

Index

M

N

U

W

Also available from

GREG KOFFORD BOOKS

Unique But Not Different: Latter-day Saints in Japan

Shinji Takagi, Conan Grames, and Meagan Rainock

Paperback, ISBN: 978-1-58958-791-5

Unique But Not Different: Latter-day Saints in Japan offers an insightful exploration into the experiences of Japanese members of The Church of Jesus Christ of Latter-day Saints, shedding light on their integration of religious identity within a predominantly non-Christian society. Through comprehensive survey data collected from active practitioners, authors Shinji Takagi, Conan Grames, and Meagan Rainock delve into the challenges and opportunities these Latter-day Saints face. In doing so, they examine the diverse social, political, and ideological backgrounds of Japanese Latter-day Saints, providing valuable insights for scholars, missionaries, Church leaders, and members alike.

With meticulous analysis, the authors navigate topics ranging from personal conversion experiences to religious beliefs and adherence to cultural practices. They examine how Japanese Latter-day Saints successfully negotiate identity conflicts and contribute to the broader societal landscape amidst Japan's evolving cultural institutions. Offering statistical profiles and key findings tailored to various stakeholders, *Unique But Not Different* serves as an indispensable resource for understanding the complex dynamics of religious identity and acculturation in Japan, while also providing valuable insights applicable to minority religious practices worldwide.

For Japanese readers, the volume also includes a Japanese Afterword and translations of the summary, findings, tables, and figures.

Mormon and Maori

Marjorie Newton

Paperback, ISBN: 978-1-58958-639-0

2015 Best International Book Award,
Mormon History Association

Praise for *The Liberal Soul*:

"*Mormon and Maori* is the result of a labor of love that reflects not years but decades of diligent research. Indeed, in combination with Newton's earlier Tiki and Temple, it constitutes the most detailed discussion in print of the fascinating 160-year saga of accommodation and adjustment between Maori culture and Mormonism. Unflinchingly honest yet unfailingly compassionate, *Mormon and Maori* is a must-read for anyone interested in the extraordinary history of the LDS experience in New Zealand."

— Grant Underwood, Professor of History, Brigham Young University

"*Mormon and Maori* offers a substantial historical account that structures and organizes *te iwi* Māori's (The Māori people's) often complex relationship and attachment to an American religion. In this respect Newton's work should be considered groundbreaking."

— Gina Colvin, *Journal of Mormon History*

For the Cause of Righteousness: A Global History of Blacks and Mormonism, 1830-2013

Russell W. Stevenson

Paperback, ISBN: 978-1-58958-529-4

2015 Best Book Award, Mormon History Association

"In Russell Stevenson's *For the Cause of Righteousness: A Global History of Blacks and Mormonism*, he extends the story of Mormonism's long-standing priesthood ban to the broader history of the Church's interaction with blacks. In so doing he introduces both relevant atmospherics and important new context. These should inform all future discussions of this surprisingly enduring subject."

— Lester E. Bush, author of "Mormonism's Negro Doctrine: An Historical Overview"

"Russell Stevenson has produced a terrific compilation. Invaluable as a historical resource, and as a troubling morality tale. The array of documents compellingly reveals the tragedy and inconsistency of racial attitudes, policies, and doctrines in the LDS tradition, and the need for eternal vigilance in negotiating a faith that must never be unmoored from humaneness."

— Terryl L. Givens, author of *Parley P. Pratt: The Apostle Paul of Mormonism* and *By the Hand of Mormon: The American Scripture that Launched a New World Religion*

"You might wonder what a White man could possibly say to two Black women about Black Mormon history. Surprisingly a whole lot! As people who consider ourselves well informed in African-American Mormon History, we found a wealth of new information in *For the Cause of Righteousness*. Russell Stevenson's well-researched exploration of Blacks and Mormonism is an informative read, not just for those interested in Black history, but American history as well."

— Tamu Smith and Zandra Vranes (a.k.a. Sistas in Zion), authors, Diary of Two Mad Black Mormons

The Latter-day Saint Image in the British Mind

Malcolm Adcock and Fred E. Woods

Paperback, ISBN: 978-1-58958-558-4

Since the coming forth of the Book of Mormon in 1830, The Church of Jesus Christ of Latter-day Saints has added millions of people to its global membership. Crucial to its initial growth were converts from Great Britain who emigrated to join with other Latter-day Saints in the United States. Many, however, also stayed in the United Kingdom in order to establish a presence of the Church there.

In *The Latter-day Saint Image in the British Mind*, authors Malcolm Adcock and Fred E. Woods explore the multifaceted perspectives of British people outside of the Latter-day Saint faith tradition and how these people's perceptions of The Church of Jesus Christ of Latter-day Saints and its members generally have improved over time. In doing so, they present historical accounts, particularly through literature, film, and media reviews depicting Latter-day Saints and their faith. In addition, they utilize over a hundred face-to-face interviews and surveys of over a thousand Brits to determine how citizens of the United Kingdom perceive the Church in the twenty-first century.

The Trek East: Mormonism Meets Japan, 1901–1968

Shinji Takagi

Paperback, ISBN: 978-1-58958-560-7
Hardcover, ISBN: 978-1-58958-561-4

2017 Best International Book Award, Mormon History Association

Praise for *The Trek East*:

"In *The Trek East*, Dr. Shinji Takagi has produced a masterful treatment of Mormonism's foundation in Japan. Takagi takes an approach that informs us of Mormonism in Japan in a manner that focuses on inputs and results, environmental conditions in Japan and cultural biases of a Mormonism informed by western assumptions."

— Meg Stout, *The Millennial Star*

"This is a wonderful book, full of historical knowledge on a lesser-known subject in LDS history. The author, who is Japanese, LDS and lives in Virginia, is deeply invested in the subject and carefully includes all sides of the history."

— Mike Whitmer, *Deseret News*

"A monumental work of scholarship. . . . I can't imagine that any future study of this period could hope to provide a more thorough and engrossing analytical study of the origins and growth of the Church in Japan. This remarkable contribution is unlikely ever to be supplanted."

— Van C. Gessel, *Journal of Mormon History*

www.ingramcontent.com/pod-product-compliance
Lightning Source LLC
LaVergne TN
LVHW051023080826
845145LV00009B/2784